Cooking with the Healthful Herbs

Cooking with the Healthful Herbs

Jean Rogers

Over 300 No-Salt Ways to
Great Taste and Better Health

Rodale Press, Emmaus, Pa.

Printed in the United States of America on recycled paper, containing a high percentage of de-inked fiber.

Book Designer: Barbara Field
Illustrator: Don Page

Library of Congress Cataloging in Publication Data

Rogers, Jean, 1948–
    Cooking with the healthful herbs.

    Includes index.
    1. Cookery (Herbs)   I. Title.
TX819.H4R6   1983   641.6'57   82-25177
ISBN 0-87857-449-2   hardcover
ISBN 0-87857-486-7   paperback

2   4   6   8   10   9   7   5   3   1   hardcover
2   4   6   8   10   9   7   5   3   1   paperback

For John and Ivy

Contents

Ingredient Notes

In an attempt to avoid repeating certain information during the recipes, I'm listing a few ingredient guidelines here.

- All the *fruits and vegetables* called for are fresh. Canning and freezing tend to lower their nutrient values, and processing often adds salt to vegetables and sugar to fruits. If fresh items are not available, choose frozen foods over canned ones. But read labels carefully to avoid unwanted ingredients!
- All *butter* used is unsalted.
- All *eggs* are large size.
- *Oil* means a vegetable oil such as corn, safflower, sunflower or soy. If olive, peanut or sesame oil is intended, the recipe will specify it.
- *Olive oil* should be of the highest quality—preferably virgin olive oil—for the best flavor.
- *Nuts* are unsalted and, unless specified, unroasted. If roasted nuts are called for, use the dry roasted to reduce calories.
- *Yogurt* is low fat.
- The *ricotta* called for contains some skim milk.
- There are three recipes for *Basic Mayonnaise* in the book, and they are different in ingredients and calorie content. When a recipe calls for mayonnaise, choose the one that best suits your diet requirements.
- *Stock* refers to chicken, beef, veal, vegetable or fish stock. In most recipes I have not specified a kind of stock because most people don't have a selection on hand and will use what's available. In general, chicken, veal and vegetable stocks are best for poultry, vegetable and other light-colored dishes, while beef stock is best for meats and other hearty foods. Of course, fish stock should be reserved for fish dishes (and is usually specified), although you can substitute chicken or vegetable stock, if necessary. Be guided by your taste and what's on hand.
- All cup and spoon *measurements* refer to standard U.S. portions and assume that the food being measured will be leveled off. Unless otherwise noted, flour is measured by dipping a dry-measure cup into the flour container and then sweeping off excess flour with the flat edge of a knife.

Chapter 1

Break the Salt and Sugar Habit

I've got a million cookbooks, more or less, and you probably do too. Why, then, when we wander into even the smallest bookshop, do dozens of new books have the power to beckon us from the shelves? What's your pleasure? French? Italian? Indonesian? No salt? No fat? There's no shortage of enticing offerings.

In recent years herb cookbooks have multiplied with an especially wild abandon. Right now I have a dozen or more staring me in the face from the bookshelves above my desk. They come in all sizes, shapes and degrees of quality. But what they all have in common is that they're already on the market. So why another? Because this is the only herb cookbook that tells you:

- why salt is a major health hazard and how to extract yourself from its grip;
- how to use herbs instead of salt to flavor food;
- why you should also enlist potassium—a common mineral—in this battle against salt;
- how to put onions and garlic to delicious use in fighting cholesterol.

It's the only herb cookbook to do all these things plus give you over 300 health-building recipes that eliminate salt while also doing away with such other harmfuls as alcohol, white flour, white rice, sugar and most processed foods.

A Salt Dossier

You're probably already aware that salt is bad for your health, but you may not know exactly why. Well, in a nutshell, most scientists who've investigated the matter believe that too much salt is the number one dietary cause of high blood pressure—a serious problem. What's worse, when our diet contains a lot of sugar as well as a lot of salt—which is often the case today—the risk may increase. But that's not the end of this mess. Salt has also been linked with other health problems, including headaches and kidney failure.

Don't misunderstand. Sodium (a good part of sodium chloride or table salt) is absolutely essential to our bodies. If you *could* experience a sodium deficiency, you'd probably complain regularly of weakness, headaches, giddiness, lack of concentration, poor memory and loss of appetite. But it's not likely that you'll ever have such a deficiency, because we need only a small amount of salt to function properly, and we get more than enough in the food we eat.

The real problem is *excess* sodium. Most of us seem addicted to salt—that's why we can't eat just one potato chip. But this craving is an acquired one, one that probably started when we were babies and ate commercial baby food that was salted to please an adult taste. Moreover, as we grew we saw family and friends pour salt on their food at the table, and we imitated them. The pattern was set.

Today in most developed countries, salt consumption far exceeds actual requirements. Figures from the Salt Institute place consumption in the United States at 10 to 12 grams per person *per day,* and that's about two teaspoons a day. Translated into the real problem, sodium, that comes to about 4,000 to 4,800 milligrams a day, about four times what many who've studied the situation recommend as a daily sodium limit.

The Salt We Don't See or Shake

Now the problem isn't just that people use the saltshaker too heavily. In fact, if we stopped salting food at the stove and the table, we'd probably cut only a gram or 2 from our daily intakes. Much of those daily 10 to 12 grams of salt comes from the processed food so prevalent in the American diet. Salt is added to almost every prepared food on your grocer's shelves—to prove it, go read some labels. You'll find salt in sardines, mustard, soups, breads, olives, cold cuts, soy sauce, snack foods, cakes, cookies and most other sweets. And if you read the instructions even on foods that don't contain much salt—foods like noodles, oatmeal and rice—you'll find that they recommend adding it during cooking. So there's no escape!

Food, of course, isn't our only source of excess sodium. Water that has been "softened" to eliminate minerals like calcium and magnesium gets a large amount of sodium added in the process. On the average, one cup of softened water contains about 100 milligrams of sodium while unsoftened water contains only 5. And the salt dumped on snow-covered roads sometimes finds it way into drinking water.

Salt and Battery

What happens to all that excess salt? Well, first it causes us to retain water, which, if it only showed up as extra pounds on the bathroom scale, wouldn't be too bad. But, when extra salt bloats our bodies, it sometimes also puts a strain on the kidneys, organs that play a vital role in regulating blood pressure. Too much salt somehow can interfere with normal kidney function and cause a rise in blood pressure. And as we know, high blood pressure (also called hypertension) is a cause for great concern.

To understand why, let's first look at what blood pressure is. Blood pressure is the force exerted by the blood on the walls of the vessels that carry it. When a physician takes your blood pressure, he is measuring that force, and his reading contains two numbers. The first and higher number is called the systolic pressure. It indicates the pressure in the arteries while your heart is pumping. The second (or diastolic) number is lower and indicates the blood's pressure while the heart is resting between beats. Both numbers are important. To be considered normal, your reading should be under 140/90. The lower your reading—in the vicinity of 120/70—the better.

A higher pressure is dangerous because the higher the pressure, the harder the blood presses against its arteries, and pressure-strained arteries tend to harden faster, growing stiff and less resilient. In the kidneys, minor blowouts of vessels can occur. When they do, kidney failure can follow and *it* can be fatal.

High blood pressure can also lead to stroke. The heart itself may be weakened by many years of pushing blood through resistant arteries. One physician has remarked that high blood pressure is "the most prevalent and most dangerous precipitating factor in the genesis of cardiovascular diseases, the leading cause of death in the United States and other industrialized countries."

Several recent studies have confirmed this link between salt consumption, high blood pressure and heart disease. For instance, Trefor O. Morgan, M.D., a doctor from Melbourne, Australia, studied 48 people with high blood pressure, half of whom had mild hypertension and half of whom had more severe hypertension. Of the 24 people with mild hypertension, 12 were put on a low-sodium diet, and 12 were told to make no changes at all. Of the 12 cutting down on sodium, 8 showed reductions in blood pressure over the two-month study. Only 3 of the 12 untreated patients had reduced pressure levels. Of the 24 people with more severe hypertension, 12 were put on a low-sodium diet, and 12 were given drug therapy. Nine of those on reduced sodium lowered their blood pressures, a record that was just as good as the results achieved with drug therapy. The doctor concluded, "Restriction of sodium intake is an effective method of reducing blood pressure and should be the first form of therapy in people with mild hypertension" (*Medical Journal of Australia,* October 17, 1981).

The Salt and Sugar Connection

If salt alone is bad for our blood pressures, salt combined with sugar may be even worse. Researchers at Louisiana State University Medical School found that taking a lot of sugar with a lot of salt may increase our risk of high blood pressure still more. They measured the responses of three groups of monkeys to high intakes of sugar and salt. The first group was fed a diet containing no added salt. The second group got a diet high in salt. And the third group had a diet high in salt *and* sugar. The amounts of salt and sugar were admittedly high, 3 percent and 38 percent of the food totals consumed, but the researchers say they were "within the range of human consumption."

The researchers found that the monkeys on the salt plus sugar diet showed worse symptoms of high blood pressure than both the other groups. And they concluded their report with this warning: ". . . the synergistic effect of dietary sodium and sucrose (sugar) on the induction of hypertension in this nonhuman primate species has a potentially important bearing on human hypertension" (*American*

Journal of Clinical Nutrition, March 1980). What they meant was that the effect of salt and sugar together gave the monkeys a higher blood pressure.

Some Ways Out of This Sweet, Salty Mess

It must be pretty clear by now that salt (and its blood pressure cohort, sugar) is bad for us. Fortunately, there are a number of things we can do to cut down on these two flies in the dietary ointment. We can change our eating habits, look out for softened water—and cook using the recipes in this book.

Breaking the shaker habit and getting over a taste for salt is not as hard as one might imagine. It's a lot easier than cutting out smoking, for instance. Begin slowly by holding back on salt when you're cooking. Then be sure that you actually taste your food before automatically salting it at the table. And when you do reach for the shaker—after making sure you absolutely can't eat the food without salt—go easy. After a short period of time—maybe two weeks—you'll notice that it takes less and less salt to satisfy you. That's when you can kick the habit entirely, for at that point your taste buds will begin to appreciate the fresh, natural flavors inherent in unprocessed fruits, vegetables and meats. Finally, you'll know you've won the salt battle when food at a restaurant or someone else's house suddenly seems too salty for you.

As I said, water that has been softened contains a lot of sodium. You can kick this sodium out of your life by asking your plumber to disconnect the link between the softener and the faucet you use for cooking and drinking water. In my first house, I had the cold-water faucet in the kitchen unhooked from the water softener. In my present house, I had the plumber add a second—and unsoftened cold water only—faucet to the kitchen sink. Either way I got soft water for cleaning purposes and unsalted water for drinking and cooking.

But this book's major strategy for dumping the shaker—into the garbage, not onto your food—is contained in its recipes. They contain no table salt whatsoever. Secondly, they employ herbs as flavor enhancers, so you won't miss the purloined salt at all. And finally, many contain pungent amounts of onions and garlic that add their own seasoning magic. Some of the recipes do contain foods that are naturally high in sodium—like cheese, milk and tamari—but the amounts used are far below those found in most cookbooks. And even those sodium-bearers do not begin to approach the amounts you'd add with the shaker.

By the way, please don't think that sea salt is an acceptable substitute for table salt, because it isn't. According to government standards, all salt permitted on American tables contains pretty much the same things, and sea salt, like table salt, contains little more than sodium chloride.

The recipes in this book are not only low in sodium, but they also go easy on sugar (or honey in this case, because I use no refined sugar). The desserts are pleasantly sweet without being overpoweringly so, and many of them get most of their sweetness from fresh and dried fruits that contribute valuable fiber while they're standing in for refined sugar.

The Problem with Hypertension Drugs

So my recipes have two special features— their good, natural taste *and* their hypertension-fighting nature. Built into that second feature, however, is a special bonus—they may help you stop taking drugs for hypertension. Now, many people find it easier to rely on drugs to lower their blood pressure than to change their diet or other health habits. But before you get the idea that these folks are right, consider these facts. The usual medical treatment for high blood pressure is diuretics, drugs that pull fluids—and sodium—from the tissues. Diuretics force the kidneys to pump water and sodium out of the tissues into the urine; in doing so, they lower blood pressure the same way a low-sodium intake does. Unfortunately, many of the drugs also come complete with a long list of possible side effects: gastrointestinal irritation, weakness, impotence, nausea, diarrhea, palpitations and blindness, to name a few. Reserpine, one drug used for hypertension, has caused cancer in laboratory animals according to a 1980 National Cancer Institute report. Even the *Lancet,* one of the world's most prestigious medical journals, favors salt restriction as a treatment for high blood pressure: "We should . . . give serious attention to the possibility of recommending salt restriction in hypertensive patients," the editors say (August 30, 1980).

Potassium, a Natural Way Out

But the problem with diuretics is that, while washing excess salt from the body, they may also drain away potassium. Potassium is a mineral necessary for the functioning of many body tissues, including the heart. New studies exploring the role of this mineral suggest that it is also a valuable ally in fighting high blood pressure. Potassium helps nerves transmit mes-

sages, aids digestive enzymes in their work, guides normal growth and serves as an electrolyte (that is, it carries tiny electrical charges that ensure the proper functioning of every muscle in the body). The trouble between potassium and diuretics begins because it is intimately linked with sodium in the body.

Trouble starts because potassium and sodium carry on a sort of tug-of-war in your body. When sodium is winning, potassium is dumped into the urine for excretion. But when potassium is winning, sodium gets dumped, an important victory.

"We'd probably see some dramatic changes in the incidence of hypertension if Americans cut their salt intake to less than three grams a day and started eating an equivalent amount of potassium," says Harold D. Battarbee, Ph.D., an associate professor of physiology at Louisiana State University School of Medicine in Shreveport.

Dr. Battarbee and an associate were searching for some hormonal "missing link" between salt and high blood pressure. They discovered that when rats were fed enough salt to give them high blood pressure, the levels of two hormones in their bodies went down. But doubling the rats' potassium intake prevented the hormones' decline—and also significantly slowed the rise in their blood pressures. After a year, the diastolic pressure of rats given added sodium ranged from 150 to 170, but the pressures of those given extra potassium averaged only 140.

Studies conducted at the London Hospital Medical College have also shown that potassium may act as a shield against sodium-induced high blood pressure. In one study, a group of 16 people with mild hypertension and a group with normal blood pressures received two different diets, each for a period of 12 weeks. During the first 12 weeks, both groups ate their normal diet plus some sodium tablets. During the second period, their normal diets were supplemented with potassium, and they were told to avoid excessively salty foods and the use of the saltshaker at the table and stove.

The high-sodium diet of the first 12 weeks produced a slow rise in both groups' blood pressure. But the high-potassium diet of the second 12 weeks had the opposite effect: " . . . both systolic and diastolic blood pressure fell sharply and significantly in the hypertensive group in contrast to small, but insignificant rises in the [normal] group."

A follow-up test one month after the end of this study — when the people had returned to their normal eating habits — revealed that the people with high blood pressures had returned to their dangerous levels. The researchers concluded that the key factor in the startling drops seen during the high potassium/low sodium diet had been the increased potassium, since the people's normal diets were only slightly higher in sodium than the test diets but were *much* lower in potassium (*Lancet,* January 10, 1981).

Other studies suggest that everybody can benefit from an increase in potassium. A study conducted during the 1960s in Evans County, Georgia, revealed that, while whites and blacks there consumed about the same amount of sodium, blacks consumed less than half the potassium of whites. And their blood pressures were considerably higher. The researchers concluded that "the only way to explain the higher prevalence of hypertension among blacks appears to be their much lower potassium intake, caused by low consumption of fresh fruit, salads, vegetables, and the traditional long cooking of meats and vegetables with loss of . . . potassium into the cooking water" (*Nutrition and Metabolism,* vol. 24, 1980).

Some Potassium Thieves

It isn't just Georgia blacks who should worry about a diet low in potassium. Canning and freezing foods cause substantial losses of potassium, and so *anyone* who relies heavily on these products may be suffering. What's more, those processing techniques actually reverse the sodium and potassium balance. A cup of raw peas, for example, contains 458 milligrams of potassium and just 3 milligrams of sodium. But when those same peas are canned, salt added during the process raises the sodium level to 588 milligrams, while the potassium level drops to 239 milligrams, roughly half of what it was before. The same thing happens to a cup of raw lima beans, which contains just 3 milligrams of sodium and a walloping 1,008 milligrams of potassium. After canning, the potassium is slashed in half (to 551 milligrams), and the sodium skyrockets to 585 milligrams.

"There need to be some changes in the way foods are processed in industry and at home," Dr. Battarbee says. That seems clear, and the effort is already underway. But what is the proper sodium/potassium ratio in a healthful diet? That's not so clear.

No recommended dietary allowance of potassium has been established by the National Research Council, although 2,500 milligrams is a commonly cited figure along with a safe range of between 2,000 and 6,000 milligrams a day. As we have said, the body requires only a tiny amount of sodium, and while 1,000 milligrams may be safe, 500 milligrams a day or even less is usually considered sufficient. Dr. Battarbee admits that he doesn't know the ideal sodium/potassium ratio but "keeping it at one-to-one would be beneficial, though . . . less sodium would be better." Author and chemist Philip S. Chen, Ph.D., claims the ratio should be closer to two-to-one.

Some Potassium-Rich Foods

Fortunately, many foods high in potassium are also low in sodium. A large banana, for instance, packs 502 milligrams of potassium and only 1 milligram of sodium. A cup of orange juice contains only 2 milligrams of sodium to 496 milligrams of potassium. Other good sources of potassium are lima beans, apricots, cantaloupes, broccoli, wheat germ, blackstrap molasses, chicken, salmon and halibut.

But you have to handle food properly to conserve its potassium. Because the mineral is water soluble, large amounts of potassium can leach out of vegetables into their cooking water. So it's a good idea to use as little water as possible when boiling vegetables, and to use that cooking water later to make soups and gravies. Better yet, steam your vegetables.

You'll find cooking methods like these throughout the book. And, of course, since the recipes use only natural foods, they're rich in potassium.

The chart that follows lists many of the foods used in the book (which have a good sodium/potassium balance) plus a few processed foods (which have a rotten balance) for contrast.

The important column is the last one, the sodium/potassium ratio expressed as a single number, the result of dividing the sodium content by the potassium content. Many scientists believe that the lower this number, the smaller the risk is that a food will raise the blood pressure. You can see from the very first two items how salting almonds affects their blood-pressure-raising potential. Unsalted almonds have a respectable ratio of 0.005; salting the nuts raises the ratio to 0.256 which is not nearly as favorable. Much worse comparisons occur when wholesome foods, like apples (ratio 0.007), are turned into extravaganzas like apple pie (ratio 3.8).

Sodium-Potassium Ratio of Selected Foods

Food	Portion Size	Sodium (milligrams)	Potassium (milligrams)	Ratio (sodium divided by potassium)
Almonds, salted, roasted	¼ cup	77.8	303.5	**0.256**
Almonds, unsalted	¼ cup	1.3	251.3	**0.005**
Apple	1 medium	1	152	**0.007**
Apple pie	⅛ pie	355	94	**3.8**
Asparagus	½ cup	0.5	132.5	**0.004**
Banana	1 medium	1	440	**0.002**
Beans, green	½ cup	2.5	94.5	**0.026**
Beans, kidney	½ cup	3	314.5	**0.01**

Sodium-Potassium Ratio of Selected Foods—*continued*

Food	Portion Size	Sodium (milligrams)	Potassium (milligrams)	Ratio (sodium divided by potassium)
Beef, lean ground	3 ounces	57	261	**0.218**
Beets	½ cup	36.5	117	**0.206**
Blueberries	½ cup	0.5	58.5	**0.009**
Broccoli, cooked	½ cup	8	207	**0.039**
Butter, salted	½ tablespoon	58.6	1.8	**32.6**
Butter, unsalted	½ tablespoon	0.8	1.8	**0.444**
Buttermilk, salted	1 cup	257	371	**0.693**
Buttermilk, unsalted	1 cup	122.5	371	**0.330**
Cabbage, shredded, cooked	½ cup	10	118	**0.085**
Carrot, raw	1 medium	34	246	**0.138**
Cashews, salted	¼ cup	70	162.5	**0.431**
Cashews, unsalted	¼ cup	5.3	162.5	**0.033**
Cauliflower, cooked	½ cup	5.5	129	**0.043**
Celery, raw	1 stalk	50	136	**0.368**
Cheese				
blue	2 ounces	792	146	**5.4**
Brie	2 ounces	356	86	**4.1**
Cheddar	2 ounces	352	56	**6.3**
cottage, creamed	½ cup	425	88.5	**4.8**
cream cheese	2 tablespoons	84	34	**2.5**
Parmesan, grated	1 tablespoon	93	5	**18.6**
ricotta, part-skim	½ cup	155	155	**1.0**
Swiss	2 ounces	148	62	**2.4**
Chicken	3 ounces	23.4	66.6	**0.351**
Cornmeal	¼ cup	0.3	86.5	**0.003**
Eggplant, diced	½ cup	1	150	**0.007**
Eggs	1 large	69	65	**1.1**
Flounder	3 ounces	201.2	498.4	**0.404**
Haddock	3 ounces	294.3	1464.9	**0.201**
Honey	1 tablespoon	1	11	**0.091**
Milk				
half-and-half	1 tablespoon	6	19	**0.316**
skim	1 cup	130	418	**0.311**
whole	1 cup	120	370	**0.324**
Mushrooms, raw sliced	½ cup	5.5	145	**0.038**
Mustard, brown	1 teaspoon	65	7	**9.3**
Oats, rolled, uncooked	½ cup	1	141	**0.007**
Onions, raw, chopped	¼ cup	4.3	66.8	**0.064**
Orange	1 medium	1	272	**0.004**

(continued)

Sodium-Potassium Ratio of Selected Foods—*continued*

Food	Portion Size	Sodium (milligrams)	Potassium (milligrams)	**Ratio (sodium divided by potassium)**
Parsley, chopped	2 teaspoons	1.3	16.7	**0.078**
Peanuts, salted, roasted, chopped	¼ cup	150.5	242.8	**0.62**
Peanuts, unsalted, roasted, chopped	¼ cup	1.8	252.3	**0.007**
Pears	1 medium	3	213	**0.014**
Peas, cooked	½ cup	1	157	**0.006**
Pepper, green, raw	1 medium	10	157	**0.064**
Potato, baked	1 medium	6	782	**0.008**
Raisins	¼ cup	9.8	276.5	**0.035**
Rice, brown, raw	¼ cup	4.5	107	**0.042**
Sour cream	1 tablespoon	6	17	**0.353**
Squash, summer, sliced	½ cup	1	127	**0.008**
Strawberries	½ cup	0.5	122	**0.004**
Tomato, raw	1 medium	4	300	**0.013**
Tuna, salted (in oil)	3 ounces	678.9	255.4	**2.7**
Tuna, salted (in water)	3 ounces	742.7	236.6	**3.1**
Tuna, unsalted (in water)	3 ounces	34.7	236.6	**0.147**
Turkey (flesh only)	3 ounces	27.6	116.4	**0.237**
Veal	3 ounces	41	190	**0.216**
Walnuts, English or Persian, chopped	¼ cup	0.5	135	**0.004**
Watercress, chopped	¼ cup	16.3	88.3	**0.185**
Whole wheat flour	¼ cup	1	111	**0.009**
Yogurt, low-fat	1 cup	159	531	**0.299**
Yogurt, whole milk	1 cup	105	351	**0.299**

SOURCES: Adapted from

Catherine F. Adams, *Nutritive Value of American Foods in Common Units,* Agriculture Handbook No. 456 (Washington, D.C.: Agricultural Research Service, U.S. Department of Agriculture, 1975).

Bernice K. Watt and Annabel L. Merrill, *Composition of Foods,* Agriculture Handbook No. 8 (Washington, D.C.: Agricultural Research Service, U.S. Department of Agriculture, 1975).

Consumer and Food Economics Institute, *Composition of Foods: Dairy and Egg Products,* Agriculture Handbook No.8-1 (Washington, D.C.: Agricultural Research Service, U.S. Department of Agriculture, 1976).

Consumer and Food Economics Institute, *Composition of Foods: Poultry Products,* Agriculture Handbook No. 8-5 (Washington, D.C.: Science and Education Administration, U.S. Department of Agriculture, 1979).

The Garlic and Onions Story

Keeping your diet low in sodium and high in potassium isn't the only way this book can help you. Many studies have shown that two prominent members of the herb family—garlic and onions—are also potent weapons against heart disease, dangerous blood clots and respiratory complaints, and so the book makes liberal use of them in its recipes.

Many scientists believe that heart disease may be caused by high levels of blood fats such as cholesterol and triglycerides, and studies show that garlic can lower those levels significantly. One comparison of the dietary habits of people in seven countries—including the United States—showed that people in garlic-loving countries like Greece and Italy had fewer coronary complaints than people in Britain, Finland, Holland and the United States—countries where garlic is often kept at arm's length (*Lancet,* January 19, 1980).

Researchers in India have also noted the protective results of garlic. When they compared the levels of cholesterol and triglycerides in the blood of three different groups of people, they found that people who ate the most garlic had the lowest levels of blood fats. And the group that ate some garlic was better protected against high fat levels than the third group, which ate none at all (*Indian Journal of Medical Research,* May 1979).

In another study, researchers actually pitted garlic against the legions of cholesterol-rich butter. They fed ten men slices of heavily buttered bread and, naturally, found that their cholesterol levels rose sharply. But when they repeated the experiment with garlic added to the menu, they found that the men's cholesterol levels remained virtually unchanged. And the best news—for those who find garlic's pungent flavor offensive—is that the garlic used in this test retained its cholesterol-fighting potency even after it had been boiled for 30 minutes (*Indian Journal of Nutrition and Dietetics,* April 1976).

In addition to its cholesterol-fighting properties, garlic also contains something that inhibits the abnormal clumping of blood platelets, a condition which can lead to dangerous blood clots. And clotting can trigger a heart attack.

In a study of garlic's anticlotting power, researchers gave garlic oil to both healthy individuals and heart attack victims for a period of three months. Then they measured the patients' "fibrinolytic activity," the blood's ability to resist clotting. The results? The healthy subjects registered a 130 percent increase in clot-fighting power. Subjects who had suffered heart attacks more than a year prior to the study also recorded an increase. But, best of all, those people who had suffered a heart attack recently—and had, in fact, begun taking garlic within 24 hours of their attack—were helped too. Their clot-resisting capacity leaped up 95.5 percent in just 20 days. That figure is especially important because the danger of a second attack is very real in the three weeks following a first crisis (*Atherosclerosis,* October 1977).

As the authors point out, there are several drugs that can increase fibrinolytic activity, but none can be used on a long-term basis to prevent heart disease. Garlic, however, produces no harmful side effects and is very affordable. Some doctors, for instance, prescribe aspirin to prevent artery-clogging clots, because it helps keep blood platelets from sticking together. Now, many of them have found that garlic can do the same thing—without aspirin's nasty side effects.

On to Onions

Onions' track record for lowering high levels of blood fats and reducing the risk of clotting is almost as impressive as garlic's. That's why you'll also find liberal amounts of onions in the recipes of this book. But before we get to cooking, let's look at some of the lowly onion's health achievements. Chemists at East Texas State University found that yellow onions contain a potent blood pressure-lowering agent. They discovered that the blood pressures of laboratory rats dropped dramatically after they were injected with this chemical (*Science,* April 1979). And a research team at George Washington School of Medicine determined that onions (along with garlic) contain a substance that inhibits platelet clumping by blocking the formation of a chemical that makes them stickier. The team's studies have shown that chemicals extracted from onion and garlic almost completely suppress the production of this clumping agent (*Prostaglandins and Medicine,* June 1979).

Like garlic, onions maintain their protective effect even after cooking. At Queen Elizabeth College in London, investigators fed healthy volunteers three different breakfasts. The first was low in calories and fat. The second was high in both — it contained cream, bacon, sausage and butter. And the third was identical to the second but also included fried onions. When the doctors measured platelet aggregation after these meals, they found that the high-fat food predictably increased blood clumping, but that the addition of onions actually neutralized it (*Lancet,* January 8, 1977).

So, we've come a long way from the beckoning cookbooks on a store's shelves, and — to many — it may seem like a way fraught with losses for us: the loss of salt's savor from our food, the loss of sugar's sweetness from our morning tea. What's worse, maybe, is that I've offered nothing more tasty than a lowered blood pressure in return. To counteract that unhappy impression, I'd like to put my argument in another way. The recipes in *Cooking with the Healthful Herbs* replace the simple tastes of salt and sugar with the complex and exotic flavors of an herb garden; in following the book's lead, we are *gaining* flavor, not losing it. And when one adds better health to the bargain, the scales definitely tip in our favor.

Chapter 2
Grow and Keep Fresh Herbs

Stocking Up

Herbs are like tomatoes and zucchini; when they're good, they're very good, and when they're plentiful, they're impossible to keep up with. Fortunately, like their vegetable companions, herbs can be stored for winter enjoyment. And although some methods preserve their fresh color and flavor better than others, all let you savor a summer crop long after winter has set in.

But first things first. No matter how you decide to preserve your herbs, there are a few basics to keep in mind. It's the volatile, aromatic oils present in the leaves that you want to preserve. Although even haphazard handling will leave *some* of these oils intact, a little care taken during harvest and processing will yield better results.

The best time to harvest herbs is just before the plants bloom. Once flowers form, the plants put all their energy into reproducing — into forming seeds — and forget about making the tender new leaves that are best for seasoning. To harvest, pinch off the top two to three inches of each stem; this not only prevents flowering and encourages bushy growth but it also preserves the most desirable leaves. If you start harvesting leaves properly early in the season, you can coax three or four crops out of your plants each summer.

An alternate method of gathering herbs is to pinch off the top two-thirds of a stem. This method provides the longer stems necessary for hanging herbs to dry. But you must be careful to leave at least one-third of a plant's stem, because taking more will weaken the plant — possibly beyond repair.

Although herbs can be harvested up until the first frost, stop large-scale cuttings from perennials a month before the first killing frost is expected to allow plants to build their strength for the long, hard winter ahead. Annuals, of course, are another story. Harvest the entire plant at season's end to salvage every last leaf.

Generally speaking, the summer's biggest harvest should come in August or early September. If you will be drying the herbs outside or in the attic, you will have plenty of warm weather to do the job, but even if you'll be using another method, this is still the best time to accomplish the task.

An herb's aromatic oils are strongest in the morning, after a night's rest. So gather leaves as early as possible in the day — after the dew has dried but before the sun gets hot enough to drive the oil into hiding. Use a sharp pair of kitchen shears to clip the stems and be careful not to bruise the tender leaves; basil is especially crushable.

If the herbs are dusty or mud splashed, wash them quickly in cool water. Hot water will destroy some of the essential oils. Remove any yellow or blemished leaves. Unless you'll be hanging the herbs by their stems or saving them for bouquets garnis, strip the leaves from the stalks. Although it's a bit time-consuming now, this procedure will save time and effort later. Keep the stems for fragrant fireplace kindling or as a nice addition to the backyard barbecue.

Drying Herbs

There are many ways to dry fresh herbs. Although dried herbs can never match the fragrance and flavor of fresh, some methods preserve the plant better than others. Bay leaves, marjoram, oregano, rosemary, savory, tarragon and thyme survive with most of their aromatic integrity intact. Sage is a borderline case that turns musty on too many occasions; it's better frozen, as are basil, chervil, chives, coriander, dill, mint and parsley.

When drying herbs — no matter what the method — remember:

- Herbs dried in direct sunlight lose some of their essential oils and hence their flavor. Always choose a shady or even dark spot for drying.
- Most dried herbs look alike. If you're drying more than one kind at a time, label the batches while you can still tell them apart.
- Herbs must be completely — that is, crisply — dry before they are stored or they may mold.
- Although herbs can be run through a sieve before bottling, they keep their flavor best if stored whole. Crumble the leaves at the time of use.
- Store your herbs in tightly closed (preferably opaque) jars. Label each with its name and the date of drying. Remember that dried herbs keep their flavor for no more than a year.
- Check your jars a few hours after closing them for any signs of moisture on the inside of the glass: This would indicate that the herbs were not completely cool and dry before the sealing. If any moisture is present, remove herbs and dry further.
- Drying concentrates an herb's flavor tremendously. Use from one-fourth to one-half *less* of a dried herb than you would of a fresh one. The exact amount will depend upon the particular herb and how long it's been stored. Start with the lesser amount and adjust to taste.

Here are some of the most-used methods of drying herbs:

Hanging. Gather long-stemmed herbs (such as marjoram, mint, oregano, rosemary, sage and savory). Tie the stems into small bunches. If the bunches are too dense, air won't be able to reach all the leaves, and they won't dry properly. Hang upside down from a rack, rope or the rafters in a warm, dry room or attic and out of direct sunlight. To ensure good air circulation, do not hang your bunches against a wall.

Let the bunches dry for one to two weeks, or until the leaves are crisp. Carefully remove the leaves from the stems and transfer to glass jars.

One disadvantage of this method is that the herbs get dusty during the drying period. Herbs can be kept dust-free by drying them inside paper bags. Using the method described above, drop the herbs into a bag and tie them at its neck. Make sure the bunches hang freely inside the bag. Cut the bottom from the bag or punch holes in the sides so that air can circulate freely. Check for dryness after two weeks.

You may also dry seed heads in paper bags. Gather anise, caraway, coriander, cumin, dill and fennel seed heads before they're ripe; that is, just as they turn from green to gray or brown. Tie the stems to the neck of the sack as with herb bunches, but, this time, leave the bottom in the bag, and punch holes in the sides of the sack instead. Your seeds should be dry in two to three weeks.

Tray Drying. Dry small herbs, large individual leaves and seed heads by the tray method. Use wire window screens, flat baskets or cheesecloth stretched over an old picture frame for the trays. Arrange herbs or seed pods in a single layer on a tray. If you're drying outdoors, cover with cheesecloth, an old sheet or another wire screen to keep off dust and to prevent the wind from blowing the herbs away. Position the trays so air can circulate freely around them, suspending between two sawhorses or over the arms of a chair, if necessary.

Place the trays in a shady spot outdoors or, in a warm, dry, airy room or attic out of direct sunlight. Either turn the trays over or gently stir the herbs every few days to promote even drying. Let stand a week or until the leaves are thoroughly brittle. One caution: When drying herbs outdoors, bring the trays inside at night so that the dew won't dampen them. Keep an eye out for summer rains, too.

To collect dried seeds, carefully rub the dried pods through your hands to loosen the seeds. Blow away the chaff (a small fan is helpful *if* it's not placed too close to the seeds) before storing in jars.

Oven Drying. Remove the leaves from their stems. Place in a single layer on trays or on sheets of brown paper into which you've cut air slits. Heat herbs in an oven at its lowest setting (about 100°F) for several hours. Leave the door ajar to allow the moisture to escape. From time to time, gently toss herbs for even drying. Check them frequently and remove the leaves as soon as they're brittle. Let them cool completely before placing in jars.

Microwaving. The obvious disadvantage of this method's small drying area is compensated for by its superfast processing time. Make sure herbs aren't damp before beginning. Place several sprigs or a handful of loose leaves between two paper towels. Turn the oven to the lowest setting, and dry the herbs for two or three minutes. If not brittle, return for another 30 seconds or so.

Using a Clothes Dryer. Although not a

very energy-conserving practice, this method does preserve the color and flavor of herbs better than some others. Strip leaves from their stems. Place them loosely in nylon net bags or large squares of cheesecloth. Tie the bags securely. Dry with moderate heat for two hours or more or until the leaves are completely crisp.

Freezing Herbs

In my experience, freezing herbs produces more satisfying results than drying. As with drying, you have a choice of methods: You can freeze herbs whole or chopped, plain or in ice, in oil or butter, singly or in combinations.

Certain herbs take exceptionally well to freezing—among them are basil, chervil, chives, coriander, dill, fennel, lovage leaves, mint, sorrel and tarragon. Since frozen herbs tend to darken and become limp when defrosted, they should be used without thawing. They can be added directly to simmering soups, stews and sauces or blended into dressings or mayonnaise. Plan on using the same amount of frozen herbs as you would fresh.

The easiest way to freeze herbs is to strip the leaves from their stems and lay them in a single layer on a cookie sheet before placing them in the freezer. When frozen, pack in heavy plastic bags or freezer containers. Seal airtight and label.

An alternate method is to chop the herbs first before freezing them on cookie sheets or directly in their bags or containers.

For easy measuring, place one or two tablespoons of chopped herbs in squares of foil or plastic wrap. Or place a similar amount in each of the sections of an ice cube tray, fill with water and freeze. When solid, remove the cubes from the tray and store them in bags or containers. To use, pop a cube or two into a pot of simmering food. To use in a salad dressing, allow a cube to thaw, pat the herbs dry and blend them into your dressing. If you'd like to freeze finely chopped herbs, blenderize them with water and fill the ice cube trays with the mixture.

Herbs can be frozen individually or in your favorite combinations. If you're freezing vegetables from the garden, you might want to tuck a sprig or two of compatible herb in the container. Savory goes well with green beans, dill or mint accents peas and rosemary complements corn.

Herbs can also be frozen in oil concentrates and in butter. Oil concentrates are very flavorful blends of herbs and oil; they're perfect for adding to marinades and dressings. Basil, rosemary, sage, tarragon and thyme take exceptionally well to this method. Just mix two cups of packed leaves with one-half cup of oil in a blender or food processor. If desired, one-half cup of parsley can be added for extra flavor. Freeze in ice cube trays. These blends are extremely concentrated: Use them sparingly.

Herb butters are invaluable for melting over broiled fish or cooked vegetables. Use them also to make herb bread, in sauces or cooked rice and over omelets or casseroles. To make them, cream one-half cup of softened butter with one-half cup of minced herbs. If you wish, add a teaspoon or two of lemon juice for extra zip.

Refrigerate the butter mixture until it's congealed enough to handle, and then form it into a log the size of a stick of butter; wrap well and freeze. You may also transfer the still-malleable butter to a pastry bag fitted with a large star tube. Use the tube to pipe rosettes of butter onto a cookie sheet lined with wax paper or foil, and refrigerate until hard. Peel the rosettes from the paper and place in bags or containers for freezing. The butter may also be formed into one-tablespoon balls before freezing.

To use either form, place a frozen rosette or ball on top of a hot food. Or thaw it for spreading on breads and biscuits. If your butter is in log form, use a sharp knife to cut off thin slices. Herb butter is purposely concentrated to save on freezer space. A little goes a long way, and you may want to dilute the effect with plain butter.

As with other methods of freezing herbs, butters can be made from single herbs or herb combinations. Here are some suggestions for useful combos. To one-half cup of butter add one of the following blends:

- two tablespoons each of basil, chives and marjoram, one tablespoon of rosemary and one tablespoon of lemon juice
- two tablespoons each of chervil, chives and parsley, and two teaspoons of tarragon
- three tablespoons each of basil and Parmesan cheese, one tablespoon of parsley and one clove of minced garlic
- three tablespoons each of dill and parsley
- three tablespoons each of tarragon and parsley
- two tablespoons each of chives, parsley and tarragon, and one-half teaspoon of dry mustard
- two tablespoons each of chervil, chives and dill, and two teaspoons of lemon juice
- three tablespoons each of chives and parsley, and two teaspoons of rosemary
- three tablespoons each of dill and oregano
- three tablespoons of parsley, one tablespoon of tarragon and two teaspoons of thyme
- two tablespoons each of chives, dill and tarragon

- one-half cup of mint and one tablespoon of lemon juice
- three tablespoons of savory and one teaspoon of dry mustard

Preserving Herbs in Oils and Vinegars

Finally, the essences of fresh herbs may also be preserved in oils and vinegars. The oils can be used for stir-frying and marinades as well as in salad dressings. The vinegars are excellent for salads and in marinades too.

To get started with this method, fill a glass jar with chopped herbs, and cover them with the desired oil. Let the mixture stand in a warm spot for a few weeks, and then strain it into a clean bottle for storage.

A slightly faster method is to place the jar of herbs and oil in a pan of gently boiling water and simmer it for 30 minutes; then, let stand for one week before straining.

To make garlic oil, add two or three crushed cloves to one pint of oil (olive oil is good). Let them steep four days before using. If you haven't used all the oil after two weeks, strain out the garlic before using the rest. Use the same method for making hot chili oil.

Remember that corn, soy, safflower and sunflower oils make a perfectly innocuous base for any herb. Some of the more flavorful herbs (such as rosemary or garlic) can stand up to the more robust olive oil. Sesame oil is rather strong and would probably overwhelm anything but garlic or chili peppers. Try light peanut oil with tarragon.

Before making an herb vinegar, make sure your herbs are completely dry. Otherwise, their moisture will dilute the vinegar. Since vinegar is acidic, use only glass containers to steep and store your vinegar, and try to use nonmetal lids to avoid a possible chemical reaction between the vinegar and the lid. If you must employ a metal lid, be sure the vinegar doesn't rise up to the lid. Check the mixture after it has been steeping a few days to make sure that the herbs are totally immersed in vinegar. Remember that the strength of the finished product will depend upon the amount of herbs used and the total steeping time. If your herb vinegar seems too strong, dilute with plain vinegar.

Almost any herb will produce a fine vinegar, although some combinations have more uses than others. Tarragon is, of course, the most widely employed. Use it in salad dressings, marinades, hollandaise sauce and in many French dishes. Certain other herbs impart both flavor and color to the finished vinegar. Purple basil gives a lovely burgundy color. For better flavor, though, use some green basil along with the purple. Both dill seed and chive flowers color vinegar a delicate pink.

Any vinegar will do as a base: Plain white, white wine, red wine, cider or rice wine vinegar are all fine. Although certain vinegars enhance certain herbs better than others, they're virtually interchangeable.

To make a flavored vinegar, fill a mason jar with chopped or bruised herbs—both the stems and leaves—and add enough vinegar to cover. Do *not* overfill the jar; the vinegar should not touch the metal lid when it is put in place. Then cap the jar, and let it stand in a sunny, warm spot for one or two weeks. Shake the jar occasionally, and strain through cheesecloth into bottles when finished. Add a fresh sprig of herb for decoration and easy identification.

Heating the vinegar before steeping the herbs speeds up the process, but it may also change the herbs' color and cause them to break down. If you're heating the vinegar, bring it just to the boiling point, pour over the herbs, cover and let the mixture steep a week. Strain as above.

To make garlic or shallot vinegar, blend several whole cloves of either herb with one cup of vinegar in a blender. Let the result stand in a covered jar in a warm spot for about two weeks and then strain it into a clean bottle. If it's too strong, dilute before using. For a hot spicy vinegar, steep several hot chili peppers in vinegar for 10 days (taking care to shake daily), and then strain into bottles.

Growing Herbs

All herbs may be divided into three categories: annuals, biennials and perennials.

Annuals have a one-year life cycle and must be planted anew each year (although a few will reseed themselves in the garden). Basil, chervil, coriander, dill and summer savory are among the most common annuals grown at home. In general, they're easily propagated by seed. Sow seeds directly in the garden or start plants indoors in pots about six weeks before the expected planting time. By starting your herbs indoors, you can get a jump on the growing season. Some annuals, like basil, root easily in water so that you can maintain your garden indoors at summer's end.

Biennials have a two-year growing cycle. They form leaves their first year and go on to make flowers and seeds the second. Even if you're raising plants for their second-year seeds, you should start new plants each year to assure an unbroken succession of harvests. Parsley and caraway are biennials and are usually propagated by seed like the annuals.

Perennials are long-lived plants that last for many years with the proper care. With the exception of French tarragon, perennials may be started from seed. However, plants grow larger sooner when propagated from cuttings, root divisions or stem layerings.

Chives, mint, oregano, sage, tarragon, thyme and winter savory are hardy perennials that will come back year after year once they've established themselves in a satisfactory spot. Marjoram, although technically a perennial, is sensitive to cold and must often be replanted each year in colder climates. Bay and rosemary are also tender perennials, and they're best potted and brought inside during the winter. When summer comes, they can either be placed on a porch or sunk in their pots in the garden and left until fall.

Cuttings, root divisions and layerings are the best ways of developing new plants. They work faster than seeds, and they're guaranteed to produce a child identical to its parent. Seeds sometimes produce a disappointing hybrid instead of the desired herb.

To take cuttings from plants like mint, rosemary and tarragon, snip the top 3 inches of a branch off with a sharp knife or kitchen shears. Then, strip off any leaves within 1½ inches of the cut. Recut the bottom at a slight angle with a clean, downward stroke. Finally, dip the cut end in rooting powder and plant the cutting in a 2¼-inch pot containing either a rooting mix (equal parts of milled sphagnum moss, crushed granite and screened compost or humus) or plain moist sand, peat moss or vermiculite. To create a hothouse atmosphere for better rooting, cover the pot

Guide to Growing Herbs

Name	Type of Plant	How to Propagate	When to Plant
Basil *Ocimum basilicum*	annual	seed	Sow outdoors after danger of frost has passed or sow indoors 6 weeks before last predicted frost.
Caraway *Carum carvi*	annual or biennial	seed (self-sowing)	Sow annual in early fall; biennial in early spring.
Chervil *Anthriscus cerefolium*	annual	seed (self-sowing)	Sow in early spring and late summer.
Chives *Allium schoenoprasum*	perennial	seed or division (self-sowing)	Sow indoors 6 to 8 weeks before last predicted frost.
Coriander *Coriandrum sativum*	annual	seed (self-sowing)	Plant in warm soil after danger of frost has passed.
Dill *Anethum graveolens*	annual	seed (self-sowing)	Sow in early spring, or may be planted all summer.

with a plastic bag. Set out of direct sunlight, and water to keep the soil from drying out. In about a month new roots should have formed.

Root division is also a simple matter. Dig up an established plant having more than one stem (like oregano, tarragon or thyme); either cut through the roots with a sharp knife or pull apart their sections; and immediately replant both halves.

Layering works with plants whose stems are flexible and fall over the ground (like rosemary, sage and tarragon). These stems often take root spontaneously and send up new plants. You can help them along by selecting a branch and bending it to the ground. About a foot from the branch's tip, scrape away a bit of the surface just below a leaf node.

Anchor this section to the ground with a hairpin, and cover with a fine, rich topsoil. Water, mulch and check in six weeks for new roots. Once it's rooted, cut the stem from the old plant, dig it up and relocate it elsewhere.

Although herbs grow wild in many parts of the world and can survive just about any environment given them, most have preferences about sun and soil. The better you can meet these preferences, the better your yield from those plants will be. The chart that follows lists the climatic tastes of some of the most commonly grown herbs.

In general, most herbs prefer a sunny, well-drained location with sandy, even gravelly, soil. Although too much fertilizer will reduce the amount of volatile oils in the leaves of

(continued on page 24)

Conditions Required	Tips for Companion Planting	Height (inches)	Color of Flower	Parts Used in Cooking
Full sun; rich soil; some wind protection	Protects tomatoes from insects and disease; plant near asparagus, but away from rue.	12–24	white	leaves
Full sun; average soil with good drainage	Plant here and there to loosen soil.	24–36	white	seeds
Full sun; partial shade; rich, moist soil	Improves growth and flavor of radishes.	12–18	white	leaves and stems
Full sun; rich soil	Plant near carrots, but away from beans and peas.	12–18	lavender	flowers and leaves
Full sun; rich loam with good drainage	Prevents fennel from setting seed; plant by itself, away from garden.	12–36	pink	seeds, leaves and stems
Full sun; good, moist soil	Plant near cabbage, cucumbers, lettuce and onions, but away from tomatoes and carrots.	24–36	yellow	seeds and leaves

(continued)

Guide to Growing Herbs—*continued*

Name	Type of Plant	How to Propagate	When to Plant
Fennel *Foeniculum vulgare*	perennial (treat as annual)	seed	Sow early in spring.
Garlic *Allium sativum*	perennial	bulb	Plant early in spring.
Marjoram *Origanum majorana*	tender perennial (treat as annual)	seed	Start indoors in March; transplant when the soil has warmed.
Mint *Mentha* spp.	perennial	seed, cutting or division	Cuttings may be taken during summer. Plant divisions in early spring.
Oregano *Origanum vulgare*	perennial	seed, cutting or division	Sow indoors in early spring; divide in spring; take cuttings in summer.
Parsley *Petroselinum crispum*	biennial (treat as annual)	seed	Sow seed in early spring.
Rosemary *Rosmarinus officinalis*	tender perennial (bring inside over winter)	seed, cutting or layering	Sprout cuttings in August. Place rooted cuttings in garden after danger of frost has passed.
Sage *Salvia officinalis*	perennial	seed, cutting or layering	Start seed indoors 6 to 8 weeks before last predicted frost or sow outdoors in April.
Summer Savory *Satureja hortensis*	annual	seed	Sow in early spring.
Winter Savory *Satureja montana*	perennial	seed	Sow in early spring.

Conditions Required	Tips for Companion Planting	Height (inches)	Color of Flower	Parts Used in Cooking
Full sun; good soil	Most plants dislike fennel; plant outside garden.	24-60	yellow	seeds and leaves
Full sun; rich, moist, sandy soil	Repels Japanese beetles; plant near potatoes, tomatoes and cabbage.	12-24	white	bulb
Full sun; dry soil	Plant throughout garden to improve flavor of vegetables	12	white or pink	leaves and flower knots
Partial shade; moist, slightly acid soil	Plant peppermint near cabbage to repel cabbage butterfly; put spearmint and peppermint near radishes and tomatoes.	12-24	purple, white, pink or lavender	leaves
Full sun; fairly dry soil	Good near vine crops such as cucumbers and melons.	12-20	pink, white, purple or lilac	leaves
Full sun, but will tolerate partial shade; average soil	Repels rose beetles and carrot flies; plant near tomatoes and asparagus.	10-15	greenish yellow	leaves and stems
Full sun; alkaline soil that is well drained. Bring indoors in winter or store dormant in cool cellar.	Repels cabbage butterfly, bean beetles and carrot flies; grows well near sage.	24-36	blue, white or pink	leaves
Full sun; sandy soil	Plant with rosemary, cabbage and carrots; keep away from cucumbers.	12-24	blue, purple or red	leaves
Full sun; rich and fairly dry soil	Plant with tomatoes, beans and onions; repels bean beetle and tomato hornworm.	12-18	pink to violet	leaves
Full sun; light, sandy soil	Plant throughout garden; general insect repeller.	12	white or purple	leaves

(continued)

Guide to Growing Herbs—*continued*

Name	Type of Plant	How to Propagate	When to Plant
French Tarragon *Artemisia dracunculus* var. *sativa*	perennial	cutting	Cuttings may be taken during midsummer. Plant cuttings after danger of frost has passed.
Thyme *Thymus vulgaris*	perennial	seed, cutting or division	Sow indoors in early spring.

many herbs, a little compost turned into the soil before planting will get most off to a better start. Most herbs like at least five hours of sun a day, although some (like chives, chervil, mint and tarragon) will tolerate partial shade better than others.

Mulch your herbs well (with cocoa hulls, grass clippings, chopped hay or straw) to conserve the soil's moisture and to keep down competition from weeds. Feed your plants occasionally with weak manure tea or fish emulsion, being careful not to feed too often.

It should be said that the chart is merely a suggestive guide to growing herbs, because it's hard to be specific about heights and flower color when you're dealing with a family as large and varied as the herb clan. I've seen as many as 15 different basils, 24 mints and 20 rosemaries offered in some nursery catalogs, and I'm sure even more are available. Heights vary from variety to variety and from garden to garden. The oregano that grows two feet high in one soil barely lifts its head from the ground in another. Flower color, of course, depends upon the specific variety of herb.

I've also included what are called companion planting traits in the chart. Companion planting is the practice of placing plants that "like" each other close together in a garden to boost growth.

By odd (or maybe not so odd) coincidence, many garden companions are kitchen buddies as well: basil and tomatoes; savory and beans; chives and carrots. For quick harvesting when mealtime comes, it pays to put those plants near each other. In addition, certain herbs are thought to repel or destroy insect pests in the garden. Although there isn't a wealth of scientific studies backing up the theory, many experienced gardeners swear it works, and so some of these pest-defenders are included.

Finally, the most important requirement of an herb garden is easy access. Try to locate it conveniently—preferably near the kitchen door—so it'll be easy to pop outside any time you need a sprig of this or that fragrant, flavorful accent to your everyday cooking.

Herbs Indoors

You can easily grow enough herbs indoors to last you through a long winter—if you respect a few of their basic requirements concerning light, humidity and soil. Most annuals

Conditions Required	Tips for Companion Planting	Height (inches)	Color of Flower	Parts Used in Cooking
Moderate sun; fertile, loamy soil; good drainage	Plant throughout garden.	24–36	whitish green	leaves
Full sun; sandy soil	Repels white cabbage butterfly and cabbage worm.	6–12	lavender, pink or white	leaves

and perennials can be grown indoors in pots. I've grown basil, chives, coriander, marjoram, mint, oregano, parsley, rosemary, sage, savory and thyme. Although yields aren't equal to those outdoors, the fresh fragrance and flavor of just-picked herbs more than compensates for the small harvest.

Herbs can be started indoors from seed, although using root cuttings taken from your garden in late August sometimes goes faster. You can also pot whole plants from the garden and cart them indoors, but that takes more preparation and tends to give less satisfactory results. Besides needing top and root pruning in August to fit into pots, these plants also need to be quarantined from other houseplants when they are brought indoors to prevent the possible spread of insect infestation.

If you are starting herb plants from seed, use a soilless potting mixture, and place it in small flats or individual peat pots. Follow the planting instructions printed on the seed packets. Then moisten the soil, and cover the containers with a plastic bag until the seeds germinate; the bag will keep in moisture and provide a hothouse environment. Transplant your new seedlings when they have grown two sets of leaves.

A point to remember when planting seeds: Do not let your enthusiasm overrule good sense! Plants seeded too thickly will soon tangle themselves into a mass of seedlings that are too delicate to transplant and too crowded to flourish.

In general, herbs indoors need a clean, porous potting mix that will hold moisture without collapsing into a hard lump. Most garden soil doesn't quite fit the bill indoors, and it is also likely to harbor undesirable weeds and insects. There are, however, suitable potting mixtures you can make yourself. Try equal parts of sterile potting soil, sand and fine peat moss. Or equal parts of fine peat moss, vermiculite and perlite. Or equal parts of sand, loam and fine compost. Or equal parts of sterile potting soil, perlite, fine peat moss and vermiculite. A problem with these potting mixtures is that they don't supply as many nutrients as garden soil does, and you must feed your indoor plants occasionally with either weak manure tea or weak fish emulsion.

Adequate light is essential for indoor gardening. Most herbs want at least 5 hours of full sunlight a day. A wide, sunny windowsill is often sufficient to keep your herbs happy, but full-spectrum fluorescent lights are even better. Give herbs grown under lights about 14 to 16 hours of light a day. Seedlings should be placed about three inches from the light source. To accommodate both tall and short plants under your lights, you may need platforms for the shorter ones. Remember that the light is most intense at the middle of these tubes and diminishes at the ends. You will have to arrange your plants along the tube's length according to their light preferences. Cuttings tend to be satisfied with a little less light and can be positioned near the ends of the tubes.

Let your herbs have a breath of fresh air now and then—especially on warm winter days. But make sure they don't have to endure constant drafts. Try to keep the temperature between 50° and 70°F.

Keep the plants evenly moist. Don't allow them to sit in water or become bone dry. Because indoor air tends to be very dry in winter, mist the leaves frequently with tepid water. For even more humidity, place bowls of water near your herbs. Or put a deep layer of pebbles in some plant trays along with enough water to fill them to just below the top of the pebbles. Set your pots on the pebbles, being careful that they aren't actually sitting in the water. Evaporation will keep the air humid around them.

A few insects (like spider mites, mealybugs, scale or whiteflies) may attack your plants. As a counterattack, you can try picking them off by hand or rinsing the foliage in soapy water. Fill a sink with lukewarm water, then add a few drops of mild dish detergent. Cover the soil with foil or plastic wrap (to avoid a sinkful of dirt); then turn the plants upside down, and swish the leaves through the water. Rinse with clear water. Repeat as necessary.

For more detailed information on growing herbs both indoors and out, see *The Rodale Herb Book* (Rodale Press, 1974) and Millie Owen's excellent book, *A Cook's Guide to Growing Herbs, Greens, and Aromatics* (Alfred A. Knopf, 1978).

Chapter 3

A Kitchen Herbal

Spicy Bits

Here's a brief introduction to most of the herbs and spices used in the recipes and some suggestions for their use.

Allspice
- Comes from a tropical evergreen tree (*Pimenta dioica*).
- Part used: the hard, dry reddish brown berries, which combine the flavors of cinnamon, cloves and nutmeg.
- Available whole and ground commercially.
- Use in tomato sauce; for poaching fish; in spicy meatballs; with carrots, eggplant, squash, sweet potatoes and tomatoes; also in pumpkin and mincemeat pies.

Anise
- An annual herb (*Pimpinella anisum*) that grows well in home gardens.
- Parts used: the small grayish brown seeds and the feathery leaves; both have a sweet, licorice taste.
- Available commercially as whole or ground seeds and in extract.
- Use in coleslaw, spicy meat mixtures, rye bread, cookies and apple pie.
- Star anise (*Illicium verum*) is the fruit of a Chinese evergreen tree and cannot be grown in home gardens. The large, smooth brown seeds are used in teas and oriental cooking.

Basil
- A bushy annual herb from the mint family; easily grown at home.
- Part used: the leaves.
- Available dried whole or crumbled commercially; sometimes found fresh.
- Use in Italian and other Mediterranean

cuisines; in tomato or vegetable soup; in tomato sauce; with fish, poultry, beef, veal or lamb; in scrambled eggs and omelets; and with green beans, broccoli, cucumbers, eggplant, peas, spinach, tomatoes and zucchini.

- The best way to preserve basil is to blend it with oil and store in the refrigerator or freezer. You can also freeze the leaves whole in plastic bags.

Bay

- Comes from a tree native to the Mediterranean area (*Laurus nobilis*); can be grown outside year-round in warm areas but must be potted and taken indoors during cold months in northern areas.
- Part used: the leaves.
- Available dried whole commercially.
- Use sparingly as its powerful flavor easily overwhelms. Use in bouquet garni, fish chowders, tomato juice and stocks; with poached fish; in hearty fish dishes; and with roast chicken, beef roasts and beef stew.
- Leaves can be used fresh, although flavor is better when leaves are dried a bit.

Caraway

- A biennial herb of Europe and Asia; can be grown at home.
- Part used: the dark brown, bow-shaped seeds.
- Available whole and sometimes ground commercially.
- Use in cabbage soup; with cabbage and on cucumber salads; in hearty meat dishes, goulash, meatballs, rye bread and cheese spreads; with green beans, carrots, potatoes and red beets; and in apple pie, cookies and cakes.

Cardamom

- Comes from a perennial plant of the ginger family; native to India.
- Part used: the small green or white pods containing the dark, reddish brown seeds.
- Available commercially as whole or ground pods or seeds; a variety with larger dark brown pods is also available in some markets.
- Use in curry dishes; with fish or poultry; in meat marinades and Swedish meatballs; in spiced punches; with cabbage, pumpkin and sweet potatoes; with apples, honeydew melons, peaches, raspberries and strawberries; also in pastries, cakes and custards.
- Cardamom holds its flavor best when stored whole; roughly 10 seeds make up one-half teaspoon when ground; "ground decorticated cardamom" indicates that the seeds were removed from their pods before grinding.

Cayenne Pepper

- Made from small, hot red peppers.
- Part used: the whole fruit.
- Available ground commercially.
- Use sparingly in soups, stews, salad, curries, Mexican dishes and sauces; and with cottage cheese, eggs and various vegetables.

Celery Seed

- Comes from wild celery, also called smallage.
- Part used: the small, brown, aromatic seeds with their strong celery flavor.
- Available whole or ground commercially.
- Use sparingly in soups, stews, salads, curry dishes, poultry stuffing, fish and meat dishes; also with eggs, breads and vegetables.

Chervil

- An annual herb with lacy leaves resembling parsley; easily grown at home.
- Parts used: the leaves and stems with their delicate anise flavor and scent.
- Available dried commercially.
- Use as a garnish and in potato, spinach and cream soups; in egg and chicken salads, salad dressings and mayonnaise; with fish, shellfish and chicken; in fish sauces and cheese spreads; with lettuce, potatoes, red beets and tomatoes, in a *fines herbes* combination.
- The delicate flavor of fresh chervil is destroyed by heat; add at the last minute to hot dishes.

Chives

- A member of the onion family; easily grown at home.
- Parts used: the slender, dark green, tubular leaves and the lavender flowers.
- Available freeze-dried or frozen commercially; sometimes found potted.
- Use with all foods but sweets. Use in cream soups and vichyssoise; with fish, chicken and lamb; in salads and cheese sauces; and with cheeses, eggs, carrots, corn, green beans, mushrooms, peas, red beets, summer squash and tomatoes.
- The flowers make an attractive garnish; use whole or divided into petals.
- The best way to store chives is to freeze them whole or chopped.

Cinnamon

- Comes from a glossy evergreen tree grown in Sri Lanka (*Cinnamomum zeylanicum*).
- Part used: the inner bark, which is peeled from the tree, rolled and dried.

- Available whole or ground commercially.
- Use in curries; with couscous, chicken, lamb and ground beef; in stews, meat and fruit combinations; with carrots, eggplant, onions, spinach, winter squash, tomatoes, apples, blueberries and pears; also in fruit compotes, rice pudding, apple pie, cakes, fruitcakes and nut breads.

Cloves

- Come from an evergreen tree (*Syzygium aromaticum*) native to the Moluccas.
- Part used: the unopened flower buds that dry into deep brown bits that resemble small nails.
- Available whole or ground commercially.
- Use in onion soup, curries, chili sauce, tomato sauce and marinades; with spicy meat, fish and poultry dishes and roast chicken; in spiced beverages; with green beans, red beets and winter squash; in puddings, preserves, applesauce, gingerbread and cakes; and with poached pears, stewed fruits and nut breads.

Coriander

- An annual herb (*Coriandrum sativum*) easily grown at home.
- Parts used: the fresh leaves and stems or the dried seeds.
- Available commercially as whole or ground seeds; the fresh leaves and occasionally the dried leaves may be found in ethnic markets.
- Use the seeds in curries and pickling spice mixtures; with lentils, lima beans, peas and potato dumplings; in biscuits, breads, lamb dishes; also in carrot cake and pies. Use the leaves in Mexican, Chinese, Indian and Moroccan dishes; in meat, rice and lentil dishes; with corn, zucchini and chicken; and in salads.

- Fresh coriander and coriander seeds are not interchangeable; their flavors differ greatly.

Cumin

- An annual of the parsley family with origins in ancient Egypt; it can be grown at home in areas where there are four warm months.
- Part used: the brown elongated seeds that follow the small white or red flowers and ripen in the fall.
- Available whole or ground commercially.
- Use in Mexican, oriental, Indian and Middle Eastern dishes; in curries, stews, chili, spicy meat and vegetable dishes; with green beans and cabbage; in deviled eggs and breads; and with cheese.

Dill

- An annual member of the parsley family native to the Mediterranean area; easily grown at home.
- Parts used: the feathery green leaves and the dried brown seeds.
- Available commercially as fresh or dried leaves and whole or ground seeds.
- Use the leaves with salads and salmon; in potato salad, rice dishes and borscht; with cottage cheese, green beans, carrots, cucumbers and potatoes. Use the seeds in salad dressings, fish soups, meat dishes, lamb stew, and egg and potato dishes; also with cabbage and in breads.

Fennel

- A tender perennial suitable for home growing. Two common varieties are sweet fennel and Florence fennel.
- Parts used: the sweet fennel seeds and leaves; the vegetable-like stalks of Florence fennel.

- Sweet fennel available commercially as whole or ground seeds; Florence fennel available fresh.
- Use sweet fennel with fish; in spicy meat mixtures; with eggs, cabbage, red beets, squash and apples; and in stuffings and breads. Use Florence fennel as a vegetable; serve raw like celery, braise, bake au gratin or turn into a cream soup.

Garlic

- A small pungent member of the onion family, easily grown at home.
- Part used: the bulb which divides into cloves.
- Available fresh commercially or dried to form garlic chips or powder.
- Use with everything but sweets. Use for soups, salads, fish, poultry, meat and egg dishes; in stews, sauces and mayonnaise; in breads and with any vegetables; and to make oil and vinegar dressing.
- Long, slow cooking softens garlic's flavor; high heat and browning turn it bitter.

Ginger

- Comes from a perennial plant (*Zingiber officinale*) indigenous to Southeast Asia.
- Part used: the root.
- Available fresh and dried commercially; the dried form is often ground.
- Use fresh ginger in oriental and Indian dishes and with fish, chicken, meats and vegetables. Use dried ginger with pot roasts, poultry, carrots, red beets, squash and sweet potatoes; also in breads, cakes, cookies, puddings, fruit salad dressings and in stewed fruit mixtures.

Horseradish
- A perennial of the mustard family that may have originated in Hungary.
- Part used: the root.
- Available fresh whole or prepared commercially; it is sometimes sold in dried granular form.
- Use in cocktail and mustard sauces; in sauces for fish, roast beef and green vegetables; in salad dressings; with boiled meats; in sandwiches; and with red beets.

Lovage
- A perennial native to the Mediterranean area with a strong celery taste; it is easily grown at home.
- Parts used: the stalks, leaves and seeds.
- Not widely available commercially; grow your own.
- Use the leaves and stalks sparingly as a celery substitute in soups, salads, potato salad, stews and stuffings; braise the stalks as a vegetable. Use the seeds in chicken salad, meat loaf, breads and herb butter.

Mace
- Comes from the same tropical evergreen tree that produces nutmeg (*Myristica fragrans*): native to the Moluccas.
- Part used: the lacy red covering of the nutmeg seed.
- Available ground and sometimes whole commercially; the whole forms are called blades.
- Use in fish and poultry dishes; in meatballs and meat loaf; with veal, cheese dishes, broccoli, brussels sprouts, cabbage, succotash and yellow vegetables; in baked goods and custards; also with stewed apricots, cherries and peaches.

Marjoram
- A tender perennial from the mint family, a first cousin to oregano and easily grown at home.
- Parts used: the leaves and knots or flower buds.
- Available commercially as dried whole, crumbled or ground leaves.
- Use in chicken soup, onion soup, tomato juice, fish recipes, fish chowders, chicken salad, beef stew, hamburgers, meat loaf, chili and tossed salad; with cottage cheese; in omelets and scrambled eggs; with cabbage, carrots, eggplant, lima beans, mushrooms, peas, spinach and tomatoes; and with cooked fruits.

Mint
- From an extensive family of perennials that includes peppermint and spearmint.
- Part used: the leaves.
- Available fresh commercially or dried in the form of whole, crumbled or ground leaves.
- Use with fruit and vegetable salads; in cucumber soup; with fish, beef, veal and lamb; with green beans, carrots, cucumbers, eggplant, peas, potatoes and spinach; in yogurt dishes; and with desserts.

Mustard
- Annual plants that grow wild in much of the world and can be grown at home.
- Part used: the seeds. Black mustard plants produce dark, reddish brown seeds that are potent in flavor; white mustard plants produce milder, pale yellow seeds.
- Available commercially as whole seeds, ground and prepared.
- Use as a pickling spice; in salad dressings

and potato salad; with creamed fish, egg dishes, deviled eggs, baked beans, cheese and chutneys; and with marinated green beans or cauliflower.

Nutmeg
- Comes from a tropical evergreen tree (*Myristica fragrans*) native to the Moluccas.
- Part used: the grayish brown, oval seed.
- Available whole or ground commercially.
- Use in fish stews and Swedish meatballs; with green beans, carrots, cauliflower, corn, onions, spinach and squash; in potato dumplings; in apple, cherry and pear pies; also in custards, pumpkin pie, cakes, cookies and nut breads.

Onion
- A large family of herbs whose members are easily grown at home. Some of the choices are yellow, white and red.
- Parts used: the bulb and sometimes the green leaves.
- Available fresh, dehydrated, frozen or as onion powder.
- Use for all dishes except sweets. Use in soups, stews, salads and egg dishes; and with fish, poultry, meat and all vegetables.

Oregano
- A perennial closely related to marjoram; easily grown at home.
- Part used: the leaves.
- Available commercially dried whole, crumbled or ground.
- Use in vegetable soups, tomato sauces, stews, meatballs, meat loaf, tomato and pasta dishes; on pizza; in potato salad, salad dressings and green salads; with omelets; in chili; also with broccoli, cabbage, mushrooms, onions, peas and potatoes.

Paprika
- Mild peppers (*Capsicum annuum*) that are widely cultivated; the Hungarian variety has the fullest flavor; the Spanish and American are the brightest red.
- Part used: the whole pepper.
- Available ground commercially.
- Use in Hungarian dishes, sauces and salad dressings; with noodles; also in chicken and veal paprika, beef stroganoff and goulash.
- Store in refrigerator to preserve flavor.

Parsley
- Biennial plant known to early Greeks and Romans; easily grown at home. The two main varieties are the curly leaved and the flat leaved (Italian) which has a fuller flavor.
- Parts used: the leaves and stems (for their stronger flavor).
- Available fresh or dried commercially.
- Use in all dishes except sweets. Use in bouquet garni, *fines herbes*, soups, stews and salads; also with fish, meat, poultry and all vegetables.
- Best frozen for at-home preservation.

Peppercorns
- Come from a perennial climbing vine (*Piper nigrum*) native to India. Available in black, white and green varieties. The pink peppercorns found in gourmet markets come from the Brazilian pepper tree and are not related to the *Piper nigrum*.
- Part used: the dried berry.
- Available commercially as whole, crushed, coarsely ground or finely ground black and white pepper; the green available dried or packed in water or vinegar.
- Use with all foods except desserts.

(continued)

Note: Some researchers believe pepper to be a mild cocarcinogen, meaning it may act together with certain more powerful substances to promote the development of cancer. Although the evidence is not conclusive, I have avoided adding pepper to recipes except where it is an integral part of an ethnic dish or spice mixture.

Poppy Seed

- Comes from a particular species of poppy (*Papaver somniferum*).
- Part used: the tiny, slate blue seeds that form after the seed pods have dried and lost their narcotic properties.
- Available whole commercially.
- Use with noodles, eggs and cheese; in dressings, coleslaw and deviled eggs; in fruit and vegetable salads, breads and rolls; with peas, rutabagas and turnips; and in cakes and pastries.
- Heat or crush the seeds to release their essential oils and to stimulate their full nutty flavor.

Rosemary

- A tender, perennial, evergreen shrub akin to mint and native to the Mediterranean area; can be grown outside year-round in warm areas but must be potted and taken indoors during cold months in northern areas.
- Part used: the narrow needlelike leaves.
- Available as the dried whole leaf commercially.
- Use in chicken soup, pea soup, stews, and poultry or fish stuffings; with poultry, roast meats and lamb; in meat marinades; with omelets and scrambled eggs; in deviled eggs; with green beans, broccoli, cauliflower, carrots, peas, spinach and zucchini; and in sour cream dips, fruit cups and breads.

Saffron

- Comes from a purple crocus (*Crocus sativus*) native to the Mediterranean area and Asia; the best saffron comes from Spain.
- Part used: the dried orange stigmata of the crocus.
- Available commercially in the form of the whole stigma (an inch long, brownish red) or ground; buy the whole stigma when possible for the best flavor.
- Use in bouillabaisse, paella and curries; with poultry and seafood; in stews and cream soups; with rice and potatoes; in scrambled eggs; also in buns and cream cheese spreads.
- One of the most expensive spices in the world. Use sparingly to avoid an overpowering flavor.

Sage

- A perennial shrub native to the northern Mediterranean area; easily grown at home
- Part used: the leaves.
- Available dried whole, crumbled or ground commercially.
- Use in poultry seasonings and stuffings; in fish chowders; with fish, veal, lamb and roast beef; in cheese spreads, chicken salad, French dressing, corn bread and omelets; and with cottage cheese, carrots, corn, eggplant, lima beans, onions, squash and tomatoes.

Savory

- Comes in two varieties and from two different plants: annual summer savory and perennial winter savory. Both are easily grown at home; many prefer summer savory for its more delicate flavor.
- Part used: the leaves.

- Available dried whole or ground commercially.
- Use in tomato juice and fish chowder; with fish, crab, meat dishes, meat loaf, meatballs and poultry seasoning; in potato salad and rice; with eggs and deviled eggs; also with cabbage, cauliflower, green beans, lentils, lima beans, peas, red beets, summer squash and onions.

Sesame Seed

- Comes from a tropical annual plant (*Sesamum indicum*); can be grown at home in the South.
- Part used: the small, creamy white seeds.
- Available commercially whole toasted or untoasted; it is also ground into a paste (tahini) or made into sesame oil.
- Use in casseroles, soups and salads; with fish, poultry, meats and eggs; and on crackers, breads, rolls and cakes. Tahini is used in confections, hummus, and Middle Eastern dishes. Sesame oil is used in Chinese cooking.
- Heating or toasting releases sesame's rich, nutlike flavor.

Shallots

- A small, brown-skinned member of the onion family whose flavor lies somewhere between onion and garlic; can be grown at home but requires about 100 days to mature.
- Part used: the bulb.
- Available fresh or freeze-dried commercially.
- Use to flavor all dishes except sweets. Good in salads, dressings, omelets, crepes and with all vegetables.

Sorrel

- A perennial prized for its sour lemon taste; easily grown at home.
- Part used: the leaves.
- Not widely available commercially; grow your own.
- Use in French cooking; in *shav* soup, potato soup and cream soups; with fish, seafood and chicken; in salads and omelets; as a piquant substitute or addition to spinach; also with tomatoes.

Tarragon

- A perennial plant native to Russia; easily grown at home. The preferred French tarragon must be propagated from cuttings.
- Part used: the leaves.
- Available dried whole, crumbled or ground commercially.
- Use in *fines herbes*, béarnaise sauce, salad dressings, tartar sauce and mayonnaise; in potato salad and green salads; with chicken, fish, shellfish, lamb, veal and turkey; in omelets and deviled eggs; with cottage cheese; and with asparagus, mushrooms, peas, baked potatoes, red beets, spinach and tomatoes.

Thyme

- A bushy, low-growing perennial native to the Mediterranean area; easily grown at home.
- Part used: the leaves.
- Available dried whole or ground commercially.
- Use in bouquet garni, fish chowders, tomato juice and poultry stuffings; with roast chicken, meat loaf, salmon and halibut; in seafood sauces and dressings; with eggs, cheese

and cottage cheese; in herb blends; with green beans, carrots, celery, mushrooms, onions, potatoes, red beets, squash, tomatoes and zucchini; and in corn bread.

Turmeric
- Comes from a tropical plant of the ginger family that is native to southern India and Indonesia.
- Part used: the root.
- Available ground commercially.
- Used as a cheap saffron substitute for its bright yellow color. Good in curries, salads, dressings and mustard; with seafood, fish, poultry and meat; in rice dishes; and with eggs.

Vanilla
- Comes from a tropical vine of the orchid family (*Vanilla planifolia*) that is native to Mexico.
- Part used: the large, dried seed pod.
- Available whole or as an extract commercially.
- Use in desserts; with fruit; and in custards, puddings, preserves, compotes, pies, cookies and cakes.

Watercress
- A perennial member of the mustard family native to the northern United States; can be grown at home near gently flowing, cool water or in containers of water that are frequently changed.
- Parts used: the leaves and stems.
- Available fresh commercially.
- Use liberally in salads, chicken salad, bean salad, potato salad and coleslaw; in tomato juice, soups and egg dishes; with cottage cheese; and in herb butter.

What Goes Well with Cabbage?

Or carrots? Or fish? Or potatoes? What herbs go best with . . . (whatever) is often the question that comes up right after, what's for dinner? While it's true that most herbs go with most foods, there are some pairings that are especially successful. On the opposite page, there is a chart of 28 common foods and some of the herbs that flatter them. Since parsley and onions perk up almost everything but sweets, I haven't always listed them. Naturally, this chart isn't meant to be the final word on the subject, but it can be a starting point for your own experiments in herbal matchmaking.

Herb and Spice Blends

Beginning on page 39, you'll find a collection of herb and spice blends that you can mix ahead and keep in the cupboard for instant seasoning. Some are all-purpose blends for use in many soups, stews, egg dishes, cottage cheese and so on, and others are more specifically wedded to certain foods.

The quantities are purposely small so that they can be stored in empty spice jars or saltshakers. For blends to be used by the spoonful at the stove, simply mix the herbs, store them in tightly capped jars and pulverize at the time of use.

For blends to be used at the table, pulverize the herbs first with a mortar and pestle or spice mill, and then pour them into shakers. For best flavor preservation, place a piece of wax paper under the lid, and store the shakers in the refrigerator between uses.

In general, store curry and chili powders in the refrigerator to keep their flavors from fading.

Traditional Kitchen Match-Ups

Beans, Dried
cumin
garlic
onions
parsley
sage
savory
thyme

Beans, Green
basil
cloves
dill
marjoram
mint
savory
thyme

Beef
basil
bay leaf
chili pepper
cumin
garlic
ginger
marjoram
onions
oregano
parsley
rosemary
sage
savory
tarragon
thyme

Bread
anise
basil
caraway
cardamom
cinnamon
coriander
cumin
dill
garlic
onions
oregano
parsley
poppy seeds
rosemary
sage
sesame seeds
thyme

Broccoli
basil
dill
garlic
nutmeg
oregano

Cabbage
basil
caraway
cayenne pepper
dill
marjoram
savory

Cakes and Pastry
allspice
anise
cardamom
cinnamon
cloves
fennel
ginger
nutmeg

Carrots
basil
chervil
chives
cinnamon
cloves
cumin
dill
ginger
marjoram
mint
parsley
savory

Cauliflower
basil
cumin
dill
garlic
marjoram
parsley
rosemary
savory
tarragon

Cheese
basil
chervil
chives
coriander
curry powder
dill
garlic
marjoram
parsley
sage
tarragon
thyme

Chicken
allspice
basil
bay leaf
cinnamon
curry powder
dill
garlic
ginger
mace
marjoram
nutmeg
onions
paprika
parsley
rosemary
saffron
sage
savory
thyme

Cottage Cheese
basil
chives
cinnamon
curry powder
dill
paprika
thyme

Eggplant
basil
cinnamon
garlic
marjoram
onions
oregano
parsley
savory
thyme

Eggs
basil
chervil
chives
coriander
curry powder
dill
fennel
marjoram
oregano
paprika
parsley
rosemary
sage
savory
tarragon
thyme

Fish
basil
chives
curry powder
dill
garlic
ginger
marjoram
oregano
parsley
sage
savory
tarragon
thyme

Fruit
anise
cinnamon
cloves
ginger
mace

(continued)

Traditional Kitchen Match-Ups—*continued*

Fruit—*continued*
mint
nutmeg
rosemary

Lamb
basil
bay leaf
cinnamon
coriander
cumin
curry powder
dill
garlic
ginger
mint
onions
parsley
rosemary
tarragon
thyme

Mushrooms
coriander
marjoram
oregano
tarragon
thyme

Parsnips
basil
curry powder
dill
marjoram
parsley
thyme

Potatoes
caraway
chives
dill
marjoram
oregano
paprika
parsley
rosemary
tarragon
thyme

Salads, Green
basil
chervil
chives
coriander
dill
garlic
marjoram

mint
oregano
parsley
rosemary
tarragon
thyme

Soups
basil
bay leaf
chives
dill
garlic
marjoram
onions
parsley
rosemary
sage
savory
thyme

Spinach
allspice
basil
chives
nutmeg
rosemary

Squash
allspice
basil
cinnamon
cloves
dill
marjoram
nutmeg
rosemary
savory

Stuffings
garlic
marjoram
parsley
onions
rosemary
sage
thyme

Tomatoes
basil
bay leaf
chives
garlic
oregano
parsley

rosemary
savory
tarragon
thyme

Turkey
basil
garlic
marjoram
onions
rosemary
saffron
sage
savory
tarragon
thyme

Veal
basil
bay leaf
chervil
marjoram
onions
parsley
rosemary
savory
thyme

Herb and Spice Blends

All-Purpose Blend I

1 tablespoon dried parsley
1½ teaspoons celery flakes
1 teaspoon ground toasted sesame seeds
½ teaspoon onion powder
½ teaspoon paprika
½ teaspoon dried thyme
½ teaspoon dried marjoram
¼ teaspoon garlic powder
⅛ teaspoon cayenne pepper

Makes about 3 tablespoons.

All-Purpose Blend II

1 teaspoon dried basil
1 teaspoon celery flakes
1 teaspoon dried chervil
1 teaspoon dried chives
1 teaspoon dried marjoram
1 teaspoon dried parsley
1 teaspoon dried tarragon
¼ teaspoon dried savory
¼ teaspoon dried thyme

Makes about 2½ tablespoons.

All-Purpose Blend III

1 tablespoon dried basil
2 teaspoons celery seed
2 teaspoons dried savory
1 teaspoon dried thyme
1 teaspoon dried marjoram

Makes 3 tablespoons.

All-Purpose Blend IV

2 teaspoons dried basil
2 teaspoons dried marjoram
2 teaspoons paprika
2 teaspoons dried thyme
1 teaspoon powdered ginger
½ teaspoon finely grated lemon rind
¼ teaspoon dry mustard
⅛ teaspoon dried sage
⅛ teaspoon cayenne pepper

Makes about 3 tablespoons.

Soup Blend

1 teaspoon dried basil
1 teaspoon celery seed
1 teaspoon dried chervil
1 teaspoon dried marjoram
1 teaspoon dried parsley
1 teaspoon dried thyme
½ teaspoon dried lemon thyme
½ teaspoon dried sage
½ teaspoon dried rosemary

Makes about 2½ tablespoons.

Egg Blend

1 tablespoon dried parsley
1 teaspoon dried basil
1 teaspoon dried chervil
1 teaspoon dried chives
1 teaspoon dried marjoram
1 teaspoon dried tarragon

Makes about 3 tablespoons.

Beef Blend

2 teaspoons dried parsley
2 teaspoons garlic powder
2 teaspoons onion powder
2 teaspoons ground black pepper

Makes about 3 tablespoons.

Fish Blend I

2 teaspoons onion powder
2 teaspoons dried basil
2 teaspoons ground black pepper

Makes 2 tablespoons.

Fish Blend II

1 teaspoon dried basil
1 teaspoon dried chervil
1 teaspoon dried marjoram
1 teaspoon dried parsley
1 teaspoon dried tarragon

Makes about 2 tablespoons.

Fish Blend III

2 teaspoons dried chives
2 teaspoons celery seed
2 teaspoons dried dill

Makes 2 tablespoons.

Poultry Blend I

2 teaspoons dried chervil
2 teaspoons garlic powder
2 teaspoons dried tarragon

Makes 2 tablespoons.

Poultry Blend II

1 teaspoon dried basil
1 teaspoon dried chervil
1 teaspoon dried marjoram
1 teaspoon dried parsley
¼ teaspoon dried thyme

Makes about 1½ tablespoons.

Lamb Blend

2 teaspoons dried parsley
2 teaspoons dried rosemary
2 teaspoons dried thyme

Makes 2 tablespoons.

Vegetable Blend

1 teaspoon dried basil
1 teaspoon dried chervil
1 teaspoon dried chives
1 teaspoon dried marjoram
1 teaspoon dried parsley
¼ teaspoon dried savory
¼ teaspoon dried thyme

Makes about 2 tablespoons.

Poultry Seasoning

3½ teaspoons ground white pepper
1½ teaspoons dried sage
1 teaspoon dried thyme
1 teaspoon dried marjoram
1 teaspoon dried savory
1 teaspoon powdered ginger
½ teaspoon ground allspice
½ teaspoon grated nutmeg

Makes about 3 tablespoons.

Chili Powder

Many commercial chili powders have salt in them. Here's a salt-free recipe.

5 dried hot chilies (2-3 inches long)
2 teaspoons cumin seeds
1 teaspoon dried oregano
1 teaspoon paprika
½ teaspoon garlic powder

Grind the chilies, cumin, oregano, paprika and garlic powder in a spice mill until they are very fine.

Makes about ¼ cup.

Curry Powder

Curry powder seems to be a Western invention. Cooks in India make up their own spice blends and, though they are called by many names, "curry powder" is not one of them. This recipe is similar to the powders sold in stores. If you are buying your curry powder, look for one designated as "Madras," since this type often has the best flavor.

TIP: *The spices in curry powder blends release their flavors best when heated. Always sauté curry powder in a little butter before adding it to a dish. This step is especially important if the ingredients are not being cooked after the curry is added.*

3½ teaspoons ground coriander
2½ teaspoons ground turmeric
1 teaspoon cumin seeds
1 teaspoon fenugreek seeds
½ teaspoon white peppercorns or ground white pepper
½ teaspoon dry mustard
½ teaspoon ground allspice
¼ teaspoon red pepper flakes
¼ teaspoon powdered ginger

Combine the coriander, turmeric, cumin, fenugreek, pepper, mustard, allspice, red pepper and ginger in a coffee or spice mill. Grind well.

Makes about 3 tablespoons.

Garam Masalla

Garam Masalla *is what many Indian cooks use instead of our curry powder. There are almost as many recipes for it as there are families in India, so this should not be taken as* the *formula for* Garam Masalla.

1 tablespoon coriander seeds
1 tablespoon black peppercorns
1 tablespoon cumin seeds
½ teaspoon turmeric
1 small dried hot chili
¼ teaspoon powdered ginger
2 whole cloves
1 allspice berry

Finely grind the coriander, peppercorns, cumin, turmeric, chili, ginger, cloves and allspice in a spice or coffee mill.

Store in an airtight container.

Makes about ¼ cup.

Pumpkin Spice

4 teaspoons ground cinnamon
2 teaspoons powdered ginger
2 teaspoons grated nutmeg
1 teaspoon ground allspice
1 teaspoon ground cloves

Makes about 3 tablespoons.

Quatre Epices

This classic French blend is used to season meats, vegetables, soups and sauces.

2 tablespoons ground cloves
2 tablespoons grated nutmeg
2 tablespoons powdered ginger
2 tablespoons ground white pepper

Makes ½ cup.

A Potpourri of Tips and Tricks

In the Cupboard

- Arrange herb and spice jars alphabetically for easy retrieval.
- Dried herbs will keep their flavor for one year if tightly sealed and stored in a cool, dry, dark place.
- Do not store herbs above or next to the stove where heat and moisture can speed their decline.
- Mark herb jars with the date of purchase and replace after one year. If your herbs have reached old age, use more than the recipe calls for.
- Do not shake herbs from the jar into a hot pot. The moisture this releases into the jar causes the herbs to stick together and mold.
- After opening jars of paprika, cayenne pepper, chili powder or curry powder, store them in the refrigerator to preserve their color and flavor.

Getting Fresh

- When harvesting fresh herbs, pinch off a growing tip of stems and leaves rather than the leaves alone. These are the most tender leaves, and picking the stems too will encourage bushy growth.
- Wash herbs only if they're visibly dirty. Look them over for insects.
- Dry fresh herbs thoroughly with paper or kitchen towels before chopping.
- If the stems are woody, strip off the leaves before chopping.
- Discard any yellow or brown leaves.

It's a Grind

- To get the best flavor from dried herbs, grind them with a mortar and pestle just before using.
- Or use a coffee mill or spice mill that you've earmarked for grinding herbs and spices only.
- Or rub dried herbs between your palms to release their volatile oils.
- Grind dried rosemary in a pepper mill.

A Few Specifics

- Never cook fresh chervil; its delicate flavor is destroyed by heat. Add it just before serving.
- Treat chives the same way.
- For added flavor, tuck a bunch of fresh coriander leaves inside a chicken before roasting.
- Or use a bay leaf, a few sprigs of thyme, or some lemon slices. These flavors will permeate the meat without overpowering it.
- The tight knots of flowers that form on marjoram plants have more flavor than the leaves; pick them while still tightly closed.
- Harvest marjoram leaves before flower knots open.
- Marigold petals are an inexpensive way to get the coloring of saffron.
- If you will not be cooking a dish after adding poppy seed, toast it before using at 350°F for 15 minutes to bring out its flavor.

- To save fresh sorrel for winter use, cut the leaves into very thin strips and then cook them briefly in butter until they wilt. Freeze in tightly sealed containers.
- Add savory while cooking cabbage to keep down its smell and to enhance the flavor.

Bouquet Garni

The bouquet garni is a bundle of herbs (most often parsley, thyme and bay leaf) that is added to soups, stews and braising meat to enhance their flavor. It should be removed before serving.

- To make removal easier, tie the herbs in a piece of washed cheesecloth. This is especially important if dried herbs are being used.
- Or place the herbs in a metal tea ball.
- Or tie herb sprigs with unwaxed dental floss or kitchen string.
- Or tie your herbs between two stalks of celery for even more flavor and tidiness.
- To make removal even easier, especially from a large pot of stock or soup, tie the bouquet's string to the pot handle.
- Add leftover leek tops, folded in half and dried, to bouquets garnis.

Garlic

- To make garlic peeling easier, smash it with the broad side of a cleaver or chef's knife first. Skin will slip right off.
- Or rinse it first with hot water.
- Parboiling the garlic for two minutes will both loosen its skin and tame its strong flavor.
- To make the removal of garlic cloves from a stew or soup easy, spear them with a toothpick before adding.

Ginger

- To store ginger root, make yourself a ginger jar: Peel the root, place it in a glass jar and cover with sherry; then cap tightly. It will keep indefinitely even at room temperature and will not soak up either the flavor or the alcohol of the sherry.

Too Hot to Handle

- Wear rubber gloves when handling hot peppers; they can produce a burning sensation if they get into open cuts. Do not touch or rub your eyes when handling hot peppers.
- Removing the seeds and inner membranes from hot peppers reduces their fire.

It's a Lemon

Lemons aren't herbs, but, like herbs, they can do marvelous things for salt-free food. If a dish needs a little zip, a few drops of lemon juice can often do the trick.

- To get the most juice from a lemon, let it warm up to room temperature or soak in hot water for 10 to 15 minutes before squeezing.
- Also roll a lemon on a hard surface, exerting pressure with your palm, to release its juice before cutting.
- To get just a few drops of lemon juice, poke a hole in one end of a lemon and squeeze out the desired amount of juice.
- Store a cut lemon unwrapped in refrigerator; wrapping tends to encourage more deterioration than it discourages.

Parsley

- Parsley stems are stronger in flavor than the leaves.
- If you're only using the leaves, save parsley stems for the stockpot.

Onion Family

- When harvesting chives, cut them at the soil line to encourage a strong replacement growth.
- To control your tears when chopping onions, refrigerate them before chopping.
- Or peel and cut them under cold running water to wash away the irritating agent.
- Or have an exhaust fan pull the fumes away from you.
- To obtain a small amount of onion juice, put a piece of onion in a garlic press and squeeze.
- Add onion skins to stock to enrich its color.

Something's Fishy

- To add flavor to a steaming fish, lay herbs across it while it's cooking. Dill, tarragon sprigs and bay leaves are especially good.

In the Fridge

- Stand fresh herbs, stems down, in a glass containing about one-half inch of water. Slip a plastic bag over the herbs and glass to retain the moisture. Remove the bag every few days and shake out the excess water to prevent leaves from spoiling.
- Blend fresh herbs with olive or other cooking oil and place in a cup or widemouthed jar. Add about one-half inch of oil and cover tightly. To use, dip out desired amount. Be sure to keep the insides of the jar clean above the oil line to discourage mold. Also be sure the oil line is above the herbs.

Freezer Space

- Chop fresh herbs, place in small freezer bags, store tightly closed in the freezer until needed.
- Snip chives and freeze them for winter use.

- Chervil, tarragon and coriander leaves freeze especially well and are more flavorful than their dried counterparts.
- To freeze *fines herbes* for winter use, combine three parts snipped chives, one part minced tarragon and one part minced chervil. Before use, add three parts minced parsley to the mixture. To avoid cooking the herbs, add to hot foods just before serving.
- Freeze pesto or other oil and herb emulsions. To use, scrape the top of the block with a knife to obtain a small amount.
- Cream equal parts of minced herbs and softened butter together. Form into a log and freeze. To use, cut off thin pieces with a sharp knife. This mixture is ideal for melting over broiled fish or cooked vegetables.
- Or shape herb butter into small, tablespoon size balls and freeze them on a baking sheet. When frozen, transfer to a container or heavy plastic bag until they're needed.

A Breath of Air

- Save and dry the woody stems of your herbs during the summer to throw into the fireplace for a fragrant winter evening.
- When herbs have passed their cooking prime, set them in a crock near the fireplace. Toss a handful onto the flames now and then.
- Spices like cloves, nutmeg and cinnamon also work.
- So do dry orange rinds.
- Freshen air by boiling one-half to one tablespoon of whole cloves in a pan of water.
- Or boil orange rind.

Chapter 4

Appetizers

Marinated Mushrooms

Delicious by themselves or added to a salad. When the mushrooms are gone, use the marinade on meat or as a salad dressing.

½ cup thinly sliced onions
3 tablespoons olive oil
2 cloves garlic, minced
¾ cup stock
2 tablespoons lemon juice
1 bay leaf
1 tablespoon chopped thyme or 1 teaspoon dried thyme
1½ teaspoons chopped marjoram or ½ teaspoon dried marjoram
½ teaspoon ground coriander
½ pound mushrooms
1 tablespoon minced parsley
1 teaspoon Dijon-style mustard

In a 2-quart saucepan slowly cook the onions in olive oil until wilted (about 10 minutes over low heat). Stir in the garlic, stock, lemon juice and bay leaf.

Tie the thyme, marjoram and coriander in a square cheesecloth, and add to the pan.

Bring liquid to a boil over high heat, then lower the temperature and simmer over medium-low heat for 5 minutes.

If mushrooms are less than an inch in diameter, leave whole. Otherwise cut in half or quarter. Add to the pan. Simmer 5 minutes.

With a slotted spoon remove the mushrooms to a shallow dish. Sprinkle with parsley.

Bring the cooking liquid back to the boil. Reduce over medium-high heat until ¼ to ⅓ cup remains. Remove bay leaf and cheesecloth. Stir in the mustard.

Pour the liquid over the mushrooms. Toss to coat. Chill about 1 hour before serving.

Makes about 2 cups.

Oregano Chicken Puffs

These whole wheat puffs come out of the oven already filled with oregano-spiced chicken. If you wish, you can add cheese to the dough.

TIP: *To make an instant pastry bag, fill a plastic bag with the dough mixture, and cut off a bottom corner to the desired size. Now, squeeze the mixture through the hole. When you've finished, throw out the bag and avoid the usual cleanup.*

1 cup stock
½ cup butter
1 cup sifted whole wheat flour
4 eggs
3 tablespoons minced shallots
2 tablespoons minced oregano or 2 teaspoons dried oregano
1 cup finely chopped cooked chicken

In a medium saucepan bring the stock and butter to a boil. Remove from heat.

Dump the flour all at once into the pan. Stir vigorously with a wooden spoon. Return to heat and cook for about 30 seconds, beating hard, until the ingredients are well blended and leave the sides of the pan. Remove from heat.

Beat in the eggs, one at a time, making sure that each egg is completely incorporated before adding the next.

Stir in shallots, oregano and chicken.

Using two spoons or a pastry bag fitted with a large plain or star tube, squeeze walnut-size mounds of dough onto greased baking sheets. Leave about 1 inch between mounds.

Preheat oven to 450°F. Bake one sheet at a time in the middle of the oven. Put a batch of puffs into the oven and immediately lower temperature to 350°F. Bake 25 to 30 minutes, until puffs are golden and are baked through. The centers will remain a little moist.

Before baking the next sheet, return temperature to 450°F. Repeat baking instructions.

Serve immediately. Puffs can be made ahead and reheated to 300°F for about 10 minutes.

Makes about 3 dozen puffs.

Festive Rice Squares

The leftovers are good reheated or even cold.

2 tablespoons butter
1 tablespoon olive oil
1½ cups finely chopped onions
½ cup finely chopped red pepper
2 cups cooked long-grain brown rice (see page 205 for cooking instructions)
⅔ cup grated Parmesan cheese
¼ cup minced parsley
2 tablespoons minced basil or 2 teaspoons dried basil
4 eggs, lightly beaten
2 tablespoons grated Parmesan cheese

Place butter and oil in a large frying pan over medium heat until the foam subsides. Add onions and red pepper. Sauté until the vegetables are soft, stirring frequently to prevent the onions from browning.

In a large bowl lightly stir the rice, ⅔ cup of Parmesan, parsley and basil until well mixed and the rice grains are coated with cheese. Fold in the onions and peppers. Stir in the eggs.

Butter or oil a 7-by-11-inch baking dish. Spread the rice mixture evenly in the pan and level the top. Sprinkle with 2 tablespoons of Parmesan.

Bake at 350°F for 40 minutes or until the mixture is set and golden brown on top. Let cool in the pan for 10 minutes before cutting into 2-inch pieces.

Serve warm.

Makes 24 pieces.

Stuffed Mushroom Caps

Savory little morsels for a party or first course. I've served these caps hot, at room temperature and even cold. Mushrooms are low in calories and sodium, and high in potassium and B vitamins.

½ pound medium mushrooms (about 1½ inches in diameter)
1 tablespoon oil
1 tablespoon butter
⅓ cup minced onions
2 tablespoons ground almonds
1 tablespoon minced parsley
1½ teaspoons minced tarragon or ½ teaspoon dried tarragon
¼ cup whole wheat breadcrumbs
3 tablespoons grated Parmesan cheese
2 tablespoons sour cream or *Cottage Cream* (see *Index*)
1 teaspoon lemon juice

Carefully remove the stems from the mushrooms. Mince stems and set aside.

Arrange caps, stem side up, in a shallow, buttered baking dish. Set aside.

In a large frying pan heat the oil and butter until foamy. Add the minced mushrooms, onions and almonds. Cook over medium heat, stirring frequently, until the onions are soft and the liquid released from the mushrooms has evaporated—about 5 minutes. Stir in parsley, tarragon, breadcrumbs, Parmesan, sour cream or *Cottage Cream* and lemon juice.

Stuff caps with filling. Bake at 375°F for 15 to 20 minutes or until caps are soft.

Makes about 14 caps.

Basil Beef Kebabs

These delicious little kebabs can be put together ahead of time and broiled just before a party. Use your very biggest basil leaves to wrap the meat and secure the leaf ends as you place it on a skewer. If you run out of large leaves, use two smaller ones for each meatball, but be careful to pin both in place.

1 pound lean ground beef
1 egg
¼ cup whole wheat breadcrumbs
¼ cup minced onion
1 tablespoon minced basil or 1 teaspoon dried basil
1 tablespoon tamari sauce
40 very large basil leaves

Combine beef, egg, breadcrumbs, onion, basil and tamari in a food processor or a heavy-duty mixer until well blended.

Form into small logs about 1½ inches long and ½ inch thick. Wrap a large basil leaf around each kebab. Pierce with a skewer to hold the leaves in place.

Place on a lightly oiled broiler rack set above a drip pan. Broil 4 inches from heat for 3 to 4 minutes. Turn and broil the other side for another 3 to 4 minutes.

Makes 40 kebabs.

Tomato Jewels

36 cherry tomatoes
1 cup *Pesto Sauce* (see *Index*)

Cut the tops off tomatoes. With a small spoon or small melon baller, scoop out and discard the seeds.

Invert and drain tomatoes on paper towels.

With a small spoon place about 1 teaspoon of *Pesto Sauce* in each tomato.

Makes 36 hors d'oeuvres.

Hard-Cooked Eggs

Although most people refer to them as hard-boiled eggs, hard-cooked eggs are not boiled at all. They're gently simmered until the whites are tender and the yolks are firm. Hard boiling often causes dark rings to form on the yolks.

There are many recipes for cooking the perfect egg, but here's the one that works best for me. Bring at least three inches of water to a boil in a deep saucepan. Gently lower the eggs into the water with a spoon. Adjust the heat until the water barely simmers, cover the pan and then cook the eggs for 15 minutes. Drain off the water, crack the eggs gently in two or three places with the back of a spoon and plunge in cold water. When the eggs are cool enough to handle, gently crack the rest of the shell and peel it off under a stream of cold, running water.

Most cookbooks caution against using eggs straight from the refrigerator because they will crack upon contact with boiling water. I hardly ever warm up my eggs, and I've seldom had an egg crack. As I think Julia Child once said, "A cold egg won't crack, but a cracked egg will." What she meant is that contact with hot water will only split open the shells that already have hairline cracks. If an egg isn't cracked, hot water won't bother it.

If you want to play safe, take your eggs out of the refrigerator at least 30 minutes before cooking. Or prick the large end of each egg with a pin to allow the air inside to escape; if it's got an escape, it won't crack the shell when suddenly heated. If, despite all these precautions, an egg does crack during boiling, add a little vinegar to the water to seal the break.

Spinach Stuffed Eggs

These are easiest made in a food processor.

½ pound spinach leaves
8 hard-cooked eggs
3 ounces softened cream cheese
1 tablespoon minced dill or 1 teaspoon dried dill
2 tablespoons snipped chives
few gratings of nutmeg
¼ cup *Basic Mayonnaise* (see *Index*)

Wash spinach in lots of cold water. Without adding water, heat the damp spinach in a large pot until the leaves wilt. Transfer to a colander or sieve to drain and cool. When it's cool enough to handle, squeeze the moisture from the spinach and chop finely, either by hand or with a blender or food processor.

Cut the eggs in half lengthwise.

Carefully remove the yolks, and set the whites aside.

In a blender or food processor mix the spinach, egg yolks, cream cheese, dill, chives, nutmeg and mayonnaise until well blended, stopping frequently to scrape down the sides of the container.

Do not overblend; the finished mixture should be flecked with green.

Transfer the filling to a pastry bag fitted with a large star tip. Fill the egg whites with the filling.

Use the extra filling to fill hollowed-out cherry tomatoes or celery stalks.

Makes 16 stuffed eggs.

Eggs *Fines Herbes*

Eggs are perfect, high-protein party fare. This variation on the deviled egg has a delicate anise taste and is best when made with fresh tarragon and chervil.

8 hard-cooked eggs
2 tablespoons minced parsley
2 tablespoons snipped chives
2 tablespoons minced chervil or 2 teaspoons
       dried chervil
1 teaspoon minced tarragon or ½ teaspoon
       dried tarragon
1 teaspoon Dijon-style mustard
½ cup *Basic Mayonnaise* (see *Index*)
   chervil or tarragon sprigs (as a garnish)

Cut the eggs in half lengthwise.
Carefully remove the yolks. Mash the yolks and combine with the parsley, chives, chervil, tarragon, mustard and enough mayonnaise to moisten fully.

Using a spoon or pastry bag fitted with a large plain or star tube, fill the whites.

Garnish each with a sprig of chervil or tarragon.

Makes 16 stuffed eggs.

Pesto Deviled Eggs

8 hard-cooked eggs
2 cloves garlic
3 tablespoons minced basil or 1 tablespoon
       dried basil
2 tablespoons pine nuts or walnuts
2 tablespoons grated Parmesan cheese
2 tablespoons minced parsley
½ cup *Basic Mayonnaise* (see *Index*)
   small basil leaves (as a garnish)

Cut the eggs in half lengthwise.
Carefully remove the yolks and set the whites aside.

Mince the garlic and then mash to a paste. Using a mortar and pestle, mash together the garlic, basil, nuts, Parmesan and parsley.

Mash the yolks thoroughly with a fork. Blend in the basil mixture and mayonnaise. If the mixture is too thick, thin it with a bit of milk or yogurt.

Using a spoon or a pastry bag fitted with a large star tube, fill the egg whites with the yolk mixture.

Garnish with tiny basil leaves.

Makes 16 stuffed eggs.

Watercress Eggs

The large amount of watercress in this recipe adds calcium and vitamin K to the eggs, and the parsley kicks in vitamins A and C.

8 hard-cooked eggs
1 cup finely chopped watercress
½ cup minced parsley
2 shallots, minced
½ teaspoon Dijon-style mustard
5 tablespoons *Basic Mayonnaise* (see *Index*)
   watercress sprigs (as a garnish)

Cut the eggs in half lengthwise.
Carefully remove the yolks. Mash the yolks and combine with the watercress, parsley, shallots, mustard and enough mayonnaise to moisten fully.

Using a spoon or pastry bag fitted with a large plain or star tube, fill the whites.

Garnish each with a sprig of watercress.

Makes 16 stuffed eggs.

Curried Eggs

8 hard-cooked eggs
2 teaspoons *Curry Powder* (see *Index*)
2 teaspoons butter
2 teaspoons snipped chives
1 tablespoon grated Parmesan cheese
½ cup *Basic Mayonnaise* (see *Index*)
1 teaspoon Dijon-style mustard
  parsley or dill sprigs (as a garnish)

Cut the eggs in half lengthwise.

Carefully remove the yolks and set the whites aside.

Mash the yolks thoroughly with a fork.

In a very small pan cook the *Curry Powder* in butter for 2 minutes to bring out its flavor. Then blend the *Curry Powder,* chives, cheese, mayonnaise and mustard. If the mixture is too thick, thin with milk.

Using a spoon or a pastry bag fitted with a large star tube, fill the egg whites.

Garnish with parsley or dill sprigs.

Makes 16 stuffed eggs.

Tarragon Lemon Dip

4 ounces softened cream cheese
½ cup sour cream or *Cottage Cream* (see *Index*)
2 tablespoons lemon juice
½ teaspoon fennel seeds, crushed
2 tablespoons minced tarragon or 2 teaspoons
  dried tarragon

Cream together the cream cheese, sour cream or *Cottage Cream* and lemon juice. Stir in the fennel and tarragon.

Refrigerate for at least an hour to blend flavors before serving.

Makes about 1⅓ cups.

Allspice

Herbalists use the oil or water of allspice to soothe indigestion and flatulence. One suggests combining it with bilberries and lemon juice for diarrhea. Others credit it with anesthetic properties. Add it to your bath, they say, to soothe away aches and pains; use it as a compress to help relieve rheumatism.

Brie in Herbed Brioche

Be sure to let these stand awhile after baking. If you don't, the hot cheese will escape.

1 recipe *Herbed Brioche* dough (see *Index*)
3 four-ounce Brie rounds
1 egg yolk beaten with 1 teaspoon water (as a glaze)

Make the *Herbed Brioche* dough through the first rise. Punch down the dough, and divide into thirds. Roll each into a circle about ¼-inch thick on a well-floured surface. (If the dough is too soft to handle, refrigerate for an hour.)

Put one brie round in the center of each dough circle. Carefully fold up the dough to enclose the cheese. Trim off the excess dough, and pinch seams well. Be careful not to stretch the dough or it will weaken it and allow the cheese to burst through during baking.

Place the dough-and-cheese bundles, seam side down, on a baking sheet. Brush with an egg glaze.

Bake at 400°F for 20 to 25 minutes or until the brioches are golden. Let cool to room temperature before cutting.

Slice thinly into wedges.

Makes 3 filled brioches.

Pepper Cheese Bread

1 cup whole wheat pastry flour
1 teaspoon *Baking Powder* (see *Index*)
½ cup shredded Swiss cheese
¼ teaspoon cayenne pepper
¼ cup butter, melted
¼ cup buttermilk
3 eggs
1 tablespoon Dijon-style mustard
2 tablespoons minced dill or 1 tablespoon dried dill
2 tablespoons minced parsley
1 onion, minced
3 cloves garlic, minced
½ green pepper, minced
½ red pepper, minced

Butter three small bread pans about 6 by 3½ inches, or coat them with equal parts of oil and liquid lecithin. Dust well with flour.

In a large bowl, sift together the flour and *Baking Powder*. Then stir in the cheese and cayenne.

In another large bowl combine the butter and buttermilk. Whisk well to combine. Add the eggs beating them in one at a time, and then stir in the mustard, dill and parsley.

Add the flour to the liquid ingredients and begin folding everything together. Sprinkle the onions, garlic and peppers over the top and complete folding. Do not overmix, but make sure that all the flour is moistened.

Spoon into prepared pans, leveling the tops with a spatula.

Bake at 375°F for 50 minutes.

Best served warm.

Makes 3 small loaves.

Herb-Stuffed Brie

Small round Bries stuffed with an herb butter and pecans make nice party food. Sliced thin and served on whole-grain crackers, they go a long way.

Make these appetizers ahead and let them warm up to room temperature to soften the butter and to bring out the full flavor of the cheese.

Feel free to substitute any other white-rind cheese, such as Camembert, Delice des Neiges *or* Secret des Moines.

TIP: *If you've stocked herb butter in the refrigerator or freezer, you'll be ahead of the game here — especially in the dead of winter when fresh herbs are in short supply.*

1 four-ounce round Brie
2 tablespoons softened butter
2 tablespoons minced chives
2 teaspoons minced parsley
2 tablespoons ground pecans

Cut Brie in half horizontally.

In a small bowl combine the butter, chives, parsley and pecans. Spread the filling on one half of the cheese. Cap with the remaining half to make a sandwich. Refrigerate until firm.

Warm up to room temperature before serving.

Cut into small wedges and serve on whole wheat crackers.

Makes 1 Brie.

Variation

1 four-ounce round Brie
2 tablespoons softened butter
2 tablespoons minced basil or 2 teaspoons dried basil
2 tablespoons chopped roasted pine nuts
½ teaspoon lemon juice

Hummus

A favorite Middle Eastern dip. Serve with warm pita bread or crisp vegetables.

2½ cups cooked chick-peas (about 1 cup dried)
4 cloves garlic, minced
½ cup tahini (sesame seed paste)
¼–¾ cup stock or water
6 tablespoons lemon juice
2 tablespoons olive oil
1 teaspoon minced coriander leaves paprika

In a blender or food processor combine the chick-peas, garlic, tahini, ¼ cup stock or water, lemon juice, olive oil and coriander leaves. Process until fairly smooth but not completely homogenized. If necessary, add more stock or water to bring the hummus to the consistency of thick mayonnaise.

Spread on a flat dish. Sprinkle with paprika.

Makes about 2½ cups.

Some Herbed Yogurts

These herbed yogurts are easy to make (just start the day ahead) and have scores of uses. Best of all, they sport less fat and calories than the butter, sour cream, mayonnaise or cream cheese they replace in many dishes. Here are a few of the possible substitutions:

- Spread them on bread in place of butter.
- Serve at parties on whole-grain crackers.
- Offer as a thick dip for sturdy *crudités* (raw vegetables) such as carrot and celery sticks or broccoli florets.
- Spoon onto baked potatoes in place of sour cream.
- With a pastry bag and a star tip, squeeze into scooped-out cherry tomatoes, celery ribs, opened snow peas and mushroom caps for hors d'oeuvres.
- Use when making deviled eggs in place of mayonnaise or cream cheese.

Variation I

2 cloves unpeeled garlic
1 tablespoon minced dill or 1 teaspoon dried dill
1 tablespoon minced savory or 1 teaspoon dried savory
1 cup yogurt

Variation II

2 cloves unpeeled garlic
1 tablespoon minced tarragon or 1 teaspoon dried tarragon
2 teaspoons minced chervil or 1 teaspoon dried chervil
1 cup yogurt

Variation III

2 cloves unpeeled garlic
1 teaspoon minced rosemary or ¼ teaspoon dried rosemary, crushed
1 tablespoon minced thyme or 1 teaspoon dried thyme
1 tablespoon minced parsley
1 cup yogurt

Variation IV

2 cloves unpeeled garlic
1 tablespoon minced dill or 1 teaspoon dried dill
1 tablespoon minced parsley
1 tablespoon minced scallions
1 cup yogurt

Variation V

1 clove unpeeled garlic
1 tablespoon minced thyme or 1 teaspoon dried thyme
5 basil leaves, minced or ½ teaspoon dried basil
1 cup yogurt

Parboil the garlic for 2 minutes. The skin will slip off easily and the garlic will be tamer. Mince, then mash to a paste.

Mix mashed garlic, herbs and yogurt and pour into a strainer lined with cheesecloth. Set over a bowl or in the sink, and allow yogurt to drain overnight. (If the weather is hot, drain in the refrigerator.)

Makes ½ cup.

Curried Chervil Dip

Creamy and tangy. Serve with whole-grain crackers or crisp vegetables.

1 teaspoon *Curry Powder* (see *Index*)
1 teaspoon butter
½ cup yogurt
½ cup sour cream or *Cottage Cream* (see *Index*)
2 teaspoons lemon juice
1 tablespoon minced parsley
1 tablespoon snipped chives
1 tablespoon minced chervil or 1 teaspoon
   dried chervil

In a small pan cook the *Curry Powder* in butter for 2 minutes to release its flavor. In a bowl whisk together the *Curry Powder,* yogurt, sour cream or *Cottage Cream,* lemon juice, parsley, chives and chervil. Chill.

Makes 1 cup.

Radish Butter Canapes

This is an interesting way to use some peppery small radishes.

10 small red radishes
½ cup softened butter
2 tablespoons minced parsley
2 teaspoons snipped chives
2 teaspoons lemon juice
1 teaspoon Dijon-style mustard
  whole-grain crackers or thinly sliced whole-
   grain bread

Mince the radishes (a food processor fitted with the grating disk works best) and squeeze out the moisture.

Beat together the butter, parsley, chives, lemon juice and mustard. Stir in the radishes.

Spread thinly on whole-grain crackers or on thinly sliced whole-grain bread cut into small squares or triangles.

Makes about 1 cup.

Anise

Anise is a spice that was relished by ancient civilizations, particularly in the Mediterranean and Middle East. The Romans ate anise-spiced cakes after rich meals to aid digestion. One herbalist writes that anise tea relieves coughs, colds, headaches and indigestion. And he claims nursing mothers use the tea to promote milk production. Warm milk mixed with anise has long enjoyed a reputation as a soothing bedtime drink.

Blue Cheese Log

An easy way to crumble blue cheese is with two forks. If you buy more blue cheese than you can use quickly, store the remainder in the freezer. To crumble your frozen cheese later, scrape it with a paring knife.

4 ounces finely shredded Cheddar cheese
4 ounces softened cream cheese
2 ounces crumbled blue cheese
3 tablespoons ground almonds or whole toasted sesame seeds
1 teaspoon minced basil or ¼ teaspoon dried basil
dash of cayenne pepper
chopped almonds or whole toasted sesame seeds

With a food processor or heavy-duty mixer, cream together the Cheddar, cream cheese, blue cheese, almonds or sesame seeds, basil and cayenne.

Wet your hands and form cheese into a log about 10 inches long and 1 inch in diameter. Roll in chopped almonds or sesame seeds.

Makes 1 log.

Pears *au Bleu*

The tangy cheese contrasts nicely with sweet pears. Either soft or crunchy pears work in this recipe, but I prefer the crunchy ones for the contrast they provide for the cheese. Be sure to squeeze lemon juice into the hollowed-out pears to keep them from discoloring. I find pears easier to fill with my fingers.

4 ounces softened cream cheese
2 ounces softened blue cheese
1 tablespoon minced parsley
1 tablespoon snipped chives
8 large pears
lemon juice

In a small bowl thoroughly mix the cream cheese, blue cheese, parsley and chives.

Core each whole pear through the bottom using a melon baller. Squeeze lemon juice into each hollow to prevent discoloration.

With a small spoon or your fingers pack the cheese mixture firmly into each pear. Wrap each pear separately in plastic. Chill for at least 2 hours.

At serving time, cut into halves or quarters.

Makes 16 to 32 servings.

V-7 Cocktail

4 cups *Tomato Juice* (see page 58)
2 tablespoons lemon juice
2 stalks celery, chopped
1 teaspoon minced parsley
1 tablespoon minced onion
2 tablespoons minced green pepper
¼ teaspoon crushed celery seed

Combine 1 cup of the *Tomato Juice*, the lemon juice, celery, parsley, onion, pepper and celery seed in blender. Blend at high speed until smooth. Add the remaining juice and blend until mixed.

Chill before serving.

Makes about 5 cups.

Cheddar-Thyme Log

Delicious! Slice thinly and serve with whole-grain crackers, crisp vegetables or apple slices. As the recipe suggests, this spread may also be thinned and piped through a pastry bag into mushroom caps or cherry tomatoes.

Tip: *If you're shredding the cheese by hand, wipe the grater with a little oil before beginning. The cleanup will be easier.*

½ pound finely shredded Cheddar cheese
⅓ cup ground pecans
2 tablespoons softened butter
1 tablespoon thyme leaves or 1 teaspoon dried thyme
⅛ teaspoon cayenne pepper
3-4 tablespoons milk
ground pecans

With a mixer or food processor cream together the cheese, pecans, butter, thyme and cayenne. Add enough milk to make a thick paste.

Form into a log about 1 inch in diameter. Roll in ground pecans. (If the cheese is too soft to mold, scrape into a bowl and refrigerate for 20 minutes or until manageable. Then form into a log.) Let it come to room temperature before serving.

As an alternative method of serving, thin the mixture with a few additional tablespoons of milk until a soft paste forms. Using two spoons or a pastry bag fitted with a medium star tube, pipe the cheese into small mushroom caps or hollowed-out cherry tomatoes.

Makes 1 log.

Basil

The name basil comes from the Greek word for "royal"; only the king himself could cut this aromatic herb. It was regarded as a dangerous and powerful plant that attracted scorpions and could draw poisons from bites. Herbalists say that basil tea is helpful for stomach problems, including cramps, vomiting and constipation. And they recommend rubbing basil oil on the forehead to relieve headaches.

Baba Ghannouj

Another Middle Eastern favorite. This one's made from eggplant, which, some studies say, can lower cholesterol. Eggplant is also low in calories, sodium and fat, but high in potassium.

1 large eggplant
2 cloves garlic, mashed to a paste
2 tablespoons tahini (sesame seed paste)
2 tablespoons lemon juice
½ cup whole wheat breadcrumbs
2 tablespoons olive oil
  cayenne pepper

Pierce the eggplant in several places with a fork. Place on a cookie sheet and broil about 6 inches from the heat until it's blackened on all sides. Set aside until cool enough to handle.

Remove the eggplant's skin, and cut the pulp into pieces. Run the pulp through a food mill or sieve to remove the seeds and transfer to a blender. Add the garlic, tahini, lemon juice and breadcrumbs and blend until smooth. With the blender running, slowly add the olive oil. Chill before serving. Sprinkle with cayenne.

Makes about 2 cups.

Tomato Juice

It's sometimes hard to find commercial tomato juice without salt; but, fortunately, it's easy to make homemade. Tomatoes are good sources of potassium, vitamins C and B6 and pectin. Make juice during the height of the summer tomato season and freeze for the winter.

Tip: *Freeze some of your juice in ice cube trays. When frozen, transfer the cubes to heavy plastic bags or freezer containers. They're ideal for perking up soups, stews, sauces and gravies.*

8 cups chopped tomatoes
½ cup chopped onion
½ cup chopped parsley
2 stalks celery, chopped
1 bay leaf
1 clove garlic, chopped
1 cup stock

Combine the tomatoes, onion, parsley, celery, bay leaf, garlic and stock in a large pot. Cover and bring to a boil. Lower the heat and simmer for 30 to 40 minutes or until the tomatoes are thoroughly soft and have given up their juice.

Strain through a sieve, pressing firmly to extract all the juice. Discard pulp.

Chill. Stir or shake before serving.

Makes about 5 cups.

Close Encounters of the Savory Kind

With their multicolored spires jutting in all directions, these extravaganzas always remind me of the mother ship in Close Encounters of the Third Kind. *Use whatever fruits are in season.*

1 whole cantaloupe
 additional cantaloupe balls
 whole strawberries
 seedless grapes
 pitted cherries
 pineapple chunks
 mint leaves

Cut off the top third of the cantaloupe; reserve it for another use. Scoop out and discard the seeds.

Place cantaloupe, cut side down, on a platter.

Using wooden skewers about 7 inches long, thread the fruit and mint leaves on each skewer. (Use about five or six pieces of fruit and a leaf or two on each skewer. If you wish, wrap leaves around the fruit before skewering.)

Arrange the skewers around the cantaloupe in a pleasing pattern.

Makes 1 edible centerpiece.

Chapter 5
Stocks and Soups

Sturdy Stock

A good stock is the foundation for full-bodied soups, stews and sauces. It adds extra flavor to marinades and perks up vegetables lightly cooked in it. A weak stock, on the other hand, leaves you with a shaky base that can topple the hoped-for end product.

In addition to its flavor contribution, a good stock can have some health bonuses. It's low in calories, fat (when properly skimmed) and sodium. And it does contain vitamins and minerals that leached out of the meat, bones and vegetables that went into the stock.

Here are a few things to keep in mind when making stock:

- Always start with cold water. Hot water sears the ingredients and seals in flavorful juices, and you want just the opposite.
- Bones—especially veal bones—contain gelatin, which gives body to the stock. For best results, hack or saw bones into small pieces (or ask your butcher to do it) to release this gelatin.
- Save vegetable and bone odds and ends of other dishes. Keep them in the freezer until there's enough to make a stock.
- Cut stock vegetables into large pieces so they won't fall apart during cooking and cloud the broth.
- For a rich, deep color, add onion skins to the stock pot.
- For more nice color, brown the bones and vegetables in the oven before adding them to the pot.
- To help draw valuable calcium from the bones, add an acidic ingredient to your stock. Tomatoes, vinegar or lemon juice (even a lemon half) will do the trick.

- To speed the removal of small spices and dried herbs, tie them in a piece of cheesecloth to keep them from floating freely in the finished stock. (A metal tea ball also works.)
- Tie fresh herb sprigs into a bundle or bouquet garni for the same reason.
- Simmer your stock over very low heat for several hours to slowly extract its maximum flavor and nutrients. (Fish stocks are the exceptions; they're usually done in less than an hour.)
- Never allow the stock liquid to boil at this early stage or it will become cloudy.
- When your stock has simmered for the required number of hours, strain it through several layers of cheesecloth or through a clean kitchen towel to remove the bones, vegetables and sediment. Do not use a coffee filter because it will strip the gelatin from the liquid.
- To avoid stirring the sediment at the bottom, use a ladle to transfer the stock from the pot to the strainer.
- Taste the stock carefully. If the flavor is weak, boil it in a clean pot until it is reduced in volume. Remember that it's better to have four quarts of full-flavored stock than six quarts of weak broth.
- Before refrigerating the stock, cool it quickly to prevent bacterial growth. Place the pot in a sink full of ice water and stir until cool. To prevent souring, do not cover a stock until it is cool.
- If you are in a hurry to use the stock, you may degrease it at this point. The easiest way is to use a measuring cup made for this purpose; it allows you to pour the stock out a spout at the bottom of the cup while the fat floats on top. Stop pouring when you reach the fat layer.
- Fat can also be skimmed off with a spoon or ladle. When you've got all you can, pull strips of paper toweling across the surface of the stock to pick up the rest.
- Or drop ice cubes into the stock. The fat will coagulate on them, but you must remove the cubes before they melt.
- When you're not in a hurry, the best way to remove fat is to refrigerate a cooled batch overnight. The fat will congeal on top and can be easily removed the next day.
- Stock will keep for several days in the refrigerator.
- For longer storage, freeze it in pint or quart containers. Label and date the containers. Stock will keep for about a year in the freezer.
- Remember to freeze some stock in ice cube trays. When frozen, remove the cubes from the trays and store in heavy bags or other containers. They're perfect for times when you need just a few tablespoons of stock.
- Before using frozen stock, bring it to a rolling boil. (This is not necessary if you add the frozen cubes to something that's cooking.)
- When you need an absolutely clear stock, clarify it in the following way: Make sure that all the fat has been removed from the stock. Beat together two egg whites and one cup of stock and bring the remaining stock to a boil in a clean pot. When it has come to a boil, whisk a cup or two of hot liquid into the egg white mixture. Then return everything to the pot. Whisk until the stock returns to a boil, then lower the heat and simmer it undisturbed for 5 to 10 minutes. Do *not* stir the egg mass

that will rise to the top during this step. Strain the stock gently through clean cheesecloth or a towel and into a deep bowl. Do not allow the stock level to reach the strainer. Let the stock drain for 5 minutes; do not wring the cloth into the stock. Your stock should now be free of any cloudiness or sediment.

Chicken Stock

  1 small butternut squash
  2 carrots
  4 stalks celery with leaves
  2 large onions
  1 leek
  ½ bunch parsley
  ½ lemon, sliced
5-6 pounds chicken bones and meat
  ½ bulb garlic, coarsely chopped
  2 bay leaves
  4 whole cloves
3-4 large sprigs thyme or 1 teaspoon dried thyme
3-4 large sprigs tarragon or 1 teaspoon dried tarragon
3-4 sprigs oregano or 1 teaspoon dried oregano
  2 large sprigs rosemary or ½ teaspoon dried rosemary
  2 large sprigs sage or ¼ teaspoon dried sage
  5 quarts cold water
  ¼ cup vinegar

Remove the seeds from the squash. Chop flesh coarsely. Chop the carrots, celery, onions and leek into large sections. Place the vegetables into a large stockpot (or divide between two smaller ones). Add the parsley, lemon and chicken.

Wrap the garlic, bay leaves, cloves, thyme, tarragon, oregano, rosemary and sage in a large square of cheesecloth. Tie securely and add to the pot.

Add the water and vinegar. The liquid should cover ingredients; if it doesn't, add more water.

Bring to a simmer. Cover partially and simmer gently for about 2 hours or until meat is thoroughly tender. Remove the chicken from the pot, take the meat off the bones and reserve for another use. Break up the bones and return to the pot. Simmer, partially covered, for another 3 to 4 hours.

Strain the stock. Taste, and, if necessary, cook over medium-high heat to reduce it to concentrate its flavor.

Makes about 4 quarts.

Fish Stock

  3 pounds fish bones, heads and tails
  1 stalk celery, sliced
  1 carrot, sliced
  1 onion, sliced
  ½ bunch parsley
  ½ lemon, sliced
  4 cloves garlic, coarsely chopped
  1 bay leaf
3-4 sprigs dill or 1½ teaspoons dried dill
3-4 sprigs thyme or 1½ teaspoons dried thyme
5-6 cups cold water

Place fish, celery, carrot, onion, parsley, lemon, garlic, bay leaf, dill and thyme in a large pot. Add water.

Bring to a simmer. Partially cover and cook about 45 minutes. Strain.

Makes 1½ quarts.

Veal Stock

1 tablespoon oil
5 pounds meaty veal bones
3 leeks, coarsely chopped
2 carrots, chopped
3 stalks celery, chopped
½ bunch parsley
2 tablespoons tomato paste
1 large bulb unpeeled garlic, coarsely chopped
2 bay leaves
3-4 large sprigs thyme or 1 teaspoon dried thyme
1-2 pounds chicken and bones (optional)
3-4 quarts cold water

Oil a large baking pan with 1 tablespoon oil, and arrange veal bones on it. Bake at 400°F for about 50 minutes, stirring occasionally, until the bones are nicely colored.

Place bones in large stockpot. Add leeks, carrots, celery, parsley and tomato paste. Tie garlic, bay leaves and thyme in a piece of cheesecloth, and add to pot. Place chicken on top for easier removal later.

Deglaze the baking pan with some of the water, and scrape the browned bits into the stockpot. Add enough cold water to just cover ingredients.

Bring to a simmer and skim off any foam that forms. Partially cover the pot and simmer for 5 hours. (Remove chicken after 1½ hours. Take meat off the bones and reserve for another use. Return the bones to the pot.)

Strain liquid into a large pot; then boil down until stock has a full, rich flavor.

Makes 2½ or 3 quarts.

Bay Leaves

In Roman mythology, the nymph Daphne was changed into a laurel tree by her father to defy the love-smitten Apollo. In response, Apollo decreed the tree sacred, wore a crown of its leaves, and used the laurel as a sign of achievement and greatness. In early times, it was regarded as a protective herb, particularly against the plague. According to some herbalists, bay leaves can stimulate appetite. They use the oil as a salve for rheumatism and skin problems and make a paste of the leaves or berries to apply to the chest for colds or breathing difficulties.

Beef Stock

- 3 pounds beef shins or other braising meat
- 5 pounds beef bones (or beef and veal bones)
- 3 onions, quartered
- 3 carrots, cut into chunks
- 3 stalks celery, cut into chunks
- 2 parsley roots, chopped (optional)
- 1 large leek, chopped
- 1 handful parsley
- 1 bulb garlic, coarsely chopped
- 2 bay leaves
- 4 whole cloves
- 3-4 sprigs thyme or 2 teaspoons dried thyme
- 3-4 sprigs marjoram or 2 teaspoons dried marjoram
- 1-2 sprigs rosemary or 1 teaspoon dried rosemary
- piece of lemon rind
- 2 tablespoons tomato paste (optional)
- 2 tablespoons lemon juice or vinegar
- 6 quarts cold water

Oil one or two large shallow baking pans. Arrange the meat, bones, onions, carrots, celery, parsley and leeks on them.

Bake at 400°F for 40 to 50 minutes or until meat and bones are nicely browned.

In a large piece of cheesecloth, tie up the parsley, garlic, bay leaves, cloves, thyme, marjoram, rosemary and lemon rind.

Transfer the meat, bones and vegetables to a large stockpot; put the meat on top for easier removal later. Add cheesecloth, tomato paste, lemon juice or vinegar and water. Deglaze the baking pans, using a little of the water, and scrape all the browned bits into the stockpot.

Slowly bring the water to simmer and skim off any foam that forms. Partially cover and simmer slowly for 6 or more hours. If you wish, remove the meat after about 4 hours, but return the bones to the pot.

Strain the stock into a large pot. Taste, and if stock is weak, boil it down to concentrate its flavor.

Makes 4 to 4½ quarts.

Beef and Barley Soup

- ½ pound beef, cut into ½-inch cubes
- whole wheat flour
- 2 tablespoons oil
- 2 cups finely chopped onions
- ½ cup finely chopped celery
- ½ cup finely chopped carrots
- 1 bay leaf
- 1½ teaspoons minced thyme or ½ teaspoon dried thyme
- 3 tablespoons uncooked barley
- 1 tablespoon tamari sauce
- 4 cups stock
- juice of ½ lemon

Dredge beef cubes in flour to coat.

Heat oil in a large saucepan. Add beef cubes and brown over medium heat. Stir in onions. Cook for several minutes to wilt onions, stirring often to prevent sticking.

Add celery, carrots, bay leaf, thyme, barley, tamari, stock and lemon juice. Cover and simmer over low heat for about 1½ hours or until beef is tender and barley is cooked.

Remove bay leaf before serving.

Serves 4 to 6.

Dilled Fish Chowder

- 1 large onion, chopped
- 3 cloves garlic, minced
- 2 tablespoons butter
- 3 cups *Fish Stock* (see page 62)
- 2 potatoes, finely chopped
- ½ pound cod or haddock fillets
- 1½ cups peas
- ¼ cup chopped dill or 2 teaspoons dried dill
- ¼ cup minced parsley
- ⅓ cup sour cream or *Cottage Cream* (see *Index*)

Using a large saucepan, slowly cook the onion and garlic in the butter until the onions are tender. Add the stock and potatoes. Cook, covered, over low heat until the potatoes are tender. Place 1 cup of vegetables and stock in blender. Process until smooth. Return to the pot.

Cut the fish into 1-inch chunks. Add to the soup along with the peas, dill and parsley. Cook until the fish is done, about 5 minutes. Remove from heat. Slowly stir in the sour cream or *Cottage Cream*.

Serves 4.

Chicken Corn Chowder

- 1 cup finely chopped onions
- 1½ teaspoons minced thyme or ½ teaspoon dried thyme
- 1 tablespoon butter
- 1 quart stock
- 2 cups corn
- 2 cups chopped cooked chicken

In a small frying pan sauté the onions and thyme in butter until onions are tender but not browned.

Combine stock, corn and chicken in a large saucepan. Heat until corn is cooked and chicken is heated through. Stir in onions.

Serves 4 to 6.

Mushroom Soup

- ½ pound mushrooms
- 2 cups stock
- 1 onion, minced
- 1 clove garlic, crushed
- 1 bouquet garni (1 bay leaf, 1 large sprig of thyme or ¼ teaspoon dried thyme and 4 parsley sprigs tied in a piece of cheesecloth)
- 1 cup mashed potatoes
- 2 tablespoons butter
- 1 tablespoon lemon juice
- 1 teaspoon thyme leaves or ¼ teaspoon dried thyme
- ¼ cup minced parsley
- ½ cup half-and-half or milk

Remove the stems from the mushrooms and chop them coarsely. Slice the caps thinly and set aside.

Combine the chopped mushroom stems in a saucepan with the stock, onion, garlic and bouquet garni. Simmer, covered, for about a half hour. Strain off the stock, pressing all the juice from the vegetables.

Whisk about ½ cup of stock into the mashed potatoes until they are smooth.

In a frying pan cook the sliced mushroom caps, butter and lemon juice over medium heat until mushrooms are limp and all the liquid has evaporated. Stir often to prevent burning.

Add the mushrooms to the reserved stock, along with the mashed potatoes, thyme, parsley and half-and-half or milk. Heat through, but do not allow mixture to boil.

Serves 4.

Bean Soup Provencale

I learned this classic recipe in classes at Roger Vergé's cooking school in Provence. Its secret is to make the soup and the garlic-flavored sauce separately and then to combine them at serving time.

The Soup
- ½ cup dried marrow or navy beans, soaked overnight
- 3½ cups water
- 1 bouquet garni (1 bay leaf, a few sprigs thyme and parsley tied together between 2 pieces of celery)
- 2 tablespoons olive oil
- 1 large onion, diced
- 1 carrot, diced
- 1 stalk celery, diced
- 1 leek, thinly sliced
- 1 thin zucchini, diced
- 1 tomato, seeded and chopped
- 4 cups stock
- 1 potato, diced

The Sauce
- 3 cloves garlic, minced
- 15 large basil leaves
- 1 tomato, seeded and diced
- ½ cup grated Parmesan cheese
- 2 tablespoons olive oil

To make the soup: Cook the beans in the water with the bouquet garni until tender, about 1 hour. Set aside.

In a large saucepan heat the oil over medium heat. Add the onion, carrot, celery, leek, zucchini, tomato and stock. Simmer for 20 minutes. Add the potato. Simmer until all the vegetables are tender.

Drain cooked beans and add to the soup. Heat to blend flavors.

To make the sauce: In a blender or food processor blend the garlic, basil, tomato and Parmesan until smooth. With machine running slowly, add the oil. Place the sauce in a small bowl. Let diners stir a spoonful into the hot soup at the table.

Serves 4.

Potato Pea Soup

- 1 pound leeks
- 1 tablespoon butter
- 1 pound potatoes, thinly sliced
- 3 cups stock
- 2 tablespoons lemon juice
- 1 cup peas
- 1 egg
- ½ cup milk
- 1 tablespoon minced parsley
- 1 tablespoon minced dill
- 2 tablespoons snipped chives

Trim the green stems of the leeks and save for future bouquets garnis. Trim off the root ends. Cut each leek in half lengthwise. Wash under cold running water to remove the dirt between its layers. Slice thinly.

Place the leeks and butter in a large pot. Cover and cook over low heat for about 20 minutes or until the leeks are soft.

Add the potatoes, stock and lemon juice to the pot. Cook, covered, until potatoes are soft. Uncover, add the peas and simmer until they are just cooked.

Puree in batches in a blender to the desired smoothness. Combine the egg and milk in a small cup, and, with the blender running, add the egg mixture to a single batch of soup. Then stir this into the remainder of pureed soup.

Sprinkle with parsley, dill and chives.

Serves 4.

Squash Bisque

The winter squash and carrot in this soup make it a rich supply of vitamin A.

TIPS: If you will be pureeing the bisque with a food mill, don't bother to peel the squash, the apple or the potato. The food mill will strain out the peels for you.

If you use a blender or food processor for pureeing, the bisque will be thicker, and you may want to add more milk.

1 small butternut squash
1 leek
1 apple
1 small potato
1 onion, chopped
1 carrot, sliced
1 stalk celery, sliced
2 cloves garlic
1 tablespoon chopped oregano or 1 teaspoon dried oregano
2 teaspoons minced rosemary or ½ teaspoon crushed rosemary
¼ cup chopped parsley
3 cups stock
½ cup milk
  oregano leaves (as a garnish)

Peel the squash and remove the seeds.

Wash the leek thoroughly to remove the sand between its layers.

Coarsely chop the squash, leek, apple and potato. Place in a large pot with the onion, carrot, celery, garlic, oregano, rosemary, parsley and stock.

Cover and cook over medium heat until vegetables are tender (40 minutes or more).

Puree in a food mill or blender. Stir in milk, adding more if bisque is too thick.

Garnish with oregano leaves.

Serves 4 to 6.

Borage

Folklore says borage is an invigorating tonic capable of restoring good spirits. Modern research may concur, suggesting that borage actually stimulates the adrenal glands. The herb is also rich in potassium, calcium and salts which, many herbalists believe, have the ability to promote kidney activity and cleanse the blood. They recommend borage tea for fevers, coughs and bronchitis and advise leaf poultices for inflammations.

Onion Soup

1½ pounds onions, thinly sliced
1 tablespoon butter
2 tablespoons oil
¼ teaspoon honey
4 cups stock
4 slices whole-grain bread
1½ tablespoons olive oil
1 clove garlic, minced
¼ cup minced parsley
¼ cup grated Parmesan cheese

In a large pot combine the onions, butter, oil and honey. Cover and cook over low heat for 30 minutes or until the onions are limp.

Remove the cover and cook over medium heat for 30 minutes or until the onions have browned, stirring frequently to prevent sticking.

Add stock. Partially cover pot and simmer for 30 minutes.

While soup is simmering, prepare croutons. Cut slices of bread in half, place on a cookie sheet and bake at 275°F for 15 minutes.

Combine the olive oil and garlic in a small cup. After croutons have baked for 15 minutes, brush them with oil, and then turn over. Bake for another 15 minutes. Brush with oil again.

To serve soup, ladle out a portion into a bowl, sprinkle with parsley and float one or two croutons on top. Sprinkle with Parmesan.

Serves 4.

Cabbage and Tomato Soup

A robust, peasanty soup with lots of fiber and vitamin C.

2 cups thinly sliced onions
1 clove garlic, minced
2 tablespoons butter
1 pound cabbage, thinly shredded
2 cups *Tomato Juice* (see *Index*)
2 cups stock
2 tablespoons minced basil or 2 teaspoons dried basil
½ cup yogurt or sour cream
¼ cup grated Parmesan cheese

In a large pot over medium-low heat, cook the onions and garlic slowly in butter for 10 minutes. Add the cabbage and cook until wilted, another 5 to 10 minutes.

Add the *Tomato Juice,* stock and basil. Cook for 15 minutes.

Serve with a dollop of yogurt or sour cream sprinkled with Parmesan in each bowl.

Serves 4 or 5.

Ella's Parsley Soup

This easy, delicious soup comes from Ella Padus of Allentown, Pennsylvania. The parsley adds vitamins A and C, while the potatoes contribute fiber, iron and potassium. It's also a low-sodium soup.

2 medium potatoes, cubed
3 cups stock
2 large onions, thinly sliced
2 tablespoons butter
¼ cup minced parsley

In a medium saucepan cook the potatoes in stock until tender, about 20 minutes.

In a frying pan over low heat, cook the onions in butter until they are tender.

Add onions and parsley to potatoes.

If desired, puree part or all of the soup.

Serves 4.

Cream of Watercress Soup

This French soup is wonderful in spring or early summer.

2 cups (lightly packed) chopped watercress
   leaves
1 tablespoon butter
2 tablespoons chopped parsley
2 tablespoons minced basil or 1 teaspoon dried
   basil
2 cups stock
¾ cup minced onion
½ cup finely diced potato
2 egg yolks
½ cup half-and-half

In a medium saucepan melt the butter and then add the watercress. Cook, covered, over low heat until the watercress wilts, about 10 minutes. Stir often. Add the parsley and basil. Set aside.

In another saucepan combine the stock, onion and potato. Cover and simmer until the potato is tender. Puree in a blender until smooth but not completely homogenized (about 20 seconds). Return to the pan.

In a small bowl beat the egg yolks and half-and-half together. Stir in about half a cup of hot stock. Blend well. Pour back into remaining hot stock and blend well. Cook over very low heat, stirring constantly, for several minutes. Do not overheat or soup will curdle.

Stir in watercress. Serve immediately.

If it is necessary to reheat the soup, do so over very low heat, stirring constantly, to prevent curdling.

Serves 4.

Cream of Carrot Soup

1 pound carrots, diced
1 large potato, diced
1 large onion, diced
1 stalk celery, diced
3 cloves garlic, minced
1 teaspoon *Curry Powder* (see *Index*)
3 cups stock
¼ cup minced parsley
1 tablespoon thyme leaves or 1 teaspoon dried
   thyme
1 tablespoon minced chervil or 1 teaspoon
   dried chervil
1 cup half-and-half or milk
  chervil sprigs (as a garnish)

Cook carrots, potato, onion, celery, garlic and *Curry Powder* in stock until the vegetables are tender. Stir in parsley, thyme and chervil; let sit 5 minutes to blend flavors.

Puree, adding half-and-half or milk, in a blender until smooth; tiny green herb specks should remain. If soup is too thick, add more milk.

Garnish with chervil sprigs.

Serves 4.

Curried Cream of Apple Soup

An unusual and velvety soup that combines the bite of curry with the sweetness of apple.

1 tablespoon butter
1½ teaspoons *Curry Powder* (see *Index*)
2 medium onions, diced
2 large tart apples (such as Granny Smiths)
1 small potato, diced
2 cups stock
1 cup half-and-half

Heat the butter in a medium saucepan until it foams. Stir in the *Curry Powder* and onions. Cook over low heat until the onions are limp.

If you wish, peel the apples and chop coarsely. Add to saucepan, along with the potato and stock.

Cover and simmer over low heat until the apples and potato are tender.

Pass through a food mill or spin in a blender until fairly smooth. Do not overblend; this soup should have a *little* texture.

Stir in half-and-half. If it's necessary to reheat after the milk has been added, do so over very low heat to prevent curdling.

Serves 4.

Cool Cucumber Soup

Simple to make and delightfully refreshing on a hot day. The mint is a nice flavor accent to the cucumbers.

2 medium cucumbers
1 cup buttermilk
¼ cup minced parsley
2 teaspoons snipped chives
1½ teaspoons minced dill or ½ teaspoon dried dill
6 mint leaves or ¼ teaspoon dried mint
¼ teaspoon minced tarragon or pinch of dried tarragon
2 teaspoons lemon juice
1½ cups yogurt

If the cucumbers have been waxed, peel them. Cut in half lengthwise and scoop out the seeds. Cut the flesh into chunks.

Place the cucumbers, buttermilk, parsley, chives, dill, mint, tarragon and lemon juice in a blender.

Blend at high speed for 10 to 15 seconds or until finely chopped.

Transfer to a bowl. Whisk in yogurt and chill before serving.

Serves 4.

Chilled Peach Soup

This chilled soup has a Scandinavian heritage. It makes a nice palate cleanser between courses and it can even be used as a dessert sauce.

  4 large peaches
1½ cups water
  2 tablespoons honey
  1 cinnamon stick
  3 whole cloves
  2 teaspoons cornstarch
  ¼ cup water
  ½ cup yogurt or sour cream

Remove the peach stones. Add peaches and 1½ cups of water to a blender. Puree until smooth.

Transfer the peach puree to a large saucepan. Add the honey, cinnamon stick and cloves. Bring to a boil and simmer for 10 minutes, stirring frequently. Remove the cinnamon stick and cloves.

Dissolve the cornstarch in a ¼ cup of water, and stir into the pot. Cook for a minute or two longer.

Chill the soup. Whisk in yogurt or sour cream before serving.

Serves 4.

Burnet

These days, burnet is more noted as a flavorful salad ingredient than an herbal medicine. But in the past it was highly regarded for its ability to heal wounds and protect against infection. One herbalist suggests using the leaves as a wash for sunburn and skin problems.

Chapter 6
Salads

Salad Tips

- To preserve their nutrients, avoid peeling salad fruits and vegetables. Instead, wash them under cold, running water and use a vegetable brush. Dry everything thoroughly.
- Never soak greens or vegetables (especially after they've been sliced). Their water-soluble nutrients will go right down the drain with the water.
- Dressings stick better to dry greens so whirl yours in a mesh basket or salad spinner.
- If you have lots of time before serving, dry salad greens by placing a single layer of leaves on a clean kitchen towel, covering them with paper towels or another towel and rolling up the whole bundle like a jelly roll. Then, slip it into a plastic bag and refrigerate it for several hours. The towels will absorb the excess moisture, but the leaves will stay crisp. Greens can be stored in this way for three days without spoiling.
- For best nutrition, bypass pale iceberg lettuce in favor of the darker greens of romaine, chicory, escarole, spinach and kale. If your family objects to their chewier textures, shred them finely.
- For variety, add celery tops, beet tops, carrot tops, turnip tops, Swiss chard, Chinese cabbage, or green and red cabbage to your salads. For more zip toss in nasturtium and violet leaves.
- Try watercress and parsley for their impressive amounts of vitamin A, calcium and potassium.
- If you're using apple, avocado, banana, peach or pear slices, brush them with pineapple or orange juice to prevent discoloring.
- Add cucumber or tomato slices at serving time to keep excess moisture from wilting greens and diluting the dressing.

- When you're using lots of heavy-weight fruits or vegetables, wait until the last minute to assemble the salad lest the bulk of these items crush the more tender greens.
- If you must assemble a salad beforehand, place the heavier items at the bottom of the bowl, and then add the dressing—if you wish—before covering them with greens. The lighter things will remain crisp above the dressing, and you can toss everything together at serving time.
- Greens will wilt if they're covered with dressing ahead of time—so toss a salad at the last minute.
- Greens will stay crisper if they're placed in the freezer for five minutes before serving.
- For a touch of garlic flavor (when there's no garlic in the dressing), rub the inside of a salad bowl with a cut clove of garlic. Or rub a dry crust of bread with garlic and toss it with the greens and dressing. Remove the bread before serving.
- For more protein and nutrients of all kinds in your salads, add seeds and sprouts. Seeds alone are good sources of minerals, and sprouting them increases their protein value as well as their stores of vitamins A, B, C, E and K. Good seeds to add directly to salads or dressings are sesame, sunflower, pumpkin, caraway and poppy. Good seeds and beans to sprout are alfalfa, mung, wheat, radish, lentil and sunflower.
- To sprout seeds, all you need is a large jar, a piece of cheesecloth and a rubber band. (And seeds too, of course!) Place a tablespoon of small seeds or a few tablespoons of larger ones in the jar. Cover with water and let stand overnight. Next morning pour off the water, rinse the seeds and drain them. Cover the jar with the cheesecloth and clamp it in place with the rubber band. Shake the jar vigorously to remove excess water from the seeds, and then lay the jar on its side on the kitchen counter. Finally, rinse and drain the sprouts three or four times a day until they reach the desired length. Sprouts from small seeds like alfalfa are good when they're two inches long. Larger seeds can be harvested when their sprouts are only a quarter of an inch long. Store your sprouts in the refrigerator in a bowl lined with a paper towel and covered with plastic. They'll keep for four to five days.

Pepper Salad

2 large green peppers
2 large red peppers
2 navel oranges (optional)
2 large shallots, minced
3 tablespoons minced parsley
1 tablespoon minced tarragon
2 teaspoons Dijon-style mustard
2 teaspoons tarragon vinegar or white wine vinegar
3 tablespoons olive oil

Cut the peppers into strips ½ inch wide.

Peel the oranges. Divide into sections and remove membranes between the sections.

Transfer the peppers and oranges to a large bowl. Sprinkle with shallots, parsley and tarragon.

In a small bowl whisk together the mustard and vinegar. Gradually whisk in oil to produce a creamy dressing.

Pour the dressing over the peppers. Toss gently with two forks to combine. Chill before serving.

Serves 4.

Oriental Chicken Salad

A high-protein lunch or light supper, there's just enough dressing here to lightly coat all the ingredients without dousing their flavor.

TIP: *If you don't have water chestnuts, substitute thinly sliced radishes.*

  2 cups cooked and shredded chicken
  2 cups sliced mushrooms
  1 cup mung bean sprouts
  ½ cup thinly sliced scallions
  ½ cup thinly sliced water chestnuts (optional)
  ½ pound broccoli florets, lightly steamed
  2 cloves garlic, minced then mashed
1-2 teaspoons grated ginger root
  4 teaspoons tamari sauce
  2 tablespoons sesame oil or oil
  4 tablespoons olive oil
    Bibb or romaine lettuce, torn into bite-size pieces

In a shallow, 9-by-13-inch pan lightly toss the chicken, mushrooms, sprouts, scallions, water chestnuts and broccoli together.

In a cup or small bowl whisk garlic, ginger, tamari, sesame oil and olive oil together.

Drizzle the dressing over the chicken and toss lightly. Cover and let marinate at room temperature for at least 30 minutes. Toss occasionally to make sure all the ingredients are coated with dressing.

Serve on torn Bibb or romaine lettuce.

Serves 4.

Curried Chicken Salad

A delicious chicken and fruit salad that's low in sodium and high in protein.

  3 cups cooked and chopped chicken
  ½ cup minced celery
  ¼ cup minced scallions
  ¼ cup minced parsley
  ¼ cup chopped roasted cashews
  1 cup seedless grapes, halved
  ½ cup *Basic Mayonnaise* (see pages 84-85)
  3 tablespoons yogurt
1½ tablespoons minced dill or 1 teaspoon dried dill
  1 tablespoon butter
  2 teaspoons *Curry Powder* (see *Index*)
    spinach leaves

Toss together the chicken, celery, scallions, parsley, cashews and grapes in a large bowl.

In a small bowl mix the mayonnaise, yogurt and dill.

In a small pan melt the butter over medium heat. Add the *Curry Powder* and stir for 1 minute to release its flavor. Add to the mayonnaise dressing.

Toss the dressing and chicken mixture. Serve on crisp spinach leaves.

Serves 4.

Avocado Salad

3 ripe avocados
  Garlic Parmesan Dressing (see page 84)
  Boston lettuce

Remove pits from the avocados. With a melon baller scoop out the avocado flesh. (Or peel and cut into chunks.)

Toss with enough dressing to coat.

Serve on Boston lettuce.

Serves 4.

North African Carrot Salad

I first came across this recipe in classes on Moroccan cooking given by Paula Wolfert in New York City. The lightly cooked carrots gain an intriguing new flavor when combined with cumin and cinnamon.

1 pound carrots
2 cloves unpeeled garlic
1 scallion, minced
2 tablespoons minced dill or 2 teaspoons dried dill
2 tablespoons minced parsley
2 tablespoons lemon juice
1 tablespoon olive oil
½ teaspoon cumin seed, crushed
¼ teaspoon sweet Hungarian paprika
⅛ teaspoon ground cinnamon
 dash of cayenne pepper

Slit carrots lengthwise; slit each half of very thick carrots to produce quarters. Remove the thick, bitter cores of the larger carrots with a paring knife.

Bring 1 inch of water to a boil in a large saucepan and add the garlic to the water. Put the carrots into a steamer basket and place it in the pan. Be sure that the water does not come above the level of the steamer. Steam the carrots, tightly covered, for 5 minutes or until just crisp-tender. Cut into half-inch pieces and put into a large bowl. Add the scallion, dill and parsley.

Remove the garlic cloves from the steaming water. Peel and then mash them into a paste. Combine with lemon juice, oil, cumin, paprika, cinnamon and cayenne in a small bowl. Pour over the hot carrots.

Refrigerate and allow to marinate until cold.

Serves 4.

Caraway

Caraway has been a household item since prehistoric times. It was reputed to have power against evil and value in love potions. The seeds are well known to herbalists for their digestive properties, in particular, as a remedy for colic. One herbalist suggests caraway for menstrual problems and as a breast-feeding aid. And chewing the seeds will freshen the breath.

Asparagus Vinaigrette

1 pound trimmed asparagus spears
1 clove garlic, minced
1 tablespoon snipped chives
2 teaspoons minced tarragon or 1 teaspoon
   dried tarragon
1 teaspoon minced rosemary or ¼ teaspoon
   dried rosemary, crushed
2 tablespoons olive oil
1 tablespoon lemon juice
1 tablespoon tarragon vinegar or white wine
   vinegar

Bring 1 inch of water to a boil in a large saucepan. Place the asparagus in a steamer basket and put it into the pan. Be sure that the water does not come above the level of the steamer. Cover tightly and steam for 5 to 7 minutes or until just tender.

Combine garlic, chives, tarragon, rosemary, oil, lemon juice and vinegar.

Transfer asparagus to a shallow dish that is just large enough to hold the spears in one layer. Pour the dressing over the asparagus, cover, and let marinate in the refrigerator for 30 minutes, turning the spears occasionally.

Serves 4.

Marinated Cauliflower Salad

Quick and delicious and low in fat and sodium. There's just enough dressing here to coat the cauliflower, and that keeps the calories down.

2 cloves unpeeled garlic
2 tablespoons olive oil
1 tablespoon thyme vinegar or white wine
   vinegar
1 tablespoon lemon juice
2 tablespoons chopped dill or 2 teaspoons dried
   dill
2 tablespoons chopped parsley
1 teaspoon thyme leaves or ¼ teaspoon dried
   thyme
1 head cauliflower
2 red onions, sliced into rings

Parboil the unpeeled garlic for 2 minutes to loosen the skins. Peel and mince.

Combine the garlic, oil, vinegar, lemon juice, dill, parsley and thyme in a blender and process until the herbs are finely chopped.

Bring about an inch of water to a boil in a medium saucepan. Separate the cauliflower into florets, place in a steamer basket and set into a pan. Make sure that the water does not come above the level of the steamer. Cover tightly and steam for 5 minutes. Place onion rings on top of the cauliflower and steam for another 2 minutes or until the cauliflower is just tender and onions are tender-crisp. Do not overcook.

Transfer the vegetables to a shallow dish which is just large enough to hold them in a single layer. Pour the dressing over the hot vegetables and turn to coat well.

Refrigerate for several hours, turning vegetables in marinade occasionally.

Serves 4.

Orange Salad

4 navel oranges
2 tablespoons minced parsley
1 tablespoon snipped chives
2 tablespoons olive oil
2 tablespoons orange juice
2 teaspoons Dijon-style mustard
Boston or Bibb lettuce

Peel and section the oranges, removing all the membranes. Place in a medium bowl. Sprinkle with parsley and chives.

In a small bowl whisk together the oil, orange juice and mustard. Pour over the oranges. Toss well and allow to marinate in the refrigerator for several hours.

Serve on tender Boston or Bibb lettuce leaves.

Serves 4.

Fruit Salad with Honey Ginger Dressing

¾ cup yogurt
1 tablespoon honey
1 teaspoon lemon juice
¼ teaspoon powdered ginger
¼ teaspoon *Vanilla Extract* (see *Index*)
1 cup blueberries
1 cup seedless grapes
1 cup cantaloupe balls or chunks
1 cup strawberries

In a small bowl whisk together the yogurt, honey, lemon juice, ginger and vanilla. Chill.

In a large bowl combine the blueberries, grapes, cantaloupe and strawberries. Just before serving, fold in enough dressing to lightly coat fruit.

Serves 4.

Tomato Yogurt Salad

This is similar to a dish Julie Sahni prepares in her Indian cooking classes. Black mustard seeds are available in some gourmet shops and ethnic stores. When they hit a hot pan, they will pop and splatter, so be sure to have a lid ready to cover the pan as soon as you dump the seeds. Naturally, this dish is best when made with the ripest summer tomatoes.

4 large tomatoes
1 hot green chili pepper
1 tablespoon oil
1 teaspoon black mustard seeds
¼ cup yogurt
2 tablespoons sour cream or *Cottage Cream* (see page 85)

Remove the cores from the tomatoes. Cut each tomato in half crosswise. Squeeze gently to remove excess juice and seeds. Chop coarsely. Transfer to a bowl.

Remove the seeds from the pepper. Chop the flesh finely. Reserve.

In a small frying pan heat the oil until hot (but not smoking). Hold the mustard seeds in one hand and the pan's lid in the other. Dump the seeds into the hot oil, and *immediately* clamp the lid on the pan. Shake the pan gently over the heat until the seeds stop popping.

Add the chili pepper to the pan. Heat for 10 seconds. Transfer the pepper and seeds to a bowl with the tomatoes.

Combine the yogurt and sour cream or *Cottage Cream*. Carefully fold into the tomatoes. Do not overmix.

Serve immediately.

Serves 4.

Julienne Salad

2 carrots
2 small zucchini
1 red pepper
1 green pepper
2 scallions, thinly sliced
2 tablespoons minced parsley
2 tablespoons minced chervil or 2 teaspoons
    dried chervil
1 teaspoon minced tarragon or ¼ teaspoon
    dried tarragon
½ cup *Basic Mayonnaise* (see pages 84-85)
2 tablespoons yogurt
2 teaspoons tarragon vinegar or white wine
    vinegar
1 teaspoon Dijon-style mustard

Cut the carrots, zucchini and peppers into julienne pieces (matchsticks about ¼ by ¼ by 2 inches). Toss together in a large bowl with scallions, parsley, chervil and tarragon.

In a small bowl whisk the mayonnaise, yogurt, vinegar and mustard together.

Pour the dressing over the vegetables and toss lightly with forks.

Serves 4.

Apricot Bulgur Salad

1 cup stock
1 cup uncooked bulgur
1 cup cooked peas
2 tablespoons minced scallions
¼ cup minced mint or 2 tablespoons dried mint
2 tablespoons minced parsley
16 apricots, coarsely diced
1 teaspoon ground coriander
¼ cup olive oil
¼ cup stock
2 tablespoons lemon juice

In a small saucepan bring 1 cup of stock to a boil and stir in bulgur. Cover and remove from heat. Let the mixture stand for 20 minutes or until the liquid is absorbed. Fluff the bulgur with two forks.

In a large bowl toss the peas, scallions, mint and parsley together. Toss in the bulgur and apricots.

Combine the coriander, olive oil, ¼ cup of stock and the lemon juice. Sprinkle over the bulgur mixture and toss to combine.

Serves 4.

Marinated Turnips

A different way to serve turnips.

1 pound turnips
1½ teaspoons white wine vinegar
1½ teaspoons lemon juice
1 teaspoon Dijon-style mustard
2 tablespoons olive oil
1 tablespoon minced shallots
1 tablespoon minced dill or 1 teaspoon dried
    dill
1 tablespoon minced parsley

Peel the turnips and cut them into sticks about ⅜ inch square.

Bring 1 inch of water to a boil in a large saucepan. Put the turnips into a steamer basket and place it in the pan. Make sure the water does not come above the level of the steamer. Cover tightly and steam for 10 minutes or until tender. Transfer to a large bowl.

In a small bowl beat the vinegar, lemon juice and mustard together. Slowly beat in the oil, whisking it until fully incorporated. Then, stir in the shallots, dill and parsley.

Pour the dressing over the hot turnips. Toss gently with two forks. Chill before serving.

Serves 4.

Tomato Pepper Salad

  2 peppers, cored, seeded and chopped
1½ cups seeded and chopped tomatoes
  2 tablespoons minced parsley
  2 scallions, minced
  2 tablespoons olive oil
  2 teaspoons minced thyme or ½ teaspoon
     dried thyme
  1 teaspoon Dijon-style mustard
  1 teaspoon basil vinegar or white wine vinegar
  ¼ teaspoon ground cumin

    Combine the peppers and tomatoes in a large bowl. Toss in the parsley and scallions.

    In a small bowl combine the oil, thyme, mustard, vinegar and cumin. Pour over the tomatoes. Mix well. Refrigerate until cold.

Serves 4.

Green Beans with Marjoram

  1 pound green beans
  3 tablespoons olive oil or oil
  4 teaspoons marjoram vinegar or white wine
     vinegar
1½ teaspoons minced marjoram or ½ teaspoon
     dried marjoram
  2 shallots, minced

    Bring 1 inch of water to a boil in a large saucepan. Put beans into a steamer basket and place it in the pan. Be sure that the water does not come above the level of the steamer. Steam beans, tightly covered, for 5 minutes or until just tender. Do not overcook.

    Transfer the beans to a shallow dish large enough to hold them in a layer that is no more than an inch deep.

    Beat together the oil, vinegar, marjoram and shallots and pour over the beans, tossing them to coat well.

    Cover, refrigerate and let marinate at least an hour. Toss occasionally.

Serves 4.

Cardamom

Cardamom is a rich, sweet spice of the East that the Greeks employed to flavor wine and make fragrant perfumes. Although it is used primarily for flavoring these days, cardamom is said to help relieve indigestion and is used by herbalists to complement other herbal remedies.

Orange Rice Salad

2 cups stock
⅔ cup uncooked long-grain brown rice
2 oranges
¼ cup minced scallions
¼ cup chopped pecans
2 tablespoons minced parsley
2 tablespoons minced dill or 2 teaspoons dried
   dill
1 tablespoon snipped chives
¼ cup olive oil
3 tablespoons orange juice
1 tablespoon tarragon vinegar or white wine
   vinegar

Combine the stock and rice in a saucepan. Cover and cook until the rice is tender and all the liquid has been absorbed, about 50 minutes.

Peel the oranges and section them, being careful to remove the membranes from between the sections. Chop coarsely. Combine the oranges with scallions, nuts, parsley, dill, chives, oil, orange juice and vinegar in a large bowl.

When the rice is cooked, fluff with two forks, and add to the bowl. Toss to combine. Serve warm.

Serves 4.

Fiesta Rice Salad

3 cups stock
1 cup uncooked brown rice
2 carrots, minced
2 scallions, minced
1 stalk celery, minced
½ red pepper, minced
½ green pepper, minced
⅓ cup chopped toasted almonds
2 tablespoons minced parsley
2 teaspoons minced oregano or 1 teaspoon
   dried oregano
1 teaspoon minced tarragon or ½ teaspoon
   dried tarragon
1 teaspoon minced sage or ½ teaspoon dried
   sage
¾ cup *Basic Mayonnaise* (see pages 84–85)

In a medium saucepan bring the stock to a boil and stir in the rice. Cover and cook over medium-low heat until the rice is tender and all the liquid is absorbed, about 50 minutes. Fluff with two forks.

Transfer to a large bowl. Toss with carrots, scallions, celery, peppers, almonds, parsley, oregano, tarragon, sage and mayonnaise.

Serve warm or at room temperature.

Serves 4.

Confetti Rice Salad

A crunchy and cold rice salad that's perfect for summer days. Hot rice absorbs dressing better and makes for a more flavorful salad.

2 cups hot cooked brown rice (see page 205 for cooking instructions)
¼ cup minced carrot
¼ cup minced celery
¼ cup minced pepper
2 tablespoons minced parsley
2 tablespoons minced shallots
2 tablespoons sunflower seeds
2 tablespoons snipped chives
1 tablespoon minced dill or 1 teaspoon dried dill
1 teaspoon minced tarragon or ¼ teaspoon dried tarragon
½ teaspoon minced rosemary or pinch dried rosemary, crushed
1 teaspoon Dijon-style mustard
1 teaspoon tamari sauce
2 tablespoons tarragon vinegar or white wine vinegar
¼ cup olive oil

With two forks toss together the rice, carrots, celery, peppers, parsley, shallots, sunflower seeds, chives, dill, tarragon and rosemary in a large bowl.

In a small bowl blend the mustard, tamari and vinegar. Beat in the oil slowly until a creamy emulsion forms.

Pour the dressing over the rice and toss to coat. Chill before serving.

Serves 4.

Cayenne

Cayenne derives its name from the Greek "to bite," presumably for its pungent assault on the tongue. Herbalists often recommend it to ease stomach and bowel pains and to stimulate appetite. Cayenne plasters tend to increase blood flow through the skin and have been used to relieve rheumatism and arthritis. Folklore also says the pepper builds excellent resistance to disease.

Tuna Shell Salad

1½ cups tiny whole wheat pasta shells,
   uncooked
1½ cups whole wheat pasta twists, uncooked
13 ounces waterpack tuna, drained and flaked
½ cup diced red pepper
 1 stalk celery, minced
 2 scallions, minced
 2 tablespoons minced parsley
 2 tablespoons minced dill or 2 teaspoons
   dried dill
½–¾ cup *Basic Mayonnaise* (see pages 84–85)
 4 teaspoons tarragon vinegar or white wine
   vinegar
 2 teaspoons Dijon-style mustard

Cook the pasta in a large pot of boiling water until tender, about 8 to 10 minutes. Do not overcook. Drain and transfer to a large bowl.

Toss the noodles together with the tuna, pepper, celery, scallions, parsley and dill.

In a small bowl combine ½ cup of mayonnaise, the vinegar and mustard. Stir the dressing into the noodles. If necessary, add more mayonnaise until the pasta is thoroughly moistened.

Serve warm or at room temperature.

Serves 4.

Tabbouleh

This classic Middle Eastern salad combines the fiber, zinc and B vitamins of the bulgur and the vitamin C of the tomatoes.

 1 cup stock
 1 cup uncooked bulgur
⅓ cup minced scallions
⅓ cup minced mint
⅓ cup minced parsley
 2 tomatoes, peeled, seeded and chopped
¼ cup lemon juice
 3 tablespoons olive oil
 1 tablespoon tamari sauce

In a small saucepan bring the stock to a boil and stir in the bulgur. Cover and remove from heat. Let the mixture sit until the liquid is absorbed, about 20 minutes.

Fluff the bulgur with two forks. Gently toss in the scallions, mint and parsley. Then toss in the tomatoes.

Whisk together the lemon juice, olive oil and tamari and drizzle over the bulgur. Toss gently with forks to moisten.

Let marinate at least 1 hour before serving.

Serves 4.

Salmon and Avocado Salad

A beautiful, high-protein salad. Make sure your avocados are ripe.

 1 cup poached and flaked salmon
 1 tablespoon snipped chives
 2 hard-cooked eggs
½ cup *Basic Mayonnaise* (see pages 84–85)
 2 tablespoons yogurt
 1 tablespoon minced dill or 1 teaspoon dried
   dill
 2 avocados
  lemon juice
  Bibb lettuce
  alfalfa sprouts

In a small bowl toss together the salmon and chives.

Cut the eggs in half. Reserve 1 yolk; finely chop the remaining eggs, and add to the salmon.

Press the reserved yolk through a sieve and set aside.

In a cup mix the mayonnaise, yogurt and dill.

Peel the avocados and slice them lengthwise into half-inch slabs. Sprinkle with lemon juice to prevent discoloration.

Arrange the lettuce and sprouts on a large platter; place the avocado slices over the lettuce and top with salmon. Spoon the mayonnaise dressing over the salmon. Sprinkle with sieved egg yolk.

Serves 4.

Ginger Garlic Dressing

Use on green salads and in oriental dishes.

½ cup oil
2 tablespoons lemon juice
1 tablespoon tamari sauce
1 tablespoon peanut butter or tahini (sesame seed paste)
1 teaspoon grated ginger root
1 clove garlic, minced

Combine the oil, lemon juice, tamari and peanut butter or tahini in blender container. Blend on medium speed for 10 seconds to combine.

With the blender running, add the ginger and garlic. Blend for 20 seconds or until the ginger and garlic are thoroughly pulverized.

Makes ¾ cup.

Creamy Tarragon Dressing

1 teaspoon Dijon-style mustard
2 tablespoons *Basic Mayonnaise* (see pages 84-85)
2 tablespoons tarragon vinegar or white wine vinegar
2 tablespoons oil
2 tablespoons olive oil
1 tablespoon minced tarragon or 1 teaspoon dried tarragon
1 tablespoon minced parsley

In a small bowl whisk together the mustard and mayonnaise. Whisk in the vinegar. Slowly whisk in the oil and olive oil to form a creamy emulsion. Stir in the tarragon and parsley.

Makes about ½ cup.

Creamy Blue Dressing

Yogurt makes for a lighter fat and calorie content in this tangy dressing. Use two forks to crumble the blue cheese.

2 tablespoons crumbled and softened blue cheese
1 tablespoon minced parsley
1 tablespoon snipped chives
1 teaspoon lemon juice
½ cup *Basic Mayonnaise* (see pages 84-85)
½ cup yogurt

In a bowl blend the blue cheese, parsley, chives and lemon juice with a fork until a paste forms. Gradually whisk in the mayonnaise to make a smooth dressing. Mix in the yogurt.

Makes 1 cup.

Basil Cottage Dressing

This dressing has the consistency of mayonnaise and can be used in its place.

½ cup cottage cheese
¼ cup milk
4 teaspoons basil vinegar or white wine vinegar
1 tablespoon minced basil or 1 teaspoon dried basil
1 teaspoon minced oregano or ¼ teaspoon dried oregano
1 clove garlic, minced
¼ cup olive oil
yogurt or milk (optional)

In a blender or food processor blend the cottage cheese, ¼ cup milk and vinegar until smooth. Add the basil, oregano and garlic. With the machine running, slowly pour in the oil.

Dressing will be thick. To thin, add yogurt or additional milk.

Makes 1 cup.

Basic Oil Mayonnaise

This is a classic, high-calorie, high-fat mayonnaise made by beating oil into an egg emulsion. To be fair, it is low in sodium and, per tablespoon, relatively low in cholesterol. However, if you're interested in lowering the fat and the calories too, try the Basic Ricotta Mayonnaise or Basic Tofu Mayonnaise recipes that follow. They both look amazingly like standard mayonnaise and taste darn near the same.

1 egg
1 tablespoon tarragon vinegar or white wine vinegar
1 teaspoon Dijon-style mustard
1 clove garlic, minced
⅓ cup olive oil
⅔ cup oil

Place the egg, vinegar, mustard and garlic into a blender or food processor. Process for 15 seconds.

With machine running, *slowly* add the olive oil. Use enough of the remaining oil to produce a thick emulsion.

Makes about 1 cup.

Basic Ricotta Mayonnaise

This version has about a third of the calories and a quarter of the fat of an oil-based mayo. However, because of its dairy content, the cholesterol is slightly higher. Use it as you would regular mayonnaise.

I find that a part-skim ricotta produces the best results.

1 egg
2 tablespoons lemon juice or tarragon vinegar
2 tablespoons oil
1 teaspoon Dijon-style mustard
1 clove garlic, minced
1 cup part-skim ricotta cheese

Put the egg, lemon juice or vinegar, oil, mustard and garlic into a blender. Blend 10 seconds on the highest speed.

Add the ricotta and blend on high until smooth, stopping often to scrape down the sides of the container.

Makes about 1½ cups.

Garlic Parmesan Dressing

1 tablespoon oregano vinegar or white wine vinegar
1 tablespoon lemon juice
1 clove garlic, minced
1½ teaspoons minced oregano or ½ teaspoon dried oregano
6 tablespoons olive oil
3 tablespoons grated Parmesan cheese

In a small bowl beat the vinegar, lemon juice, garlic and oregano with a wire whisk until combined. Slowly beat in the oil to form a creamy dressing. Beat in the cheese.

Makes about ¾ cup.

Basic Tofu Mayonnaise

Tofu is a soybean product that is low in calories and fat and high in protein. Because it has little taste of its own, it easily takes on the "mayonnaise taste" of the mustard and garlic. Compared to a regular, oil-based dressing, this version has about a quarter of the calories and a fifth of the fat. Because there's egg used, the cholesterol is the same.

1 egg
2 tablespoons lemon juice or tarragon vinegar
2 tablespoons oil
1 teaspoon Dijon-style mustard
1 clove garlic, minced
8 ounces tofu, mashed with a fork

Put the egg, lemon juice or vinegar, oil, mustard and garlic into a blender. Blend 10 seconds on the highest speed.

Add the tofu and blend on high until smooth, stopping often to scrape down the sides of the container.

Makes about 1½ cups.

Cottage Cream

This sour cream substitute tastes and looks like the real thing, but it has about one-half the calories, one-fifth the fat, and one-third of the cholesterol. Be aware, though, that unless you use a low-sodium cottage cheese, this substitute will contain more sodium than sour cream.

2 tablespoons milk
1 tablespoon lemon juice
1 cup cottage cheese

Put the milk and lemon juice into a blender container. Add the cottage cheese. Blend on the highest speed, stopping often to scrape down the sides of the container, until the mixture is completely smooth.

Makes 1 cup.

Chervil

Chervil, one of the oldest seasonings known in Europe, figures prominently in French cuisine and is one of the classic *fines herbes* used in many dishes. The Romans favored chervil vinegar for hiccups. Herbalists ascribe blood cleansing and digestive properties to the herb and have used it to increase perspiration during colds and fevers and to lower blood pressure. A wash of chervil is said to clear the skin.

Chapter 7

Breads and Butters

Bread Basics

The most important thing I can tell you about making bread is that it's not an exact science. Bread recipes are not sacred, nor are they carved in stone. At best, they give a rough approximation of the amount of flour needed, the dough's rising time, and its baking time. Humidity, room temperature, altitude, the particular flour you're using, your oven—all can play havoc with a recipe's approximations. The best bread makers are the ones who are familiar enough with the process to do it by feel.

For maximum health value, always use whole wheat flour in your baked goods. It contains all the fiber-rich bran and vitamin-packed wheat germ of the original wheat kernel. When the whole wheat grain is milled into white flour, those important components are removed, leaving only its nutrient-poor, starchy center—increased shelf life is achieved at the expense of health-giving elements. And although industrial millers brag that they "enrich" their white flour, they actually return only a few of the nutrients to their original levels.

Making whole wheat bread is a tad trickier than white bread because it's heavier and somewhat less inclined to produce an elastic dough. Whole wheat dough is also stickier to knead and harder to get out of the pan after baking. But, as a result, it's more satisfying to turn out perfect whole wheat loaves, and they're a lot better for your health. Here are some things to keep in mind to ensure your success.

Regular whole wheat flour comes from hard wheat, which contains a substance called gluten that produces the elasticity necessary for yeast-risen breads. Whole wheat pastry flour is milled from soft spring wheat, which is lower in gluten and more suited for delicate pies, pastries and quick breads. Occasionally the two are combined in a recipe to give both lightness and elasticity to a dough. The bran and wheat germ present in whole wheat flours impart a golden brown color and hearty texture to baked goods.

Keep whole wheat flours in moisture-proof containers, and store them in a cool, dry place, preferably the refrigerator or freezer. Stir the flour lightly before using. If a recipe calls for sifting, be sure to add any bran left in the sifter to the dough or batter.

Most breads rise through the action of baking yeast. Yeast is a living organism—actually, lots of tiny organisms. When activated by warmth and moisture, it releases carbon dioxide, a process that enables dough to rise. You can buy yeast in dry granular form or in compressed cakes. Dry yeast has a very long shelf life if it is stored properly. I buy it in four-ounce packages at the health food store. Once a package has been opened, I transfer the yeast to a jar and place it, tightly closed, in the refrigerator—where it keeps for up to a year with no problems. Larger packages are more economical than individual packets, and so if you're using bulk yeast, figure that one table-spoon can successfully take the place of each individual packet.

I seldom use cake yeast because it has a much shorter life and requires more effort to store. As a result, all the recipes in this book call for dry yeast. If you prefer compressed yeast, substitute one cake (two-thirds of an ounce) for each tablespoon of dry yeast.

As I said, yeast is activated by warmth and moisture. Lower temperatures slow its activity, and excessive heat kills it. To "proof" or activate dry yeast, dissolve it in a lukewarm liquid (whose temperature is somewhere between 100° and 120°F), and give it a bit of honey to feed on. If it's still alive, the yeast will bubble up after several minutes.

Before starting your dough, make sure all the ingredients are at room temperature. If the flour has been in the refrigerator, speed up the process by warming it in the oven at 250°F for about 20 minutes (stirring occasionally). Heat any liquids to lukewarm and make sure eggs and other ingredients are at the proper temperature. Cool ingredients can retard the yeast's activity and prolong the rising periods.

The initial mixing phase of any recipe starts to activate the gluten in the flour and forms the dough into a mass suitable for kneading. Kneading evenly distributes the gas bubbles formed by the yeast throughout the dough and develops the gluten to its maximum elasticity. Every baker has his or her own kneading technique, but most are variations on this one: Fold the dough over toward you, and, pressing with the heel of your hand, push it away; then, give the whole mass a slight turn and repeat the process with another section of the dough.

Whole wheat dough requires at least 10 minutes of vigorous hand kneading to properly develop its gluten and distribute the yeast bubbles. If the dough begins sticking to the kneading surface, scrape it clean, flour it lightly and then continue. If the dough sticks to your hands, dust them with flour or oil them lightly. But go as easy as you can on the flour. The lightest loaves contain only enough flour to dry the dough and to keep it from sticking. When you've kneaded sufficiently, your dough will be smooth and satiny, and it will bounce back when you push it.

Bread dough does not have to be kneaded by hand. A properly equipped food processor or a heavy-duty mixer with a dough hook will also do a good job and save you a lot of exertion. However, even with a machine, you may want to knead the dough a minute or two by hand to ensure that its consistency is right.

After kneading, transfer the dough to a clean, lightly oiled bowl to rise. To keep it moist, turn the dough in the bowl to coat it with oil. Cover the bowl with a damp towel and place it in a warm (80° to 85°F), humid, draft-free spot. If that isn't your kitchen, place the dough near a gas stove's pilot light. Or set an electric oven at its lowest temperature, warm it slightly and then place the dough inside. To raise humidity, you might place a bowl of water close to the rising dough.

In general, let the dough rise until it has doubled in bulk—however long that may take. A good way to tell if the dough has risen sufficiently is to press two fingers into it and withdraw them. If the depressions remain, punch the dough down with your fist, knead briefly and then shape it into loaves.

Most bread recipes call for two risings: one in the bowl and one in the pan. That's because the more times a dough rises, the finer the texture of the bread will be.

Whole-grain dough is apt to stick to its pan while baking, so grease pans generously. Butter them well or use a mixture of oil and liquid lecithin. I keep a blend of two tablespoons of each in the cupboard and use it for greasing all pans. The mix combines easily with a fork and won't separate as it sits. Because the lecithin is a bit sticky, I use a crumpled piece of wax paper to spread the mixture and avoid getting it on my hands. By the way, I find that oil alone won't keep whole wheat bread from sticking to the pan.

When filling a baking pan, remember that your dough will rise a bit more in the oven. Do not overfill the pan. If the recipe calls for it, place the dough-filled pans in a warm spot and let them rise until they double in bulk.

To bake, place filled pans in the middle of the oven to allow air to circulate freely around them. If you know that your oven has hot spots, move the pans around during baking to ensure even browning. A loaf of bread is done when it's golden on top and sounds hollow when tapped with the fingers. To double-check, turn your loaf out of its pan onto a pot holder or towel. Push a skewer through the bottom until it nearly reaches the top. Pull it out. If the skewer comes out clean, the loaf is done. If it's covered with moist dough, return the loaf to the oven and check it again in five minutes. If the top gets too brown, cover it with foil.

Allow bread to cool before cutting it.

For more detailed information on bread making, see *Bread Winners* by Mel London (Rodale Press, 1979).

Quick Breads

Quick breads don't rise before baking and are placed in the oven as soon as they're mixed. The leavening agents most often used in them are baking powder and baking soda, and there lies a problem. Many commercial baking powders contain aluminum salts that can be harmful, so look for aluminum-free baking powder in a health food store, or make your own with the following recipe. Use it as you would commercial baking powder.

Baking Powder

2 tablespoons cream of tartar
2 tablespoons arrowroot
1 tablespoon baking soda

Mix the cream of tartar, arrowroot and baking soda in a small bowl until they're smooth. If lumps develop, pass the mixture through a sieve. Seal tightly and store in a cool, dry place.

Makes about ¼ cup.

If a recipe calls for baking soda alone, the batter will require an acid ingredient to activate it. Molasses, buttermilk, yogurt, sour cream or orange juice all will work.

Garlic Dill Bread

Six cloves of garlic may seem like a lot for one loaf of bread, but the flavor they produce is just right. The cottage cheese adds extra calcium, some protein, and a wonderful tang to the bread.

¼ cup lukewarm water
4 teaspoons dry yeast
1 teaspoon honey
6 cloves garlic, minced
1 cup cottage cheese, pureed until smooth
2 tablespoons softened butter
3 tablespoons chopped dill or 1 tablespoon dried dill
1 egg
2½-3 cups whole wheat flour
1 egg beaten with 1 teaspoon milk (as a glaze)

Combine the water, yeast and honey in a cup. Set aside for 10 minutes to proof (yeast will become foamy).

In a large bowl combine the garlic, cottage cheese, butter, dill and egg. Beat until smooth. Add the yeast mixture.

Stir in 1 cup flour. Beat well to combine. Add additional flour, a half cup at a time, beating continuously after you add, until a kneadable dough forms.

Turn out onto a floured surface and knead about 15 minutes or until smooth and elastic. Add only enough additional flour to prevent sticking.

Transfer dough to a lightly greased bowl, turning dough to coat on all sides. Cover and let rise in a warm place until doubled in bulk, perhaps 45 minutes to an hour.

Punch down dough. Knead briefly and form into a loaf. Butter a 9-by-5-inch bread pan, or coat pan with equal parts of oil and liquid lecithin, and place loaf in pan. Let rise until doubled in bulk, 30 to 45 minutes. Brush top lightly with egg glaze.

Bake at 350°F for 40 to 50 minutes or until top is browned and loaf sounds hollow when tapped. If you wish, remove the loaf from the pan and return to the oven for 5 minutes to brown bottom.

Makes 1 loaf.

That's Italian! Bread

Tomato juice and Italian herbs make this low-sodium bread come on like pizza.

⅔ cup lukewarm water
4 teaspoons dry yeast
1 tablespoon honey
1 cup *Tomato Juice* (see *Index*)
1 tablespoon minced oregano or 1 teaspoon dried oregano
1 tablespoon minced basil or 1 teaspoon dried basil
2 teaspoons thyme leaves or ½ teaspoon dried thyme
2 teaspoons minced savory or ½ teaspoon dried savory
1 cup lukewarm water
6-7 cups whole wheat flour
1 egg beaten with 1 tablespoon milk (as a glaze)

Combine the ⅔ cup water, yeast and honey in a cup. Set aside for 10 minutes to proof (yeast will become foamy).

Heat the *Tomato Juice* to lukewarm.

In a large bowl combine the yeast, *Tomato Juice,* oregano, basil, thyme, savory and 1 cup water. Mix well. Add the flour, 1 cup at a time, until a kneadable dough forms.

Knead until smooth and elastic, about 15 minutes. Add more flour as necessary to prevent sticking during kneading.

Transfer dough to an oiled bowl. Turn dough to coat on all sides. Cover, set in a warm place, and let rise until doubled in bulk, perhaps 45 to 60 minutes.

Punch dough down and divide in half. Roll each half into a rectangle about 9 by 11 inches. Then roll up each rectangle along its short side. Pinch the seams shut.

Butter two 8½-by-4½-inch loaf pans, or coat with equal parts of oil and liquid lecithin.

Put dough into pans, seam side down. Cover and let rise until doubled in bulk, about 30 to 45 minutes.

Brush tops lightly with the egg glaze.

Bake at 375°F for about 40 minutes, or until the crust is browned and the loaf sounds hollow when tapped.

Makes 2 loaves.

Dill Seed Loaf

Dill seeds add a crunchy goodness to this easy bread.

¼ cup lukewarm water
1 tablespoon dry yeast
1 tablespoon honey
1 cup lukewarm milk
⅛ teaspoon baking soda
2 tablespoons dill seeds
2½ cups whole wheat flour
1 egg beaten with 1 teaspoon water (as a glaze)
dill seeds (as a topping)

Combine the water, yeast and honey in a cup. Set aside for 10 minutes to proof (yeast will become foamy).

Transfer to a large bowl and add the milk, baking soda, dill seeds and 1 cup of flour. Beat well to combine. Stir in remaining flour, a half cup at a time. Combine well. The dough will be sticky, but do not knead.

Butter an 8½-by-4½-inch loaf pan, or coat it with equal parts of oil and liquid lecithin. Transfer dough to the pan.

Cover and let rise in a warm place until doubled in bulk, about 45 minutes.

Brush the top with egg glaze. Sprinkle with dill seeds. Bake at 400°F for 25 minutes.

Best served while still warm or reheated.

Makes 1 loaf.

Parsley Bread

The big bunch of parsley adds a whopping dose of vitamin A.

    ½ cup lukewarm water
    1 tablespoon dry yeast
    1 teaspoon honey
    ½ cup sour cream or yogurt
    1 egg
    1 cup minced parsley
    2 cloves garlic, minced
2-2½ cups whole wheat flour

Combine the water, yeast and honey in a cup. Set aside for 10 minutes to proof (yeast will become foamy).

Combine the sour cream or yogurt, egg, parsley and garlic in a large bowl. Stir in yeast mixture. Beat in 1 cup of flour.

Gradually beat in enough additional flour to make a soft, kneadable dough. Turn out onto a floured surface. Knead until smooth and elastic, about 10 to 15 minutes. Use only enough additional flour to prevent sticking.

Transfer dough to an oiled bowl. Turn to coat dough. Cover and let rise in a warm place until doubled in bulk, from 30 to 60 minutes.

Punch down dough. Pat out into a rectangle about 8 inches wide and then roll up like a jelly roll. Pinch the seams tightly.

Butter an 8½-by-4½-inch loaf pan, or coat it with equal parts of oil and liquid lecithin. Place dough in the pan, seam side down.

Cover and let rise until doubled in bulk, about 30 to 45 minutes.

Bake at 375°F for 40 to 45 minutes or until the loaf is golden on top and sounds hollow when tapped.

Makes 1 loaf.

Cinnamon

Cinnamon has always been a spice of great value. The ancient Egyptians used it for medicinal and embalming purposes. And explorers like Columbus discovered new worlds in their search for better sea routes to sources of cinnamon and other spices. Herbalists recommend cinnamon for indigestion and colds. They also claim it to have antiseptic properties and value as a mouthwash. Some say cinnamon is beneficial for female complaints, such as nausea during pregnancy.

Sage Bread

This is a whole wheat version of a traditional Italian bread I watched Judith Olney prepare in her classes at Pinehurst, North Carolina. It's flat like a pizza and best eaten warm. I don't recommend using dried sage unless you are absolutely sure it doesn't have a musty flavor. The chestnuts are optional, but they do add a rich flavor to the bread.

¼ cup lukewarm water
2 teaspoons dry yeast
2 teaspoons honey
1¼ cups lukewarm stock
2 tablespoons olive oil
½ cup minced sage
¼ teaspoon celery seed, crushed
1 cup cooked and chopped chestnuts (optional)
¼ cup grated Parmesan cheese
3-3½ cups whole wheat flour
1 egg yolk beaten with 1 teaspoon water (as a glaze)
1 small sprig of sage leaves (as a garnish)

Combine the water, yeast and honey in a cup. Set aside for 10 minutes to proof (yeast will become foamy).

In a large bowl combine the yeast mixture, stock, oil, sage, celery seed, chestnuts, Parmesan and 1 cup of flour. Mix well.

Add flour, a half cup at a time, until you have a soft, kneadable dough.

Turn out onto a floured surface and knead until smooth and elastic, about 15 minutes. Add only enough additional flour to prevent sticking.

Transfer dough to an oiled bowl. Turn to coat with oil. Cover and let rise until doubled in bulk, about 1 hour.

Punch down dough. Butter a baking sheet or 12-inch pizza pan, or coat it with equal parts of oil and liquid lecithin. Roll or press the dough into a 12-inch circle on the pan. With your finger poke random indentations on the surface of the dough.

Brush with the glaze. Press the sage sprig into place at the center of the dough.

Let rise, uncovered, in a warm place until doubled in bulk, about 30 minutes.

Bake at 350°F for about 35 minutes, or until bread is golden and sounds hollow when tapped.

Serve warm.

Makes 1 round loaf.

Mushroom Swirl Bread

The Dough
½ cup lukewarm water
2 tablespoons dry yeast
1 tablespoon honey
1½ cups warm buttermilk
1 cup warm water
6-7 cups whole wheat flour

The Filling
2 tablespoons butter
½ cup minced scallions
½ pound mushrooms, thinly sliced
½ cup sour cream or *Cottage Cream* (see *Index*)
2 tablespoons minced fennel or 2 teaspoons dried fennel
¼ cup grated Parmesan cheese
¼ cup minced parsley

1 egg beaten with 1 teaspoon water (as a glaze)

To make the dough: Combine ½ cup lukewarm water, yeast and honey in a cup. Set aside for 10 minutes to proof (yeast will become foamy).

In a large bowl (a mixer will make this job easier) combine the yeast mixture, buttermilk and 1 cup of warm water. Gradually beat in enough flour to make a kneadable dough.

Knead on a floured surface or by machine for 10 to 15 minutes or until the dough is

Mushroom Swirl Bread—*continued*

smooth and elastic. Try not to use more flour than is necessary to keep the dough from sticking.

Transfer to an oiled bowl. Turn the dough to coat it. Cover and set in a warm place to rise until it's doubled in bulk, from 30 to 60 minutes.

While dough is rising, make the filling.

To make the filling: Heat the butter in a large frying pan until foamy. Add the scallions and mushrooms. Sauté over low heat until they are soft. Sauté a few minutes more, stirring constantly, until the liquid given up by the mushrooms has evaporated.

Let the mushrooms cool slightly. Stir in the sour cream or *Cottage Cream,* fennel, Parmesan and parsley. Set the filling mixture aside until the dough has doubled in bulk.

When the dough has risen, punch it down, and divide in half. On a floured surface, roll each half into a rectangle about 10 to 15 inches.

Brush the entire surface of the dough with the egg glaze. Spread half of the mushroom filling over each portion of dough, leaving a border of about an inch all around.

Using the 10-inch side, roll each piece into a log and pinch the seams closed. Transfer, seam side down, to 9-by-5-inch, well-buttered bread pans.

Cover and let rise in a warm place until doubled in bulk, about 30 to 45 minutes. Brush with the egg glaze.

Bake at 375°F for about 40 minutes, or until the loaves are golden on top and sound hollow when tapped.

Makes 2 loaves.

Cloves

Cloves are the highly aromatic flower buds of an evergreen tree native to the Moluccas. Their sweet scent led to their use as an ingredient in body and sachet powders and in potpourri to freshen the air. Folklore regards cloves as helpful for indigestion, nausea and flatulence, and credits their antiseptic and numbing properties for relieving toothaches.

Rosemary Butter Bread

An easy, no-knead bread.

½ cup lukewarm water
1 tablespoon dry yeast
1 tablespoon honey
½ cup warm water
1 egg
2 tablespoons honey
2 tablespoons oil
2 cups whole wheat flour
1 cup minced or finely shredded carrots
1 cup minced onion
½ cup minced celery
2 tablespoons minced parsley
2 teaspoons minced rosemary or 1 teaspoon crushed dried rosemary
1½ cups whole wheat flour
1 teaspoon oil

In a cup combine the ½ cup lukewarm water, yeast and 1 tablespoon honey. Set aside for 10 mintues to proof (yeast will become foamy).

In a large bowl (a mixer makes this job easier) combine the ½ cup warm water, egg, 2 tablespoons honey, 2 tablespoons oil and 2 cups flour. Add yeast to mixture. Beat until well mixed. Then beat for 3 minutes.

Add the carrots, onion, celery, parsley, rosemary and 1½ cups of flour. Mix with hands, if necessary, to combine, but do not knead. The dough will be sticky.

Butter a 2-quart casserole or coat it with equal parts of oil and liquid lecithin. Transfer dough to the dish, and brush the top with 1 teaspoon oil.

Cover and set in a warm place until doubled in bulk, about 1 to 1½ hours.

Bake at 350°F for 60 minutes. If the top becomes too brown during baking, cover it lightly with foil.

Makes 1 loaf.

Pesto Bread

Make this loaf in midsummer when you've got lots of fresh basil in the garden.

The Dough
½ cup lukewarm water
1 tablespoon dry yeast
1 tablespoon honey
½ cup lukewarm water
¼ cup olive oil
1 egg
1 cup rolled oats
2½-3 cups whole wheat flour

The Filling
½ cup (packed) basil leaves
2 tablespoons parsley leaves
¼ cup grated Parmesan cheese
¼ cup pine nuts
2 cloves garlic, minced
2 tablespoons olive oil

1 egg beaten with 1 teaspoon water (as a glaze)

To make the dough: In a cup combine the ½ cup water, yeast and honey. Let proof for 10 minutes (yeast will become foamy). Transfer to a large bowl.

Stir in the ½ cup water, oil, egg and rolled oats. Stir in the flour, half a cup at a time, until a kneadable dough is formed.

Turn out onto a lightly floured surface and knead 10 to 15 minutes or until the dough is smooth and elastic. Use only enough additional flour to keep the dough from sticking.

Transfer to an oiled bowl. Turn to coat the dough. Cover and set in a warm place to rise until doubled in bulk, about 1 hour.

While dough is rising, make the filling.

To make the filling: In a food processor or blender combine the basil, parsley, Parmesan, pine nuts and garlic. Blend until finely chopped. Add the oil and continue blending until a thick,

Pesto Bread–*continued*

fine paste is formed. Set the filling mixture aside until the dough has doubled in bulk.

When the dough has risen, punch it down. Roll out on a lightly floured surface to form a rectangle about 9 by 13 inches.

With a flexible metal spatula, spread the filling evenly over the dough rectangle, leaving a 1-inch border all around. Roll up, starting at one 9-inch side, and pinch the seams closed. Tuck side seams under.

Butter an 8½-by-4½-inch loaf pan, or coat it with equal parts of oil and liquid lecithin. Transfer dough to the pan, seam side down. Cover and let rise in a warm place until doubled in bulk, about 45 minutes.

Brush top with the egg glaze.

Bake at 375°F for about 40 minutes, until the top is golden and loaf sounds hollow when tapped.

Makes 1 loaf.

Herbed Brioche

This dough is particularly silky to handle because of the butter, and the finished bread will be firm and a bit dry in texture.

- ½ cup lukewarm water
- 1 tablespoon dry yeast
- 2 teaspoons honey
- 3 eggs
- ¼ cup butter, melted
- 2 cloves garlic, minced
- 2 tablespoons minced basil or 1 tablespoon dried basil
- ⅓ cup minced parsley
- ⅓ cup minced dill or 2 tablespoons dried dill
- 3-4 cups whole wheat pastry flour
- 1 egg yolk beaten with 1 teaspoon water (as a glaze)

Combine the water, yeast and honey in a cup, and set aside to proof for 10 minutes (the yeast will become foamy).

Beat in the eggs, butter, garlic, basil, parsley, dill and 1 cup of flour. Beat well to combine. Gradually stir in enough flour to make a soft, kneadable dough. Turn out onto a well-floured surface and knead until smooth and elastic. Add more flour, if necessary, but try not to add more than you really need.

Place in a greased bowl and turn to coat the dough. Cover and let rise in a warm place for about 1½ hours, or until it's doubled in bulk. Then, punch down.

Dough will produce one 2-quart brioche, two 1-quart brioches or four 2-cup brioches. Divide dough into appropriately sized pieces, and reserve one-third of each piece for a top knot.

Put the larger piece of dough into a well-buttered brioche pan or any deep, round pan. With a sharp knive cut an *X* about an inch deep in the top of the dough. Form the smaller, reserved piece into a teardrop shape, and put its pointed end into the *X*. Cover and let rise until doubled in size, about 1 hour.

Brush with the egg glaze and bake.

For the 2-quart size: Bake at 425°F for 5 minutes, then at 375°F for 40 to 45 minutes, or until the top is well browned and the brioche sounds hollow when tapped.

For the 1-quart size: Bake at 425°F for 5 minutes, then at 375°F for 30 to 35 minutes.

For the 2-cup size: Bake at 425°F for 5 minutes, then at 375°F for 20 to 25 minutes.

Makes 1 2-quart brioche,
2 1-quart brioches,
or 4 2-cup brioches.

Basil Buttermilk Buns

¼ cup lukewarm water
1 tablespoon dry yeast
1 tablespoon honey
½ cup lukewarm buttermilk
3 cloves garlic, minced
1½ tablespoons minced basil or 2 teaspoons dried basil
1 tablespoon minced rosemary or 1½ teaspoons dried rosemary, crushed
1 tablespoon sesame seeds
1 egg
½ cup grated Parmesan cheese
2-2½ cups whole wheat flour
1 egg beaten with 1 teaspoon water (as a glaze)
1 tablespoon sesame seeds (as a topping)

Combine the water, yeast and honey in a cup, and set aside to proof for 10 minutes (the yeast will become foamy).

Combine the yeast mixture, buttermilk, garlic, basil, rosemary, 1 tablespoon sesame seeds and 1 egg in a large bowl. Beat well to combine.

Beat in the Parmesan and 1 cup of flour with a wooden spoon. Then stir in enough additional flour to make a soft, kneadable dough.

Turn the dough out onto a lightly floured surface and knead for about 10 minutes or until smooth and elastic. The dough may be slightly tacky, but add only enough flour to prevent actual sticking.

Form dough into a ball, place in an oiled bowl and turn to coat dough on all sides. Cover and let rise in a warm place until doubled in bulk, from 30 to 60 minutes.

Punch down the dough and turn out onto a lightly floured surface. Knead briefly, and then form into a log about 12 inches long. Cut the log into 12 equal pieces and form each piece into a small, smooth ball.

Butter, oil or coat a 9-inch cake pan with equal parts of oil and liquid lecithin. Form a square with four of the dough balls in the center of the pan, and then arrange the remaining balls around it. It is not necessary that they all touch. Cover lightly and let rise in a warm place until doubled in bulk, from 30 to 60 minutes.

Very carefully brush the dough balls with the egg glaze and sprinkle them with sesame seeds. Bake at 350°F for about 25 minutes, or until the buns are golden and sound hollow when tapped. Unmold the rolls and return them to the oven for 5 minutes to crisp their bottoms.

Serve warm or reheated.

Makes 1 dozen buns.

Rich Yeast Dough

The butter in this dough makes it especially easy to handle. This recipe yields two large loaves, one to go with the cinnamon apricot filling that follows and the other to use with the cardamom prune filling offered. Both are delicious at breakfast.

¼ cup lukewarm water
4 teaspoons dry yeast
3 tablespoons honey
3 eggs
½ cup butter, melted
½ cup yogurt
¼ teaspoon almond extract (optional)
1 teaspoon *Vanilla Extract* (see *Index*)
1 cup whole wheat pastry flour
2-2½ cups whole wheat flour
Apricot Filling (see opposite page)
Prune Filling (see opposite page)
1 egg beaten with 1 teaspoon milk (as a glaze)

Combine the water, yeast and honey in a cup. Set aside to proof (the yeast will become foamy).

Transfer to a large bowl. Beat in the eggs, butter, yogurt, almond extract and vanilla until they are well combined. Beat in the whole wheat

Rich Yeast Dough—*continued*

pastry flour. Gradually stir in enough additional flour to make a soft, kneadable dough.

Turn the dough out onto a floured surface. Knead until smooth and elastic, about 10 minutes. Try not to add more flour than necessary to prevent sticking.

Form the dough into a ball and transfer to an oiled bowl. Turn it to coat the top. Cover and let rise in a warm place until doubled in bulk, about 1 hour.

Punch the dough down and divide in half. Your dough is now ready to be filled.

On a lightly floured surface roll out each piece into a rectangle measuring about 9 by 18 inches. Turn it so that a 9-inch edge is facing you. Spread either the apricot or prune filling over two-thirds of the dough and leave a half-inch border at the top and sides.

Fold the dough into thirds like a business letter: Bring the bottom third up to cover half the filling, and fold the top third down to cover the other.

Pinch the seams to seal the letter.

Carefully transfer each piece to a lightly buttered cookie sheet. With a sharp knife make seven cuts across piece of dough, starting at one 9-inch edge and cutting to within 1 inch of the other side. Separate these strips slightly, but leave them attached at the folded edge.

Cover loosely and let rise until doubled in bulk, about 1 hour.

Brush each loaf with the egg glaze. Bake at 350°F for 25 to 30 minutes, or until golden. Cool on wire racks.

Makes 2 filled breads.

Apricot Filling

½ cup dried apricots
1 cup water
2 tablespoons honey
¼ cup wheat germ
¼ cup chopped pecans or walnuts
½ teaspoon ground cinnamon
grated rind of 1 orange

Bring the apricots and water to a simmer in a small saucepan. Cover and cook for about 10 minutes. Then drain the apricots, and force through a sieve or puree in a food mill or food processor.

Beat in the honey, wheat germ, nuts, cinnamon and orange rind.

Prune Filling

¾ cup pitted prunes
¾ cup water
¼ cup raisins
1 tablespoon honey
½ teaspoon ground cardamom
⅛ teaspoon grated nutmeg
grated rind of 1 lemon

Bring the prunes and water to a simmer in a small saucepan. Cover and cook for about 10 minutes. Then drain the prunes, and force through a sieve or puree in a food mill or food processor.

Stir in the raisins, honey, cardamom, nutmeg and lemon rind.

Buttermilk Biscuits

1¾ cups *sifted* whole wheat pastry flour
  2 teaspoons *Baking Powder* (see page 89)
  ¼ teaspoon baking soda
  ¼ cup cold butter
  1 tablespoon minced tarragon or
      1½ teaspoons dried tarragon
  ¼ cup minced dill or 2 tablespoons dried dill
⅔-¾ cup buttermilk
  1 egg beaten with 1 teaspoon water (as a
      glaze)

Resift flour this time adding *Baking Powder* and baking soda.

With two knives or a pastry blender cut cold butter into the flour mixture to form a coarse meal. Stir in the tarragon and dill.

With a fork stir in enough buttermilk to make a soft, kneadable dough. Turn it out onto a lightly floured surface and knead gently about 20 times to form a smooth dough. Do not overhandle.

Roll out to ½ inch thick, and cut into rounds with a 2-inch biscuit cutter.

Place on an ungreased cookie sheet. Brush with the egg glaze. Bake at 425°F for about 15 minutes, until puffed, crisp and lightly browned.

Serve immediately.

Makes about 15 biscuits.

Mini Coriander Biscuits

Be careful not to overbake these tasty coriander morsels.

  2 cups whole wheat pastry flour
  1 tablespoon *Baking Powder* (see page 89)
  2 teaspoons ground coriander
  2 tablespoons sesame seeds
  2 tablespoons grated Parmesan cheese
  2 tablespoons snipped chives
  ¼ cup cold butter
  1 cup milk
  1 egg beaten with 1 teaspoon milk (as a glaze)
      sesame seeds (as a topping)

In a large bowl combine the flour, *Baking Powder*, coriander, sesame seeds, Parmesan and chives. Then, cut in the butter with a pastry blender or two knives until the mixture forms a coarse meal.

With a fork stir in the milk until the mixture forms a soft dough and leaves the sides of the bowl.

Turn the dough out onto a lightly floured surface, and, with floured hands, form it into a log about 1½ inches thick.

With a sharp knife cut into pieces about ¾ inch thick. Arrange the pieces on their sides on a lightly greased baking sheet, leaving about an inch between each biscuit.

Brush with egg glaze and sprinkle with sesame seeds. Bake at 375°F for 20 minutes, or until the biscuits are puffed and lightly browned. Serve warm.

Makes 14 to 16 biscuits.

Sage-Dill Cornmeal Muffins

These quick muffins can be ready to go anytime you need them. Just premix the dry ingredients, and keep them in a tightly closed container; by enclosing a note listing the wet ingredients and baking directions, you'll be creating your own muffin mix.

⅔ cup *sifted* whole wheat pastry flour
⅔ cup cornmeal
2 teaspoons *Baking Powder* (see page 89)
1 teaspoon baking soda
2 tablespoons butter, melted
⅔ cup buttermilk
3 tablespoons honey
2 eggs
2 tablespoons minced sage or 2 teaspoons
   dried sage
2 tablespoons minced dill or 1 tablespoon
   dried dill

Butter 12 muffin cups or coat with a mixture of equal parts of oil and liquid lecithin. Set aside.

Resift the flour, this time adding the cornmeal, *Baking Powder* and baking soda.

In another bowl use a whisk to beat together the butter, buttermilk, honey and eggs until they are smooth. Stir in the sage and dill.

Then, add the liquid ingredients to the dry ones, mixing just until the flour is moistened. Do not overmix.

Spoon the batter into prepared muffin cups, filling each to about two-thirds.

Bake at 350°F for 20 minutes, or until the muffins are puffed and golden.

Serve warm.

Makes 1 dozen muffins.

Coriander

Coriander's name comes from the Greek word for "bug," in reference to its rather unpleasant odor. That aspect aside, coriander seeds have been a popular ingredient in medicine and food since early times. The Chinese thought coriander had the power to confer immortality, and they still believe it is invested with the ability to treat stomachaches, nausea and measles. Herbalists use it to relieve colic and indigestion and apply it externally to soothe painful joints.

Potato Thyme Rolls

These are particularly light rolls thanks to the mashed potatoes in them. To make sure yours are as light as they should be, do not knead in any more flour than is absolutely necessary. The dough should remain soft.

You may form the dough into clover leaf rolls as described, or vary the recipe slightly by cutting each rope of dough into 12 pieces and placing 2 in each muffin cup.

¼ cup lukewarm water
1 tablespoon dry yeast
2 tablespoons honey
½ cup mashed potatoes
½ cup buttermilk
3 tablespoons butter
3 tablespoons minced thyme or 1 tablespoon dried thyme
1 egg
3-4 cups whole wheat flour
1 egg beaten with 1 teaspoon milk (as a glaze)

Combine the water, yeast and honey in a cup. Set aside to proof for 10 minutes (the yeast will become foamy).

In a small saucepan combine the potatoes, buttermilk, butter and thyme. Heat to luke-warm. Combine with the yeast mixture and an egg in a large bowl. Stir in 1 cup of flour and beat well. Stir in another cup of flour, half a cup at a time. If necessary, add a little more flour to form a soft but kneadable dough. Do not add more flour than is necessary to work the dough. Knead until smooth and elastic.

Transfer the dough to an oiled bowl and turn to coat it with oil. Let rise until double in bulk, about an hour.

Punch the dough down and turn it out onto a lightly floured surface. Divide it into thirds. With your palms roll each piece into an 18-inch rope. Cut each rope into 18 pieces, and shape each piece into a smooth ball.

Butter 18 muffin cups. Place 3 balls in each cup. Let them rise in a warm place until they're doubled in bulk and fill the muffin cups. Then, brush gently with the egg glaze.

Bake at 400°F for 12 to 15 minutes, or until rolls are lightly browned. Serve warm.

Makes 18 rolls.

Honey Raisin Bread

½ cup lukewarm water
2 teaspoons dry yeast
1 tablespoon honey
½ cup warm water
¼ cup oil
1 egg
3 tablespoons honey
1 cup rolled oats
1 cup whole wheat pastry flour
2 teaspoons ground cinnamon
¼ teaspoon ground cardamom
1½-2 cups whole wheat flour
½ cup golden raisins
1 egg beaten with 1 teaspoon water (as a glaze)

Combine the ½ cup lukewarm water, yeast and 1 tablespoon of honey in a cup. Set aside to proof (the yeast will become foamy).

In a large bowl combine the ½ cup water, oil, egg, 3 tablespoons honey, oats, pastry flour, cinnamon and cardamom. Stir in the yeast mixture.

Beat for 2 minutes, stirring in enough flour to make a soft, kneadable dough. Turn out onto a floured surface, and knead for 10 minutes, or until the dough is smooth and elastic. Try not to knead in more flour than is necessary to prevent sticking.

Transfer the dough to an oiled bowl. Turn the dough to coat it with oil. Cover and set in a warm place to rise. Let rise until doubled in bulk, about 1½ hours.

Punch the dough down. Turn it out onto a lightly floured surface, and knead in raisins. Work the dough until the raisins are well distributed, about 5 minutes.

Honey Raisin Bread—*continued*

Form into a loaf. Transfer to a buttered 8½-by-4½-inch bread pan or one that has been coated with equal parts of oil and liquid lecithin.

Let rise until doubled in bulk, from 30 to 60 minutes.

Brush the top with the egg glaze.

Bake at 350°F for 35 to 40 minutes, or until the top is golden and the loaf sounds hollow when tapped with the fingers.

Makes 1 loaf.

Cardamom Tea Ring

This tasty sweet bread is best when served warm straight from the oven, although it can be successfully reheated later on.

The Dough
¼ cup lukewarm water
1 tablespoon dry yeast
¼ cup milk
¼ cup butter
¼ cup honey
1 teaspoon cardamom seeds, crushed
1 egg yolk
½ cup whole wheat pastry flour
1-2 cups whole wheat flour

The Filling
2 tablespoons orange juice
2 tablespoons honey
⅓ cup milk
¼ teaspoon almond extract
¼ teaspoon *Vanilla Extract* (see *Index*)
½ cup almonds

1 egg white beaten with 1 tablespoon water (as a glaze)
¼ cup currants
¼ cup chopped golden raisins

To make the dough: Combine the water and yeast in a cup. Set aside to proof (the yeast will become foamy).

In a small saucepan, heat the milk, butter and honey until the butter melts. Cool to luke-warm, and stir in the yeast mixture.

Transfer to a large bowl. Stir in the carda-mom and egg yolk. Beat in the pastry flour. Add the whole wheat flour, a half cup at a time, until a soft kneadable dough forms.

Turn out onto a lightly floured surface and knead until smooth, about 10 minutes. Then transfer to an oiled bowl, turning to coat the top. Cover and let rise in a warm place until doubled in bulk, about 1½ hours.

To make the filling: Combine the orange juice, honey, milk, almond extract, vanilla and half the almonds in a blender or food processor, and process until fairly smooth. Add the remaining almonds and continue processing until a paste forms. Set aside.

To assemble: When the dough has risen, punch it down and knead briefly. On a lightly floured surface, roll the dough into a rectangle about 13 by 20 inches. Make sure the sides are even.

Brush the surface of the dough with the egg glaze, and spread the filling to within ½ inch of the edges. Sprinkle with currants and raisins.

Roll up the dough lengthwise like a jelly roll, and transfer it to a buttered cookie sheet, seam side down. Then, form it into a ring, tuck one end into the other, and pinch the seams shut.

With a sharp knife or scissors, slash the dough at 1-inch intervals to within ½ inch of the ring's center. Twist each segment slightly to expose filling.

Cover loosely and let rise in a warm place until doubled in bulk, about 1½ hours.

Brush the ring with the egg glaze, and bake at 350°F for about 30 minutes, or until the top is golden and the bread sounds hollow when tapped. If the top browns too rapidly, cover it loosely with foil.

Carefully transfer to a wire rack to cool.

Makes 1 ring.

Zucchini Cheddar Bread

This moist, cheesy loaf is a wonderful thing to make with an unmanageably large harvest of zucchini.

2¼ cups whole wheat pastry flour
 2 teaspoons *Baking Powder* (see page 89)
 1 teaspoon baking soda
 1 tablespoon minced basil or 1 teaspoon
   dried basil
 1 tablespoon minced thyme or 1 teaspoon
   dried thyme
 1 cup minced onion
 2 tablespoons butter
 1 cup milk
 3 eggs
 1 cup shredded zucchini
 1 cup shredded Cheddar cheese

Sift the flour, *Baking Powder* and baking soda together, and stir in the basil and thyme.

In a frying pan sauté the onion in butter until soft.

In a large bowl beat the milk and eggs together until smooth. Stir in the flour until well blended. Then, fold in the onions. zucchini and Cheddar.

Butter a 9-inch, round cake pan or coat it with equal parts of oil and liquid lecithin.

Spoon the batter into the pan, and bake at 400°F for about 30 minutes, or until a toothpick inserted into the center comes out clean and the top is golden. Serve warm.

Makes 1 loaf.

Apricot Carrot Loaf

A scrumptious dessert bread.

⅓ cup dried apricots
1½ cups whole wheat pastry flour
 1 tablespoon *Baking Powder* (see page 89)
 ½ teaspoon ground cinnamon
 ¼ teaspoon grated nutmeg
 ¼ teaspoon powdered ginger
 ½ cup bran
 ⅓ cup oil
 ⅓ cup honey
 ½ cup buttermilk
 2 eggs
 1 cup shredded carrots
   grated rind of 1 lemon
 ¼ cup sunflower seeds
 ⅓ cup golden raisins

Butter a 9-by-5-inch loaf pan or grease it with equal parts of oil and liquid lecithin. Set aside.

If the apricots are soft, chop them into pieces about the size of raisins. Otherwise, put the dried apricots into a small saucepan and cover with water. Bring to a boil and cook over medium heat for 10 minutes, or until they are soft. Drain, dry on paper towels and chop into raisin-size pieces. Set aside.

Sift together the flour, *Baking Powder*, cinnamon, nutmeg and ginger. Stir in the bran.

In a large bowl beat the oil, honey, buttermilk and eggs together with a whisk until they are well blended. Then, stir in the carrots, lemon rind and apricots.

Stir in the flour mixture, sunflower seeds and raisins. Blend until all flour is just moistened. Do not overbeat.

Pour into the prepared pan. Bake at 350°F for 40 to 50 minutes, or until a toothpick inserted into the center of the loaf comes out clean.

Remove from the pan and cool on a wire rack.

Makes 1 loaf.

Sage Corn Bread

Fresh sage is best in this corn bread which can also be baked in a 9-inch, cast-iron skillet.

  1 cup whole wheat pastry flour
  ¾ cup cornmeal
  1½ teaspoons *Baking Powder* (see page 89)
  ½ teaspoon baking soda
  2 tablespoons minced sage or 1 teaspoon
        dried sage
  1 cup buttermilk
  2 tablespoons honey
  2 eggs
  3 tablespoons butter, melted

Butter an 8-inch-square pan or coat it with equal parts of oil and liquid lecithin.

Sift the flour, cornmeal, *Baking Powder* and baking soda into a large bowl. Stir in the sage.

In a smaller bowl beat the buttermilk, honey, eggs and butter together until well blended.

Stir the liquid ingredients into the dry ones with just enough strokes to moisten the flour. Do not overmix.

Pour the batter into the prepared pan, and bake at 425°F for 25 to 30 minutes, or until the top is golden and a toothpick inserted into the center comes out clean.

Serve warm.

Makes 1 corn bread.

Cumin

Cumin, an ancient plant native to Egypt, is currently noted more for its spicy flavor than for its medicinal value. It was esteemed for its ability to relieve colic and was considered beneficial for flatulence and headache from indigestion. The seeds in the form of a plaster were also recommended to relieve pain.

Savory Potato Bread

⅔ cup lukewarm water
4 teaspoons dry yeast
3 tablespoons honey
2 cups lukewarm buttermilk
3 tablespoons oil
⅔ cup mashed potatoes
2 tablespoons minced savory or 2 teaspoons
    dried savory
2 teaspoons dill seed
2 cloves garlic, minced
1 cup whole wheat pastry flour
5-5½ cups whole wheat flour

Combine the water, yeast and honey in a cup. Set aside for 10 minutes to proof (yeast will become foamy).

In a large bowl beat together the buttermilk, oil, potatoes, savory, dill and garlic until well combined. Stir in the yeast mixture.

Add 1 cup of whole wheat pastry flour and beat vigorously until well mixed. Beat in 2 cups of whole wheat flour, one at a time, until they're well mixed.

Stir in enough additional flour, using a wooden spoon, to produce a soft, kneadable dough.

Turn the dough out onto a floured surface. Knead vigorously for about 10 to 15 minutes, or until the dough is smooth and elastic. Add only enough additional flour to prevent sticking. The finished dough will remain a bit sticky.

Transfer to an oiled bowl. Turn dough to coat. Cover the bowl and set in a warm place to rise. Let rise until doubled in bulk, about 40 to 60 minutes.

Punch down dough and divide into two pieces. Form each piece into a loaf.

Butter two 8½-by-4½-inch loaf pans, or coat them with equal parts of oil and liquid lecithin. Transfer dough to the pans.

Cover loosely and set in a warm place to rise until doubled in bulk, about 40 to 60 minutes.

Bake at 375°F for about 40 minutes, or until the loaves sound hollow when tapped with the fingers.

Makes 2 loaves.

Sweet Zucchini Bread

1½ cups whole wheat pastry flour
1 teaspoon baking soda
¼ teaspoon *Baking Powder* (see page 89)
1½ teaspoons ground cinnamon
¼ teaspoon grated nutmeg
⅓ cup oil
½ cup honey
⅓ cup buttermilk
2 eggs
2 teaspoons *Vanilla Extract* (see *Index*)
1 cup (packed) squeezed dry shredded
    zucchini
⅓ cup raisins

Butter an 8½-by-4½-inch loaf pan or coat it with equal parts of oil and liquid lecithin.

Sift the flour, baking soda, *Baking Powder,* cinnamon and nutmeg into a large bowl.

In a smaller bowl beat the oil, honey, buttermilk, eggs and vanilla together until they are smooth.

Pour the liquid ingredients into the flour. Stir them to combine. Do not overbeat. Then, fold in the zucchini and raisins.

Pour into the prepared pan. Bake at 350°F for about 50 minutes, or until a toothpick inserted in the center comes out clean.

Makes 1 loaf.

Sparky's Banana Bread

This delicious loaf gets its extra fiber from the bran and gets B6, potassium and magnesium from the bananas.

TIP: When bananas are cheap, buy extra, mash them and freeze the pulp in one-cup containers; they'll make this bread an even quicker affair than it already is.

1½ cups whole wheat pastry flour
 1 teaspoon baking soda
 1 teaspoon ground cinnamon
⅛ teaspoon ground cloves
½ cup bran
½ cup chopped nuts or sunflower seeds
 1 cup mashed ripe bananas (about 2 or 3)
 1 egg
⅓ cup oil
⅓ cup honey
⅓ cup orange juice
 2 teaspoons *Vanilla Extract* (see *Index*)

Butter an 8½-by-4½-inch loaf pan or coat it with equal parts of oil and liquid lecithin.

In a large bowl sift together the flour, baking soda, cinnamon and cloves. Stir in the bran and nuts or sunflower seeds.

In another bowl beat together the bananas, egg, oil, honey, orange juice and vanilla until smooth. Stir into the dry ingredients just until they are blended.

Pour the batter into the prepared pan. Bake at 350°F for 50 to 60 minutes, or until a skewer inserted in the middle comes out clean.

Makes 1 loaf.

Dandelion

Dandelion (from the French *dent de lion*) is a nutritionally wholesome plant that has been valued through the ages, sometimes as a means of survival. All parts of the plant, especially the root, are rich in vitamins and minerals, which warrants its reputation as an all-purpose tonic. Herbalists recommend dandelion juice or tea for diuretic purposes, to relieve liver ailments and constipation, to improve appetite and to promote sleep.

Better Butters for Better Health

I call these "Better Butters" because they better butter in several important concerns, especially calories, fat and cholesterol. *Better Butter I*, for instance, has about half the cholesterol and only 80 percent of the fat and calories of regular butter. And *Better Butter II* is lower in all these areas too. The exact reductions in each case will depend on which *Basic Mayonnaise* you begin with. *Basic Tofu Mayonnaise* yields the lowest figures; that is, about half the calories, 40 percent of the fat and half the cholesterol of butter.

Use these butters as spreads and as toppings on baked potatoes or other dishes. I wouldn't recommend sautéing with them or freezing them.

To make these into Better Butters, stir in minced herbs in any combination. For suggestions, see the section in *Chapter 2* on herb butters.

Better Butter I

½ cup softened butter
¼ cup yogurt
¼ cup oil

Beat the butter, yogurt and oil together.

Makes 1 cup.

Better Butter II

⅓ cup softened butter
⅓ cup yogurt
⅓ cup *Basic Mayonnaise* (see *Index*)

Beat the butter, yogurt and mayonnaise together.

Makes 1 cup.

Garlic Butter

There's an extra measure of garlic in this butter, but it won't overwhelm you. If that statement doesn't reassure you, remember that parboiling garlic for a few minutes tames its flavor.

1 bulb unpeeled garlic
½ cup softened butter
2 tablespoons grated Parmesan cheese
2 tablespoons minced parsley
2 teaspoons lemon juice

Separate the garlic into individual cloves. Drop into boiling water and cook for 2 to 3 minutes. The skins will then slip off easily, and the garlic will not be quite as powerful. Mince and then mash into a paste.

Beat the butter, garlic, Parmesan, parsley and lemon juice together until they are well combined.

Transfer the mixture to a small dish or crock for serving. Or put it into a pastry bag fitted with a large star tube, and then pipe rosettes of the butter onto a cookie sheet lined with wax paper. Refrigerate to harden, peel the rosettes from the paper and store in a tightly closed container.

Makes about ¾ cup.

Chapter 8
Vegetarian Entrees

Beans

Everyone makes rude jokes about them, but if you care beans about your health, you should give them a prominent place in your diet. Why? Because — besides being cheap and filling — they are high in vitamins, minerals and fiber.

Beans contain a wonderfully balanced mixture of the major nutrients; they are about 20 percent protein, 65 percent carbohydrates, have very little fat and no cholesterol. What's more, they're good sources of the B vitamins, riboflavin, niacin and B6, and they supply the important minerals, calcium and iron. Perhaps best of all, a single serving of beans supplies half the Recommended Dietary Allowance of iron for men and a third of the RDA for women.

Beans are also rich in potassium and low in sodium — an ideal combination for people on low-sodium, high-potassium diets — like those with high blood pressure. And they're high in fiber, which goes a long way toward keeping your digestive system in good working order. Not only that, but studies have shown that fiber can lower blood cholesterol, and that can reduce the risk of heart disease. Not bad credentials for an abused vegetable.

Of course, nobody's perfect, and beans are no exception. Although they are high in protein, their protein is incomplete — meaning that it does not supply *all* the essential amino acids in *just* the right proportions for human use. But that shortcoming is easily remedied. Combining beans with grains like rice, corn or wheat completes their protein in short order. And adding small amounts of meat, eggs or milk also raises the protein quality of beans markedly.

Here are some common beans that you should care about and use often:

- Black-eyed beans (also called black-eyed peas or cow peas) have a pealike flavor and buttery texture; use as a main dish.
- Black beans (turtle beans) are ebony-colored beans that are delicious in casseroles and soups; bring out their flavor with cumin, garlic, bay leaves and tomatoes.
- Chick-peas (garbanzos) have a nutlike flavor that makes them ideal for salads, dips, soups and casseroles.
- Large limas (butter beans) possess a rich buttery flavor which makes them excellent in main dishes; try them in casseroles.
- Red kidney beans are an all-purpose favorite and can be used in any recipe calling for colored beans.
- Mung beans are an olive green variety that can be used in purees, soups or stews; they're ideal for sprouting.
- Navy beans are medium-size white beans that are wonderful baked, or use in soups and stews.
- Pinto beans are either beige colored or speckled; they're popular in chili, refried beans and other Mexican dishes.

Except for lentils and split peas, all dried beans must be soaked in water before using. But before you submerge them, make sure you discard the small stones and other unwelcome fellow travelers that sometimes get mixed in with beans. Throw out any discolored or badly broken beans too. The easiest way to do this weeding out is to spread the beans out on a clean (preferably solid color) kitchen towel and look at the whole batch all at once. When you've removed the offenders, gather up the towel and pour the beans into a strainer for a quick rinse.

There are several methods for soaking beans and the one you use will depend on how much time you have. The easiest method is to put the beans in a large bowl, cover them with lots of cold water and let them stand, uncovered and at room temperature, overnight.

With less time, an alternate approach is to place the beans in a pot, cover them with water and then bring the combination to a boil. Then reduce the heat and simmer the beans for two minutes. Remove the pot from the stove, cover it, and let the beans soak for one hour.

Finally, we'll have to face those rude comments: Beans cause gas. That's because they contain certain sugars that the body cannot break down during digestion. Fortunately, those carbohydrates are water soluble and your digestion can be aided by proper cooking. Soak your beans as outlined above, and then discard the soaking water. Now cook the beans in fresh water for half an hour, and then discard that water, too. Finally, finish cooking your batch in still more fresh water. By that time much of the resistant sugar will have leached out of the beans, but of course, you'll also be throwing out some of their nutrients with all that cooking water. But you can help compensate for these losses by adding one teaspoon of brewer's yeast to the finished beans for each half cup of dried beans.

Unless they will receive further preparation, beans should always be cooked until tender. One test for doneness is to blow on a few hot beans on a spoon; if the skins burst, they're done.

Inca Beans and Rice

Here's a spicy bean dish from South America that combines beans and rice to produce complete protein.

    2 cups stock
    ⅔ cup uncooked long-grain brown rice
    2 cups diced onions
    2 cloves garlic, minced
  1–2 hot chili peppers, minced
    2 teaspoons ground cumin
    2 tablespoons oil
    2 cups cooked red beans
    ½ cup *Tomato Juice* (see *Index*)
    3 tablespoons minced basil or 1 tablespoon
        dried basil
    2 tablespoons minced parsley
    1 tablespoon minced oregano or 1 teaspoon
        dried oregano
    1 cup yogurt

In a medium saucepan bring the stock and rice to a boil. Cover and cook over low heat until the rice is tender and all the liquid has been absorbed, about 45 to 50 minutes.

In a large frying pan over low heat, sauté the onions, garlic, chili peppers and cumin in oil until they're tender, about 10 minutes.

When the rice is done, transfer it to a 2-quart casserole dish, and fold in the onion mixture, beans, *Tomato Juice*, basil, parsley and oregano. Cover and bake at 350°F for 30 minutes. Serve with yogurt.

Serves 4.

Caribbean Beans and Rice

The Beans
    ½ cup adzuki beans
    1 onion, minced
    2 cloves garlic, minced
    1 tablespoon oil
    1 red or green chili pepper, minced
    1 bay leaf
    ¾ cup *Tomato Juice* (see *Index*)
    ¾ cup stock

The Rice
    2 cups stock
    ⅔ cup uncooked long-grain brown rice

The Assembly
    ¼ cup *Tomato Juice* (see *Index*)
    2 ounces mild cheese, sliced

To make the beans: Bring several cups of water to a boil in a large saucepan. Add the beans and boil for 2 minutes. Cover and let stand for 30 minutes away from the heat. Drain, and transfer to a bowl.

In the same pan, lightly sauté the onion and garlic in oil until they're limp. Do *not* let the garlic brown. Add the chili pepper, bay leaf, *Tomato Juice*, stock and beans; cover and simmer over low heat for 1½ hours, or until the beans are tender. If necessary, add a little more liquid. Remove the bay leaf.

To make the rice: Bring the stock and rice to a boil in a medium saucepan. Cover and cook over low heat until the rice is tender and the liquid is absorbed, about 50 minutes.

To assemble: Transfer the rice to a 2-quart casserole dish. Pour the *Tomato Juice* over the rice, and spoon the beans on top. Cover with cheese. Place under the broiler for a few minutes to melt the cheese.

Serves 4.

Lentil Tacos

Lentils give these tacos a meaty taste, but they have less fat and calories than beef.

The Filling
1½ cups minced onions
 ½ cup minced celery
 ½ cup minced pepper
 2 cloves garlic, minced
 2 tablespoons oil
 ¼ cup minced parsley
 2 tablespoons *Chili Powder* (see *Index*)
 ½ teaspoon ground cumin
 ¼ teaspoon cayenne pepper (or to taste)
 1 bay leaf
 1 cup lentils
 1 cup *Tomato Juice* (see *Index*)
 1 cup chopped tomatoes
 1 cup stock
 2 teaspoons blackstrap molasses
 2 teaspoons tamari sauce
 2 tablespoons raisins

The Assembly
 8 corn tortillas
 shredded cheese
 shredded lettuce
 chopped tomatoes

To make the filling: In a large frying pan cook the onions, celery, pepper and garlic in oil over low heat until the onions are wilted. Add the rest of the ingredients and cook over low heat for 1 hour. Uncover and continue cooking, stirring frequently, until the mixture is thick.

To assemble: Heat the tortillas at 350°F for 5 to 8 minutes or until crisp. Fill with lentils, cheese, lettuce and tomatoes.

Serves 4.

Vegetable Chili

I like to use adzuki beans in this meatless chili, because they're smaller than kidney beans and cook faster.

 1 cup adzuki beans
 2 tablespoons oil
 2 cups finely chopped onions
 2 cups diced celery
 2 cups diced carrots
 4 cloves garlic, minced
 1 pepper, diced
 1 tablespoon *Chili Powder* (see *Index*)
 2 tablespoons whole wheat flour
1½ cups stock
 4 cups crushed tomatoes
 3 cups hot cooked brown rice (see page 205 for cooking instructions)

In a saucepan bring 4 cups of water to a boil, and then stir in the beans. Cover, remove from heat and let stand for 30 minutes. Drain and set aside.

In a large pot heat the oil over a medium-low flame. Add the onions, celery, carrots, garlic and pepper. Sauté for 5 to 10 minutes, or until the onions and peppers are tender.

Stir in the *Chili Powder* and flour. Add the stock, tomatoes and beans. Cover and simmer for 30 minutes. Then, remove the lid and simmer 30 minutes more, or until the vegetables and beans are tender and the liquid has thickened.

Serve over hot brown rice.

Serves 4 to 6.

Falafel Pockets

A favorite Middle East sandwich with a bean and bulgur filling and a spicy sauce.

The Falafel
  ½ cup chick-peas, soaked overnight
  ⅓ cup stock
  ⅓ cup uncooked bulgur
  1½ tablespoons butter
    pinch of ground cinnamon
  3 cloves garlic, minced
  ⅓ cup stock
  4½ teaspoons whole wheat pastry flour
  1 small dried hot pepper, ground
  ½ teaspoon ground cumin
  2 tablespoons minced coriander leaves
  2 tablespoons tahini (sesame seed paste)
  1 tablespoon lemon juice
  ½ cup whole wheat breadcrumbs

The Assembly
  1 egg
  1 tablespoon water
1-1½ cups whole wheat breadcrumbs
1-2 tablespoons butter
1-2 tablespoons oil
4-6 whole wheat pita breads, cut in half
    chopped tomatoes
  1 cup yogurt
  ⅛ teaspoon cayenne pepper
    alfalfa sprouts

To make the falafel: Bring 4 cups of water to a boil in a large saucepan. Add the soaked chick-peas, cover and cook them over medium heat for 1 to 1½ hours or until tender. Drain. Puree with a food mill or food processor.

Bring ⅓ cup of stock to a boil in a small saucepan and stir in the bulgur. Cover, remove from the heat and let it stand for 20 minutes. When the liquid is absorbed, fluff with two forks.

In a small saucepan heat the butter over medium-low heat until it foams. Stir in the cinnamon and garlic and cook, stirring constantly, for several minutes to soften the garlic. Do not let the garlic brown.

In a small saucepan heat the ⅓ cup of stock.

Stir the flour into the butter mixture. Cook, stirring constantly, for 2 minutes, and then add the hot stock all at once. Beat with a wire whisk to combine. Cook, stirring all the while, until the sauce comes to a boil and becomes very thick. Stir in the pepper and cumin.

In a large bowl beat together the chick-pea puree, the bulgur, sauce, coriander, tahini, lemon juice and breadcrumbs until they're thoroughly mixed. Refrigerate at least 1 hour.

To assemble: Form the falafel mixture into patties about ½ inch thick and 2 inches in diameter.

Lightly beat the egg and water together in a shallow bowl. Dip the patties into the egg, then the breadcrumbs, to coat them completely.

Heat 1 tablespoon of butter and 1 tablespoon of oil in a large frying pan over medium heat. Add the falafel patties and cook until they're golden on both sides. If necessary, use more butter and oil.

Serve the patties in warm pita pockets. Top with tomatoes, yogurt mixed with cayenne and sprouts.

Serves 4.

Making Crepes

The whole wheat crepes that follow are amazingly light and delicate—they rival any white flour crepe around. Although crepe making has become quite popular in recent years, a bit of mystery still clings to the process. Many people who toss off pancakes with ease remain intimidated by crepes, but the technique is quite simple and, with a little practice, almost anyone can master it. Follow these guidelines:

- Make sure that the whole wheat flour is finely ground. You may use either regular or pastry flour; however, the delicate crepes made with pastry flour often give beginners trouble.
- Mix the batter by hand, with a mixer or in a blender. The blender seems the easiest to me. Just add all the ingredients and process until they are smooth, stopping once or twice to scrape down the sides of the container.
- Cover the batter and refrigerate it for at least an hour before proceeding. This allows the flour to expand and absorb all the liquid. It also permits any trapped air bubbles to collapse. If you have mixed the batter by hand, strain it before using just to be sure it's perfectly smooth.
- The chilled batter should have the consistency of heavy cream. If it is too thick, thin it with a little milk or water. If it is too thin, whisk in a bit of flour and then let the batter rest again.
- The batter will naturally thicken during the cooking period (especially as you near the bottom of the bowl). Thin it as necessary with water or milk.

- Use a pan with a bottom six or eight inches in diameter. Although a special pan is not necessary for crepes, a well-seasoned, iron crepe or omelet pan is ideal. However, I've also had excellent results with aluminum-bottomed stainless steel, no-stick and well-seasoned, cast-iron pans.
- The heat of the pan is crucial. Too hot a pan will produce burned and rippled crepes, and too cool a pan leaves you with tough crepes. Test the pan by dashing a few drops of water onto it. If the drops disappear immediately, the pan is too hot. If they go up in steam, it's too cool. If they dance across the surface before disappearing, it's just right.
- Grease the pan for the first few crepes to avoid sticking. Moisten a paper towel with oil (or a mixture of oil and liquid lecithin), and wipe the hot pan. If the pan is properly seasoned, the butter in the crepes will be sufficient to prevent sticking after this initial wipe.
- If the crepes stick during cooking, wipe the pan clean again with the oiled towel. If the troublesome spots don't come off, pour in a bit of salt and rub them away with a paper towel. Wipe off the salt with a clean towel and moisten the pan with the oiled towel.
- Make your first crepe a test, and be prepared to discard it. Pour a small amount of batter into the pan. If it sizzles, erupts in little bubbles on the surface, and then browns quickly, you're ready to continue.
- Use a small ladle to add a scant quarter cup of batter into the pan for each crepe and then quickly tilt the pan in all directions to coat the bottom with batter. If there is any excess, pour it back into the batter bowl.

(continued)

Making Crepes—*continued*

- Cook the crepe for just a minute or two, or until the top is dry and the bottom is golden. Then, lift the edges with a spatula and flip it over. Let the bottom brown for about a half minute.
- As it is finished, place each crepe on a square of wax paper, cover with another and then place the next crepe on top of that to keep them from sticking together.
- If you're not going to use the crepes immediately, wrap them in foil or plastic wrap and refrigerate; they'll keep for several days.
- For longer storage, freeze them. Wrap enough crepes for a meal (bundles of eight are usually good) in foil and then in freezer paper. Date and label the bundles.
- Allow crepes to thaw at least 15 minutes before separating.
- You can also freeze filled crepes for use as an oven-ready meal. If your favorites have a runny filling, bake them before freezing.

'Tis the Seasoning

A well-seasoned pan is essential for making crepes, omelets and frittatas successfully. If you have a no-stick pan, you're all set. But if you don't, you must prepare the pan you'll use for best performance.

- Scrub the pan with soap and steel wool and rinse well.
- Dry the pan, and then heat on top of the stove until it is too hot to touch. Remove from heat.
- Rub it thoroughly with a paper towel moistened with oil to coat the surface.

- Let the pan stand overnight.
- Now, heat it again, and then wipe it with a paper towel to remove the oil.
- It's now ready to use, but be sure to add a little butter or oil to the pan each time you use it.
- If you use the pan just for crepes, omelets and frittatas, you need only wipe it clean after each use and rinse with warm water. You should, however, dry it thoroughly over low heat, and rub with a bit of oil before putting it away. Before using it again, heat it briefly, and wipe away the oil with a paper towel.
- If food sticks to a seasoned pan, try rubbing the spot with salt and a paper towel. If that does the trick, just wipe the pan clean and proceed. But if the spot needs scouring, you'll have to reseason the pan.

Whole Wheat Crepes

⅔ cup milk
3 eggs
2 tablespoons butter, melted
⅓ cup whole wheat flour

Put the milk, eggs, butter and flour into a blender in that order. Process them until smooth, stopping a few times to scrape down the sides of the container.

Let the batter rest at least 1 hour before proceeding, and stir before using.

Oil a 6- or 8-inch crepe pan or frying pan. Heat until a little water dropped onto the pan sputters across the surface.

Quickly pour in a few tablespoons of batter, and swirl the pan to evenly coat the bottom.

Cook a minute or two over medium heat until the crepe is nicely browned on the bottom, and the top looks dry. Now, turn it over and cook the other side for about 30 seconds.

Whole Wheat Crepes—*continued*

Stack crepes on a plate, with a piece of wax paper between each one.

Makes about 14 6½-inch crepes.

Pesto Crepes

The Filling
¾ cup chopped basil
¼ cup minced parsley
¼ cup grated Parmesan cheese
2 tablespoons pine nuts
2 tablespoons olive oil
1 cup ricotta cheese
1 egg
¼ cup whole wheat breadcrumbs

The Sauce
1 cup milk
2 tablespoons butter
2 tablespoons whole wheat pastry flour
¼ cup grated Parmesan cheese
few gratings of nutmeg

The Assembly
8 *Whole Wheat Crepes* (see opposite page)

To make the filling: In a blender or food processor blend together the basil, parsley, Parmesan, pine nuts and olive oil until a thick paste forms. Add the ricotta, egg and breadcrumbs and process until well mixed.

To make the sauce: Heat the milk. Melt the butter in a small saucepan and then stir in the flour and cook, stirring constantly, until the sauce thickens and comes to a boil. Remove from the heat, and stir in the Parmesan and nutmeg.

To assemble: Place about 3 tablespoons of filling along one edge of each crepe and roll it up like a jelly roll. Arrange the crepes, seam side down, in a buttered 9-by-13-inch baking dish.

Cover with the sauce and bake at 350°F for 30 minutes.

Serves 4.

Dill

Dill dates back to ancient Egypt where it was buried with the dead to protect them against hunger in the afterlife. Its name comes from an old Norse word meaning "to lull," in reference to the herb's mild sedative effect. Early Americans chewed the seeds in church during the boredom of long sermons, hence the nickname "meetin' seeds." Herbalists recommend dill tea for indigestion and colic in babies and to promote the flow of milk in nursing mothers. Old herbals acclaimed dill as especially helpful in curing hiccups.

Rainbow Crepes

The inspiration for these crepes was a recipe I saw demonstrated at La Varenne cooking school in Paris. The scheduled demonstration for the day was crepes gratte-ceil *(skyscraper crepes); however, when the chef took a hasty look at the schedule (which was made up a month in advance), he thought the program called for* crepes arc-en-ciel *(rainbow crepes). With that in mind, he chose fillings with diverse colors and added them to the many skyscraper layers.*

This version is truly a rainbow from top to bottom. The carrot layer is orange, the spinach is bright green and the red cabbage adds a vibrant purple blue. If this cabbage color is a bit avant-garde for your taste, you may substitute a green cabbage. In that case I would probably re-order the layers, using the spinach first, then the carrot and finally the cabbage.

The whole wheat crepes and the vegetables add fiber and lots of vitamins to this dish. If you can stand the calories, you may use sour cream (or Cottage Cream, *a lower-calorie version) instead of ricotta in the sauce.*

The Sauce
1 egg
2 tablespoons lemon juice
1 cup ricotta cheese
¼ cup yogurt
1 tablespoon olive oil
¼ cup minced parsley
1 tablespoon minced dill or 1 teaspoon dried dill
1 tablespoon thyme leaves or 1 teaspoon dried thyme
1 scallion, minced

The Base
2 large onions, minced
1 tablespoon butter
¼ cup stock
3 cloves garlic, minced

The Carrot Layer
2 carrots, finely shredded
1 tablespoon butter
¼ cup stock
2 tablespoons *Tomato Sauce* (see *Index*)
1 tablespoon thyme leaves or 1 teaspoon dried thyme

The Spinach Layer
1 pound spinach
1 cup chopped mushrooms
1 tablespoon butter
few gratings of nutmeg

The Cabbage Layer
½ medium red cabbage, finely grated
1 tablespoon butter
¼ cup stock
1 tablespoon minced dill or 1 teaspoon dried dill

The Assembly
12 6-inch *Whole Wheat Crepes* (see page 114)

To make the sauce: Combine the egg and lemon juice in a blender, and process for 10 seconds to combine. Add the ricotta and yogurt, and process until smooth, stopping frequently to scrape down the sides of the container. Add the olive oil and process until it is combined.

Take ¼ cup of sauce and set aside for use with the spinach and cabbage layers.

Stir the parsley, dill, thyme and scallion into the remaining sauce. Refrigerate.

To make the base: Combine the onions, butter, stock and garlic in a large frying pan and cook, covered, over low heat until the onions are very tender. Remove the lid and cook uncovered until the liquid evaporates, stirring frequently to prevent sticking. Transfer to a bowl and set aside.

To make the carrot layer: Combine the carrots, butter and stock in a large frying pan and cook, covered, until the liquid evaporates. Stir in ⅓ of the onion base, the *Tomato Sauce* and thyme; transfer to a bowl and set aside.

Rainbow Crepes—*continued*

To make the spinach layer: Wash the spinach in plenty of cold water, and cook in a large pot using only the water left clinging to the leaves; cook only until the spinach wilts. Transfer to a colander or sieve to cool and drain. When the spinach is cool enough to handle, squeeze out the moisture, and chop finely. Set aside.

In a large frying pan sauté the mushrooms in butter until they are tender and all the liquid has evaporated. Remove from the heat and stir in the spinach, nutmeg, 1/3 of the onion base and half of the reserved ricotta sauce. Set aside.

To make the cabbage layer: Combine the cabbage, butter and stock in a large frying pan and cook, uncovered, over low heat until the cabbage is softened and the liquid evaporates. Stir in the final ⅓ of the onion base, the other half of the reserved ricotta sauce and dill.

To assemble: Butter a soufflé dish about 6 inches in diameter, cut a round of wax paper to fit the bottom and butter it well.

Place one crepe into the bottom of the dish, spotty side up. Line the sides of the dish with four overlapping crepes, making sure that there are no gaps at the bottom of the pan. Place four more crepes at the intersections of the first layers.

Spoon the carrot mixture into the dish, and cover it with a crepe.

Spoon the spinach mixture into the dish, and cover it with a crepe.

Now, spoon the cabbage into the dish, and fold the crepes in over it.

Cover with one more crepe. Then top the dish with a piece of buttered wax paper, and then with a piece of aluminum foil.

Bake at 400°F for 30 minutes. Remove from the oven and let stand for 15 minutes.

Carefully run a thin knife around the sides of the dish to loosen the crepes, and unmold onto a serving dish.

Serve with the cold sauce.

Serves 4.

Fennel

It was once thought that fennel suppressed evil and obesity alike. The plant was said to dull the appetite, which made it highly desirable for both dieting and overcoming hunger during fasts. Nowadays herbalists recommend fennel for colic, abdominal cramps, coughs and hoarseness. It also has a long tradition as a remedy for eye irritation and eyestrain.

Spinach Crepes

The Filling
1 pound spinach
1 cup ricotta cheese
½ cup grated Parmesan cheese
1 egg
1 teaspoon minced basil or ¼ teaspoon dried
   basil
¼ teaspoon grated nutmeg

The Sauce
⅔ cup minced onion
⅔ cup thinly sliced mushrooms
1 tablespoon butter
1 cup milk
2 tablespoons butter
2 tablespoons whole wheat pastry flour
¼ cup grated Parmesan cheese
   few gratings of nutmeg

The Assembly
8 *Whole Wheat Crepes* (see page 114)

To make the filling: Wash the spinach in plenty of cold water, and cook it in a large pot using only the water left clinging to the leaves; cook only until the spinach wilts. Transfer to a colander or sieve to cool and drain. When the spinach is cool enough to handle, squeeze out the moisture, and chop it finely, either by hand or using a food processor.

Combine the spinach, ricotta, Parmesan, egg, basil and nutmeg, and set aside.

To make the sauce: In a 2-quart saucepan over medium-low heat, cook the onions and mushrooms in 1 tablespoon of butter until they are tender and all the liquid has evaporated. Transfer to a small bowl.

In a small saucepan heat the milk.

In the same saucepan used for cooking the onions and mushrooms, melt 2 tablespoons of butter, add the flour and whisk them together for 2 minutes. Add the hot milk all at once, and whisk vigorously to combine. Over medium heat cook the sauce, stirring constantly until it thickens and comes to a boil. Remove from the heat.

Stir the onions and mushrooms into the sauce, and add the Parmesan and nutmeg.

To assemble: Place a heaping spoonful of filling at one end of each crepe, and roll it like a jelly roll.

Butter a 9-by-13-inch baking dish, and arrange the crepes, seam side down, in it. Cover with the sauce.

Bake at 350°F for 30 minutes.

Serves 4.

Speckled Sage Crepes

A green-speckled filling best made with fresh sage.

The Filling
1 cup ricotta cheese
½ cup shredded mozzarella cheese
1 egg
3 tablespoons minced sage or 1 teaspoon dried
   sage

The Sauce
1 cup thinly sliced mushrooms
1 tablespoon butter
2 tablespoons cornstarch
2 tablespoons cold water
1 cup stock
1 teaspoon tamari sauce

The Assembly
8 *Whole Wheat Crepes* (see page 114)

   To make the filling: Beat together or mix in a food processor the ricotta, mozzarella, egg and sage.

   To make the sauce: In a small frying pan sauté the mushrooms in butter until they are tender.

   In a small saucepan combine the cornstarch and water until well dissolved. Stir in the stock and tamari.

   Cook over medium heat, stirring constantly, until the sauce clears and thickens; continue until it comes to a boil. Remove from the heat and stir in the mushrooms.

   To assemble: Place a heaping spoonful of filling at one end of each crepe, and roll it up like a jelly roll.

   Butter a 9-by-13-inch baking dish, and arrange the crepes seam side down in the dish. Cover with the mushroom sauce.

   Bake at 350°F for 30 minutes.

Serves 4.

Garlic

In countries all over the world, garlic has long been prized for its power against disease and evil. Herbals describe this pungent herb as an effective remedy for poor digestion. They also credit it with improving circulation and reducing high blood pressure, as do some modern scientists. Herbalists use its antiseptic properties to treat wounds and prevent colds, bronchitis or intestinal infections.

Whole Wheat Pasta

Whole wheat pasta, like whole wheat bread, has a nutritional edge over its white flour version because the bran and wheat germ are still present along with their fiber, vitamins and minerals. Still many people turn their noses up at whole wheat pasta because they've had bad experiences with it. Either it was as tough and tasteless as cardboard when they tried it, or it was too hard to make from scratch. I think the following recipe eliminates both problems.

The way to light, tender whole wheat noodles has two steps: First, you must add extra oil to the dough to tenderize it and make it easier to handle. And second, you must roll them as thin as you can—I use the thinnest setting on my machine.

Of course, you don't need a pasta machine to make noodles, but you'll find that a machine makes the process easier. Still, while rolling by hand is more time-consuming and strenuous, anyone with a little patience can manage to do a good job.

The dough should also rest a little (well covered) before rolling. And the rolled pieces should dry slightly before cutting. Let them dry to the texture of supple leather, but do not let them become brittle, or the cutting will go badly. After the noodles are cut, they can be cooked immediately, or stored indefinitely. If you are going to hold onto the noodles for awhile, toss them with flour, twist into loose bundles and arrange them on a cloth. Then cover them with another cloth.

Fresh pasta cooks much faster than dry or store-bought pasta. To cook it, bring a large pot of water to a boil, and add a tablespoon of oil to keep the noodles from sticking together. Now, add the noodles and stir once or twice with a wooden fork to keep them from settling to the bottom and sticking.

Cook until the noodles are *al dente*—tender but still firm enough to offer a bit of resistance to the teeth when bitten. Do *not* let them overcook! Stand over the pot and start testing fresh noodles after only a minute or two of boiling.

Remove the pasta from the water with a wooden fork to keep the strands from sticking together. If you prefer a sieve or colander, pour gently to prevent sticking.

Always plan to cook pasta at the last moment before serving. If there should be an unavoidable delay after the noodles are cooked, they can be held for a short time by tossing them with a little butter or oil, covering the bowl with foil and setting it in a warm oven; do not try to hold noodles more than 30 minutes.

Whole Wheat Noodles

1 cup whole wheat flour
2 large eggs
2 tablespoons olive oil

Pile the flour in a medium bowl and form a well in the center of the mound.

In a separate cup beat the eggs and oil together until well blended, and pour them into the flour well.

With your fingers or a fork, start working the flour into the eggs, and continue until all the flour has been incorporated and a soft dough has formed.

Turn the dough out onto a lightly floured surface, and, if necessary, add a little more flour to produce a kneadable dough. Knead until smooth and satiny, about 5 minutes. Wrap the dough in plastic and let it rest for 10 minutes.

Whole Wheat Noodles—*continued*

To roll by hand: Divide the dough into thirds, and work it one piece at a time, keeping the others wrapped in plastic.

Spread a clean sheet or tablecloth over a table or large counter space, and flour it lightly. Roll the dough into a large and very thin circle; it should be thin enough to see the weave of the cloth through the dough.

As it is finished, set each circle aside to dry (try draping it over a broom handle suspended between two chairs) for 20 to 30 minutes, or until the dough has dried to the texture of supple leather.

Roll each piece into a long cylinder, and with a sharp knife cut across the cylinder into noodles of whatever width you prefer.

Unroll the noodles, and toss them with a little flour. Now, cook immediately, or let them dry completely.

To roll by machine: Divide the dough in half, and work it one piece at a time, keeping the other piece wrapped in plastic.

Flour the dough and flatten slightly. Set the machine's rollers at their widest setting and pass the dough through them several times at that setting. Fold dough into thirds and lightly flour it between the rollings.

Narrow the rollers one notch, and roll the dough through again. If it shows the slightest bit of stickiness, flour it lightly. *Do not fold the dough from this point on.* Continue to roll the dough through the machine, narrowing the rollers one notch after each pass.

When the dough becomes too long to handle easily, cut it in half. Continue to pass the dough through the machine's rollers down to the last notch.

Now, set the dough strips aside to dry; you may lay them out on a floured cloth or hang them over a special pasta rack or a broomstick suspended between two chairs. Allow the dough to dry for 10 to 20 minutes, or until it has the texture of supple leather.

Using the cutting blades of your machine, cut the dough into noodles of whatever width you wish. Toss the noodles lightly with flour. Now cook them immediately or let them dry completely.

To cook: In a very large pot, bring about 6 quarts of water to a boil, and add 1 tablespoon of oil to the water. Add the noodles, and cook for a *very short* time, until the noodles are *al dente* (meaning just barely tender and still offering a bit of resistance to the teeth when bitten). Drain carefully.

Makes about 8 ounces
of noodles, serving 4.

Herbed Poppy Seed Noodles

1½ cups thinly sliced mushrooms
½ cup minced shallots
¼ cup stock
1 tablespoon butter
1 tablespoon poppy seeds
8 ounces *Whole Wheat Noodles* (see opposite page)
1½ cups cottage cheese
¼ cup grated Parmesan cheese
3 tablespoons minced parsley
yogurt (optional)

Combine the mushrooms, shallots, stock and butter in a large frying pan. Cover and cook over low heat until the vegetables are tender. Now remove the cover and cook over medium heat until any remaining liquid evaporates, stirring frequently to prevent sticking. Add the poppy seeds and stir a minute longer to bring out their flavor.

Cook the noodles in a large pot of boiling water until they are just tender. Drain.

Toss the noodles with the mushroom mixture, cottage cheese, Parmesan and parsley. If desired, serve with yogurt.

Serves 4.

Soba Noodles with Mushroom Sauce

Soba noodles are Japanese buckwheat noodles that look like thin brown spaghetti. Buckwheat resembles a grain, but technically it is a fruit. It has no germ or bran and consists of only the shell and its kernel. The kernel, or edible portion, is called a groat. Nutritionally, buckweat is superb. Its protein content is the best of the grains, and it's also rich in B6, riboflavin, thiamine, iron and potassium.

Buckwheat is commonly sold in stores as kasha (the roasted groats whole or ground to various textures) and buckwheat flour (both light and dark). But soba noodles are also available in some large groceries and health food stores as well as many oriental markets.

Tip: *Fresh marjoram enhances the flavor of this dish.*

1 onion, thinly sliced
½ pound mushrooms, thinly sliced
1 clove garlic, minced
¼ cup stock
1 tablespoon lemon juice
2 cups milk
2 tablespoons butter
2 tablespoons cornstarch
2 teaspoons tamari sauce
8 ounces soba noodles
1 tablespoon minced marjoram or 1 teaspoon dried marjoram
1 tablespoon snipped chives
1 tablespoon minced dill or 1 teaspoon dried dill
2 tablespoons grated Parmesan cheese

Combine the onion, mushrooms, garlic, stock and lemon juice in a large frying pan. Cook until the onions are wilted and all the liquid has evaporated from the pan. Stir the mixture frequently; be careful that the onions and garlic do not brown.

In a small saucepan heat the milk.

In a medium saucepan melt the butter and then stir in the cornstarch until the mixture is smooth. Slowly stir in the hot milk, beating constantly with a wire whisk. Bring to a boil and cook for 2 minutes, stirring constantly. Add the tamari and the cooked mushrooms.

Bring a few quarts of water to a boil in a large kettle. Add the noodles and cook until they are tender, about 6 to 8 minutes. Drain the noodles and mix in the mushroom sauce. Sprinkle with marjoram, chives, dill and Parmesan.

Serves 4.

Shells Stuffed with Spinach

The Stuffing
1 pound spinach
1 egg
⅓ cup minced celery
⅓ cup minced shallots
⅔ cup minced mushrooms
2 tablespoons butter
2 cups ricotta cheese
½ cup grated Parmesan cheese
⅛ teaspoon grated nutmeg

The Assembly
20 jumbo pasta shells (about ½ pound)
2 cups *Marinara Sauce* (see page 125)

To make the stuffing: Wash the spinach in plenty of cold water. Cook in a large pot with no more water than is left clinging to the leaves. Cook only until the spinach wilts. Transfer to a colander or sieve to cool and drain. When the spinach is cool enough to handle, squeeze out the remaining moisture. Place the spinach and egg in a blender. Process until spinach is finely chopped, and then transfer to a large bowl.

In a small frying pan over medium heat, sauté the celery, shallots and mushrooms in butter until they are dry. Stir them frequently to prevent sticking.

Add the mushrooms, ricotta, Parmesan and nutmeg to the bowl containing the spinach. Stir to mix well.

Shells Stuffed with Spinach—*continued*

To assemble: Cook the shells in a very large pot of boiling water according to the package directions for *al dente*. Drain them on paper towels.

When the shells are cool enough to handle, divide the filling among them using about 1½ tablespoons per shell.

Lightly butter a 7-by-11-inch baking dish. Spread about ½ cup of sauce over the bottom. Fill the pan with rows of shells, filling side up. Cover with the remaining sauce.

Lightly cover the pan and bake at 350°F for 30 minutes. Remove the cover and bake another 10 minutes.

Serves 4.

Butternut Shells

  2 cups mashed cooked butternut squash
½ cup grated Parmesan cheese
  2 tablespoons minced parsley
½ teaspoon grated nutmeg
20 jumbo pasta shells (about ½ pound)
  2 cups *Marinara Sauce* (see page 125)
¼ cup grated Parmesan cheese

Combine the squash, ½ cup of Parmesan, the parsley and nutmeg.

Cook the pasta shells in a very large pot of boiling water following the package directions for *al dente*. Arrange them on paper towels until they are cool enough to handle.

Lightly butter a 7-by-11-inch baking dish. Spread about ½ cup of sauce in the bottom.

Stuff the shells with the butternut mixture, using about 1½ tablespoons of stuffing per shell.

Arrange the stuffed shells in the pan in even rows. Top with the remaining sauce. Sprinkle with ¼ cup of Parmesan.

Lightly cover the pan and bake at 350°F for 15 minutes. Remove the cover and bake for another 10 minutes.

Serves 4.

Geranium

Geranium is useful in the treatment of diarrhea and hemorrhage, according to herbalists. They also claim the root may effectively stop external bleeding. Some write of geranium as a mouthwash and gargle, others as a hemorrhoid remedy. Recent research suggests that geranium extracts may lower blood pressure.

Pesto Sauce

This is a long-time Italian favorite that's become very popular here in recent years. It's great served over hot noodles. Or in a cold noodle dish. Or stuffed into cherry tomatoes as an appetizer. Or spread on a tomato sandwich.

Pesto keeps well in the refrigerator when it's covered with half an inch of olive oil. To use it, scoop out the desired amount, and then re-cover the remaining sauce with oil. Be sure to keep the inside of the container above the oil line clean to prevent the growth of mold.

For longer storage, pesto may be frozen in serving-size containers. Thaw before using, unless you're stirring the sauce into a simmering soup, stew or sauce.

1 cup (tightly packed) basil leaves
½ cup (packed) parsley leaves
½ cup grated Parmesan cheese
¼ cup pine nuts
4 cloves garlic, minced
½ cup olive oil (best quality)

Combine the basil, parsley, Parmesan, pine nuts and garlic in a blender or food processor and process until they're well chopped. While the machine is running, slowly add the oil until it is all incorporated. Scrape down the container as necessary. Continue blending until the ingredients are finely chopped and formed into a thick sauce.

Makes about 1 cup.

Tomato Sauce

2 tablespoons olive oil
⅔ cup chopped onions
⅔ cup chopped carrots
½ cup chopped celery
2 tablespoons whole wheat flour
2 cloves garlic, chopped
6 cups chopped tomatoes
2 cup stock
⅓ cup chopped parsley
¼ cup chopped basil or 1 tablespoon dried basil
2 tablespoons chopped thyme or 2 teaspoons dried thyme
1 tablespoon tamari sauce
1 tablespoon chopped fennel
1 bay leaf
¼ teaspoon honey
2 tablespoons tomato paste (optional)
¼ cup grated Parmesan cheese

In a large pot heat the oil over medium heat. Add the onions, carrots and celery and, stirring constantly, cook until the onions soften. Stir in the flour and garlic.

Now add the tomatoes, stock, parsley, basil, thyme, tamari, fennel, bay leaf and honey. Cover and cook the sauce over low heat until the tomatoes are soft and have given up their liquid. Uncover, continue cooking for about 1½ hours, stirring frequently.

Puree the sauce with a food mill and return it to the pot. Stir in the tomato paste if it needs more color, and add the Parmesan. Continue to cook and stir over low heat until the sauce has reached the desired thickness.

Remove the bay leaf before serving.

Makes about 3 cups of thick sauce.

Marinara Sauce

¼ cup olive oil
2½ cups finely chopped onions
2 cloves garlic, minced
4 cups pureed tomatoes
2 cups stock
1 bay leaf
¼ cup minced parsley
2 tablespoons minced basil or 2 teaspoons dried basil
1 tablespoon minced sage or ½ teaspoon dried sage
2 teaspoons minced marjoram or ½ teaspoon dried marjoram
1 teaspoon minced oregano or ¼ teaspoon dried oregano
1 tablespoon tamari sauce

Heat the oil in a large saucepan. Add the onions and sauté over medium heat until they are soft; stir occasionally. Do not let the onions brown.

Add the garlic and stir for 1 minute. Then, add the tomatoes, stock, bay leaf, parsley, basil, sage, marjoram, oregano and tamari and bring to a boil. Cook over medium heat for about 40 minutes or until thickened, stirring frequently to prevent scorching. As the sauce thickens, reduce the heat to prevent sticking.

Remove the bay leaf.

Makes about 3 cups.

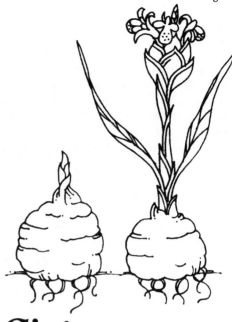

Ginger

Ginger has a rich, pungent flavor that is often used by herbalists to mask the bitter taste of other herbs. Herbals recommend the tea for promoting perspiration and bringing on menstruation. They also suggest it as a warming and soothing remedy for colds and coughs. One source says that ginger was used during the plague because of its antiseptic properties.

Whole Wheat Pie Shell

This recipe produces an excellent, all-purpose whole wheat pie shell. Use the leftover pastry scraps to make a lattice top for a 9-inch shell. If you're using an 8-inch pie plate, you will have enough dough to make both a top and a bottom crust.

Although there are probably as many ways to roll out pie dough as there are cooks, I've come upon a favorite method through trial and error. It works extremely well with whole wheat, which tends to be a little more finicky than white flour dough.

After trying to roll out dough directly on my Formica counter, I tried rolling it between two sheets of wax paper. The counter method always produced stuck dough at some point, and I could never prevent the paper from wrinkling my crusts. So I was delighted to discover that the old-fashioned pastry cloth method really does the job. Best of all, I find that any clean, smooth-weave dish towel (not terry cloth, in other words) works perfectly.

Prepare the cloth by rubbing a handful of flour into the fabric to prevent sticking and to avoid flouring the dough as you work. I find I can roll the dough in each direction three or four times before flipping it over, and that the cloth helps me turn the fragile dough without tearing it.

1⅓ cups whole wheat pastry flour
  6 tablespoons cold butter
  ice water

Place the flour in a large bowl. Cut in the butter with two knives or a pastry blender and work until the mixture resembles a coarse meal.

Sprinkle ice water over the flour a tablespoon at a time. With two forks, toss the flour to moisten it, being careful not to add more liquid than is necessary to moisten all the flour.

Wrap the dough in plastic and refrigerate it for at least 30 minutes.

Then, roll out the dough until it is about ⅛ inch thick and about 15 inches in diameter.

Fit into a 9-inch pie plate; do *not* stretch the dough. Trim off the excess, leaving a 1-inch overhang and then fold this overhang double all around the circumference; crimp with your fingers or a fork. Prick the surface of the crust with a fork.

To bake the crust: Press a piece of aluminum foil onto the dough and mold to pie plate. Weight the foil down with pie weights or dried rice or beans you have reserved for the purpose. The foil and weights will keep the crust from buckling as it bakes.

Bake at 400°F for 15 minutes, or until the sides seem firm enough to stand without the foil and weights. Remove the foil.

Return the shell to the oven and bake for another 5 to 7 minutes, or until the shell is lightly browned and thoroughly baked.

Cool on a wire rack before filling.

Makes 1 9-inch pie shell.

Mushroom Parsnip Quiche

Parsnips are low in sodium but high in potassium, a desirable combination, and they also have handsome amounts of B vitamins and calcium. Despite their relative mystery, parsnips have a pleasing, sweet taste and a texture that seems to combine carrots and sweet potatoes.

1 cup shredded parsnips
1 cup sliced mushrooms
1 onion, sliced
1 tablespoon butter
¼ cup stock
4 eggs
1 cup milk
⅓ cup grated Parmesan cheese
2 tablespoons minced dill or 2 teaspoons dried dill
2 tablespoons minced parsley
1 9-inch *Whole Wheat Pie Shell*, baked (see above)

Mushroom Parsnip Quiche—*continued*

Combine the parsnips, mushrooms, onion, butter and stock in a large frying pan. Cover and cook the ingredients over low heat until they're tender. Then, uncover and cook until the excess liquid evaporates; stir to prevent sticking.

Beat the eggs and milk together until they are smooth. Stir in the Parmesan, dill and parsley.

Spread the parsnip mixture in the pie shell. Pour the egg and cheese filling over it.

Transfer the pie plate to a cookie sheet. Bake at 350°F for 40 to 45 minutes, or until a knife inserted in the center comes out clean.

Serves 4.

Broccoli Quiche

1 cup chopped broccoli
1 cup thinly sliced mushrooms
1 large onion, sliced
¼ cup stock
1 tablespoon butter
3 eggs
1 cup milk
½ cup shredded cheese
2 tablespoons minced parsley
2 tablespoons minced dill or 2 teaspoons dried dill
1 9-inch *Whole Wheat Pie Shell,* baked (see opposite page)

In a large frying pan combine the broccoli, mushrooms, onion, stock and butter. Cover and cook over low heat until the vegetables are tender. Remove the cover and cook over medium heat, stirring frequently, until the liquid evaporates.

Beat the eggs and milk together until they are smooth. Stir in the cheese, parsley and dill.

Spread the broccoli mixture in the pie shell and pour the egg mixture over it.

Bake at 350°F for 30 to 40 minutes, or until the quiche is puffed and golden; it is done when a knife inserted in the center comes out clean.

Serves 4.

Cabbage Quiche

Cabbage, and other members of its vegetable family, have been shown to fight against colon cancer. Cabbage is also low in sodium and high in vitamins C and K.

1 large onion, thinly sliced
2 cups thinly sliced cabbage
1 tablespoon butter
¼ cup stock
1 teaspoon tamari sauce
3 eggs
1 cup milk
2 teaspoons minced marjoram or 1 teaspoon dried marjoram
½ cup shredded Cheddar cheese
1 9-inch *Whole Wheat Pie Shell,* baked (see opposite page)

Combine the onion, cabbage, butter, stock and tamari in a large frying pan. Cover and cook over medium heat until the cabbage wilts and the onion softens. Remove the cover and cook until the excess liquid evaporates. Stir to prevent sticking.

Beat the eggs and milk together until they are smooth. Stir in the marjoram and cheese, and fold in the cabbage.

Pour the mixture into the pie shell, and bake at 350°F for 30 to 40 minutes, or until the quiche is puffed and golden; it is done when a knife inserted in the center comes out clean.

Serves 4.

Red Pepper Quiche

This dish makes a pretty and surprising picture; the strips of peeled red pepper are arranged on top of the quiche to mimic a French apple tart or a large open flower.

3 large red peppers
3 eggs
¾ cup ricotta cheese
¾ cup milk
2 ounces feta cheese, crumbled
¼ cup chopped basil or 1 tablespoon dried basil
2 tablespoons snipped chives
1 teaspoon dry mustard
1 9-inch *Whole Wheat Pie Shell*, baked (see page 126)
1 tablespoon butter, melted

Broil the peppers about 6 inches from the heat until they are black on all sides, and then transfer them to a plastic or paper bag. Close the bag tightly and let the peppers stand for 10 minutes while the skins steam loose. When they are cool enough to handle, peel off the skins and discard the core and the seeds. Cut the flesh into half-inch strips and set aside.

Combine the eggs, ricotta, milk, feta, basil, chives and mustard in a blender or food processor and blend until smooth.

Pour into a pie shell, set on a cookie sheet, and bake at 375°F for 40 to 45 minutes or until a knife inserted in the center comes out clean. Do not overbake.

Remove the quiche from the oven and raise the temperature to 425°F.

Meanwhile, arrange the pepper strips on top of the quiche in a pattern like that for a French apple tart; that is, start at the outside edge of the pie, curl each strip into a semicircle and place the curled pieces side by side until you have circled the quiche. Then, start a second row that overlaps the first slightly. Continue until you have filled in the entire surface of the quiche and curl one last strip into a complete circle for the center. Brush the pattern with melted butter.

Return the quiche to the oven and bake 5 minutes to warm the peppers.

Serves 4.

Ricotta Vegetable Pie

The Cabbage Layer
1 tablespoon butter
3 cups thinly shredded cabbage
2 tablespoons minced dill or 2 teaspoons dried dill

The Mushroom Layer
1 tablespoon butter
1 large onion, thinly sliced
1½ cups thinly sliced mushrooms
1 tablespoon minced tarragon or 1 teaspoon dried tarragon
1 tablespoon minced basil or 1 teaspoon dried basil

The Cheese Layer
½ cup sour cream or *Cottage Cream* (see *Index*)
⅓ cup ricotta cheese
1 egg
2 tablespoons grated Parmesan cheese

The Assembly
1 9-inch *Whole Wheat Pie Shell*, baked (see page 126)
2 hard-cooked eggs, thinly sliced
2 tablespoons grated Parmesan cheese

To make the cabbage layer: Heat the butter in a large frying pan until it foams. Add the cabbage and dill and sauté over medium heat until the cabbage wilts; do not overcook. Transfer to a bowl.

To make the mushroom layer: In the same frying pan, heat more butter until it foams. Add the onion, mushrooms, tarragon and basil, and sauté until the onion and mushrooms are soft. Let the liquid in the pan evaporate.

Ricotta Vegetable Pie—*continued*

To make the cheese layer: In a bowl or food processor blend the sour cream or *Cottage Cream*, ricotta, egg and Parmesan until they are thoroughly combined and smooth.

To assemble: Spread the cabbage in the pie shell. Cover with the egg slices and then the mushrooms. Pour the cheese mixture over all. Sprinkle with Parmesan.

Bake at 350°F for 30 minutes, or until the top is set and golden brown.

Serves 4.

Carrot Quiche

3 carrots, cut in thin strips
1 large onion, thinly sliced
1 teaspoon butter
3 tablespoons stock
4 eggs
1 cup milk
⅓ cup shredded Cheddar cheese
1 9-inch *Whole Wheat Pie Shell*, baked (see page 126)

Combine the carrots, onion, butter and stock in a frying pan. Cover and cook them over low heat until they are tender. Remove the cover and allow the excess liquid to cook away while stirring to prevent scorching.

Beat the eggs and milk together until they are smooth. Stir in the Cheddar cheese.

Spread the cooked vegetables in the pie shell. Pour the egg mixture over them.

Transfer the pie pan to a cookie sheet. Bake at 350°F for 40 to 45 minutes, or until a knife inserted in the center comes out clean. Do not overbake.

Serves 4.

Horseradish

Herbalists describe horseradish as the plant that "gets the juices flowing." They regard this fiery but flavorful root as an excellent aid to digestion, in moderate quantities, and as a diuretic. Herbals also note its stimulating and warming effects, which warrant its use in poultices to increase blood flow and relieve rheumatic pain. Steeped in milk, the root is recommended by herbalists as a wash for clearing and freshening the skin.

Spinach Ricotta Pie

A pretty, easy, high-fiber quiche with a simple wheat germ "crust" (really just a light coating). Delicious cold.

    2 tablespoons wheat germ
    1 pound spinach
    1 large onion, minced
    ¼ cup stock
    1 cup sliced mushrooms
    1 tablespoon lemon juice
    3 cloves garlic, minced
    3 eggs
 1½ cups ricotta cheese
    2 tablespoons chopped dill or 1 tablespoon
         dried dill
    2 tablespoons minced parsley
    2 tablespoons whole wheat breadcrumbs
    2 tablespoons grated Parmesan cheese
 1½ teaspoons minced mint or ½ teaspoon
         dried mint

Butter a 9-inch pie pan and then coat it with wheat germ. Set aside.

Wash the spinach in plenty of cold water. Place in a large pot and cook using only the water left clinging to the leaves; remove the pot from the heat as soon as the spinach wilts, and transfer it to a colander or sieve to cool and drain. When cool enough to handle, squeeze *all* the moisture from the spinach and set aside.

In a large, covered frying pan cook the onions in stock over low heat until they are soft. Then, remove the lid, add the mushrooms, lemon juice and garlic, and cook until the mushrooms are limp. Raise the heat and cook, stirring constantly, until all the moisture has evaporated. Set aside.

Place the eggs, ricotta, dill, parsley, breadcumbs, Parmesan, mint and spinach in a blender container. Process until they are smooth, stopping frequently to scrape down the sides of the container. Stir in the mushroom and onion mixture.

Pour the mixture into the prepared pie pan. Place on a cookie sheet and bake at 350°F for 45 to 50 minutes, or until the pie puffs slightly. A knife inserted into the center should come out clean.

Serves 4.

Asparagus Carrot Quiche

A crustless quiche to make when you don't have time for a pie shell.

    2 medium carrots
    1 large onion, thinly sliced
    1 tablespoon butter
    ¼ cup stock
    ½ pound asparagus, lightly cooked
    ½ cup shredded Cheddar cheese
    4 eggs
    1 teaspoon minced tarragon or ¼ teaspoon
         dried tarragon
    1 tablespoon butter, melted
    ½ cup whole wheat breadcrumbs

Cut the carrots into julienne pieces (matchsticks about ⅛ by ⅛ by 2 inches). Place them in large frying pan with the onion, 1 tablespoon of butter and the stock. Cover and cook over low heat until they are tender. Remove the cover and allow the excess liquid to boil away. Stir to prevent burning.

Butter a 9-inch pie pan and add the carrot and onion mixture.

Cut the asparagus into 1-inch pieces, and scatter them over the carrots. Sprinkle with Cheddar.

In a small bowl beat the eggs until they are well combined. Stir in the tarragon and pour the egg mixture over the asparagus.

In a small bowl combine 1 tablespoon melted butter with the breadcrumbs, and sprinkle it over the eggs.

Bake at 350°F for 35 minutes, or until the eggs are set and puffed. Serve hot.

Serves 4.

Tomato Onion Quiche

1 cup minced onion
1 clove garlic, minced
1 tablespoon olive oil
1 tablespoon butter
1½ cups chopped tomatoes
3 tablespoons minced parsley
2 tablespoons minced basil or 1 teaspoon dried basil
4 eggs
1 cup milk
½ cup shredded cheese
1 9-inch *Whole Wheat Pie Shell*, baked (see page 126)
2 tablespoons grated Parmesan cheese

In a large frying pan and over medium-low heat, sauté the onions and garlic in oil and butter until they are soft.

Add the tomatoes, parsley and basil, and cover. Cook over medium heat until the tomatoes have softened and given up their juices.

Remove the lid and cook, stirring frequently, until the excess liquid has evaporated. Do not let the tomatoes scorch. Then, let the mixture cool for 5 minutes.

In a large bowl beat the eggs and milk together until they are thoroughly blended. Stir in ½ cup of cheese and the tomato mixture.

Sprinkle the pie shell with Parmesan and pour in the tomato mixture.

Bake at 375°F for 30 to 40 minutes, or until the quiche is puffed and golden and a knife inserted in the center comes out clean.

Serves 4.

Cheese and Dill Quiche

I like this quiche because most of the mixing is done in the blender, so there's very little effort or clean up. The ricotta blended with milk tastes a bit like heavy cream but has less fat and calories. Other herbs may be substituted for the dill, making this an all-purpose recipe.

Start testing this quiche after 30 minutes of baking, and leave it in the oven only until a knife inserted in the center comes out clean. Overbaking robs the quiche of its creamy texture.

3 eggs
¾ cup ricotta cheese
¾ cup milk
3 tablespoons chopped dill or 2 teaspoons dried dill
2 tablespoons snipped chives
1 teaspoon *Curry Powder* (see *Index*)
few gratings of nutmeg
3 ounces Gruyère or Swiss cheese, shredded
2 tablespoons grated Parmesan cheese
1 9-inch *Whole Wheat Pie Shell*, baked (see page 126)

Combine the eggs, ricotta, milk, dill, chives, *Curry Powder* and nutmeg in a blender or food processor. Blend until they are smooth, and then stir in the Gruyère or Swiss and Parmesan.

Pour into the pie shell. Place the quiche on a cookie sheet and bake at 375°F for 30 to 40 minutes, or until a knife inserted in the center comes out clean.

Serves 4.

French Omelets

French omelets are always a good idea, because they're fast, inexpensive and easy. With a little practice almost anyone can turn out a perfect omelet for a quick breakfast, lunch or dinner.

Although there are lots of methods for making successful omelets, I prefer the way Mmes. Child, Bertholle and Beck teach in their *Mastering the Art of French Cooking, Volume I* (Alfred A. Knopf, 1966). It's a two-part operation—somewhat like patting your head while rubbing your tummy—but it's more easily learned; more about that later.

The *first* thing you should think of is your omelet pan. Although you can use almost any pan—including those with a no-stick surface—an iron omelet or crepe pan with sloping sides and a six- or seven-inch bottom diameter is the best. This kind of pan is easy to season so the eggs don't stick; it can take the high temperatures required to quick-cook eggs; and it's the ideal size and shape for a one-serving omelet. (It's also a good idea to reserve a pan exclusively for omelets, frittatas—Italian omelets—and crepes. I find that if I cook anything else in mine it produces sticking, and I have to reseason the pan. For that reason I recommend making an omelet's filling—if it needs cooking—in a separate pan. This practice also helps when making more than one omelet, and you need more filling than an omelet pan will hold.)

Because omelet cooking time is short—as it is in Chinese stir-frying—you must have all the ingredients ready before starting the process itself:

- Have the filling chopped or cooked and next to the stove.

- Have the eggs beaten in a bowl and at hand.
- Have the pan heated to the proper temperature.
- Only then should you melt the butter and pour the eggs into the pan.

Note: The recipes that follow are for just one serving. If you're feeding more people, increase the filling ingredients and make a single, large batch. But be sure to beat the eggs and water for each omelet separately.

Omelet Instructions

- Heat an omelet pan over medium heat until a drop of water dances across its surface. Add one teaspoon of butter to the hot pan and tilt the pan until the butter is evenly distributed over the bottom.
- Add the eggs all at once and let them sit for 10 seconds.
- Hold the handle of the pan with one hand, with your thumb on top, and immediately start to slide the pan back and forth over the heating element.
- At the same time, with a fork held in your other hand so that its tines are parallel to the bottom of the pan, stir the *top* layer of eggs, being careful not to disturb the bottom "set" layer of eggs. This step will keep the center of the omelet creamy while the bottom browns. Remember to keep the pan sliding back and forth on the element while you're stirring with the fork.
- After about a minute, most of the egg mixture will have become set and creamy. At this point add the filling. If the filling is substantial, spread it over half the omelet, fold the other half over it and turn the omelet out onto a serving plate.
- If the filling is very light—like chopped herbs or grated cheese—sprinkle it evenly over the surface and roll up the omelet

using a fork. As before, turn the finished omelet out onto a serving plate.
- Serve immediately.

Curried Carrot Omelet

The Filling
- 1 small onion
- ½ carrot
- ¼ cup shredded cabbage
- 1 tablespoon stock
- 1½ teaspoons snipped chives
- 1 teaspoon butter
- ¼ teaspoon minced marjoram or pinch dried marjoram
- ¼ teaspoon *Curry Powder* (see *Index*)
- 1 tablespoon shredded Cheddar cheese

The Omelet
- 2 eggs
- 1 tablespoon water
- 1 teaspoon butter (for the pan)

To make the filling: Slice the onion thinly. Cut the carrot into julienne strips (matchsticks about ⅛ by ⅛ by 2 inches).

Combine the onion, carrot, cabbage, stock, chives, butter, marjoram and *Curry Powder* in a small frying pan. Cover and cook until the carrots are tender. Remove the lid and let the remaining liquid cook away. Do not let the vegetables scorch. Sprinkle with Cheddar.

To make the omelet: Beat the eggs and water together with about 20 strokes of a fork. Then proceed with the Omelet Instructions (see page opposite).

When the eggs are set, spread two-thirds of the filling over half the omelet and fold it in half. Garnish with the remaining vegetables.

Serves 1.

Carrot Dill Omelet

The Filling
- ½ large carrot
- 1 scallion
- 1 tablespoon stock
- 1 teaspoon butter
- 1 tablespoon minced dill or 1 teaspoon dried dill

The Omelet
- 2 eggs
- 1 tablespoon water
- 1 teaspoon butter (for the pan)

- 1 tablespoon shredded Swiss or Gruyère cheese

To make the filling: Cut the carrot and scallion into julienne strips (matchsticks about ⅛ by ⅛ by 2 inches).

Combine the vegetables with the stock and butter in a small pan. Cover and cook over low heat until they are tender. Then, remove the lid and let any remaining liquid cook away. Do not let the vegetables scorch. Stir in the dill.

To make the omelet: Beat the eggs and water together with about 20 strokes of a fork. Then proceed with the Omelet Instructions (see page opposite).

When the eggs are set, spread about two-thirds of the vegetables and all of the cheese on half the omelet. Fold it in half. Garnish with the remaining vegetables.

Serves 1.

Swiss Herb Omelet

The Filling
½ teaspoon minced oregano or ¼ teaspoon
    dried oregano
½ teaspoon minced marjoram or ¼ teaspoon
    dried marjoram
1 tablespoon snipped chives
2 tablespoons shredded Swiss cheese

The Omelet
2 eggs
1 tablespoon water
1 teaspoon butter (for the pan)

To make the filling: If you are using fresh
oregano and marjoram, combine them with the
chives and cheese in a small cup and set aside.

If you are using dried oregano and marjoram, add to the eggs before cooking. Combine
the chives and the Swiss separately in a cup and
set aside.

To make the omelet: Beat the eggs and water
together with about 20 strokes of a fork.
Then proceed with the Omelet Instructions
(see page 132).

When the eggs are set, sprinkle the filling
over them. Fold the omelet in half or roll it up.
Serves 1.

Tarragon Chive Omelet

The Filling
½ teaspoon minced tarragon or ¼ teaspoon
    dried tarragon
¼ teaspoon minced rosemary or pinch dried
    rosemary, crushed
1 tablespoon snipped chives
2 tablespoons crumbled feta cheese

The Omelet
2 eggs
1 tablespoon water
1 teaspoon butter (for the pan)

To make the filling: If you are using fresh
tarragon and rosemary, combine them with the
chives and feta in a small cup and set aside.

If you are using dried tarragon and rosemary, add them to the eggs before cooking.
Combine the chives and feta separately in a cup
and set aside.

To make the omelet: Beat the eggs and water
together with about 20 strokes of a fork.
Then proceed with the Omelet Instructions
(see page 132).

When the eggs are set, sprinkle the filling
over them. Fold the omelet in half or roll it up.
Serves 1.

Sorrel Mushroom Omelet

The Filling
1 shallot, minced
2 mushrooms, thinly sliced
1 tablespoon stock
1 teaspoon butter
¼ cup thinly sliced sorrel

The Omelet
2 eggs
1 tablespoon water
1 teaspoon butter (for the pan)

To make the filling: Combine the shallot,
mushrooms, stock and butter in a small pan.
Cook until the mushrooms are tender and all
the liquid has evaporated, stirring frequently to
prevent scorching.

Add the sorrel and stir a few minutes until
it softens.

To make the omelet: Beat the eggs and water
together with about 20 strokes of a fork.
Then proceed with the Omelet Instructions (see
page 132).

When the eggs are set, spoon the sorrel
mixture over half the omelet and fold it in half.
Serves 1.

Asparagus Omelet

The Filling
- 2 stalks asparagus, trimmed
- 2 shallots, thinly sliced
- 1 mushroom, thinly sliced
- 1 tablespoon stock
- 1 teaspoon butter
- 1 slice colby cheese, diced
- 1½ teaspoons minced chervil or ½ teaspoon dried chervil
- 1½ teaspoons snipped chives

The Omelet
- 2 eggs
- 1 tablespoon water
- 1 teaspoon butter (for the pan)

To make the filling: Cut the asparagus into 1-inch pieces and then steam it, tightly covered, until it's tender, about 5 to 7 minutes. Set aside and keep warm.

In a small frying pan combine the shallots, mushroom, stock and butter, and cook until the mushrooms are tender. Stir in the colby, chervil, chives and asparagus.

To make the omelet: Beat the eggs and water together with about 20 strokes of a fork. Then proceed with the Omelet Instructions (see page 132).

When the eggs are set, distribute the filling over half the omelet and fold the other half over it.

Serves 1.

Pesto Omelet

The Filling
- ½ cup sliced mushrooms
- 1 teaspoon butter
- 1 tablespoon *Pesto Sauce* (see page 124)

The Omelet
- 2 eggs
- 1 tablespoon water
- 1 teaspoon butter (for the pan)

- 1 tablespoon yogurt or sour cream (as a garnish)
- 2 small basil leaves (as a garnish)

To make the filling: In a small frying pan cook the mushrooms along with the butter and the *Pesto Sauce* for about 5 minutes, or until the mushrooms are tender.

To make the omelet: Beat the eggs and water together with about 20 strokes of a fork. Then proceed with the Omelet Instructions (see page 132).

When the eggs are set, spoon the mushrooms over them. Fold the omelet in half and garnish with yogurt or sour cream and the basil leaves.

Serves 1.

Frittatas

Frittatas are Italian omelets, but they differ from their French cousins in several basic ways: Their fillings are combined with the eggs *before* cooking. The eggs are cooked without stirring. And frittatas are served flat and cut into halves or wedges. Like omelets, frittatas can be eaten hot, warm or cold.

There are two basic methods for cooking frittatas, and they're equally effective. The technique that I prefer—and describe in the recipes that follow—suggests that you:

- Pour the egg mixture into a pan.
- Lift the sides of the cooking egg occasionally so that uncooked portions can flow underneath. Frittatas should be cooked until the edges are set and the bottom is golden.
- Broil a frittata until the top is set and browned.

The second method, which is the one taught in France, does everything on top of the stove. It asks you to:

- Pour the egg mixture into a pan.
- Stir it once with a fork, and then allow the eggs to cook undisturbed until the top is just set.
- Sprinkle the frittata with breadcrumbs (and, if you wish, drizzle on a little oil).
- Place a heatproof plate upside down on top of the pan.

- Then, invert both the plate and the pan so that the eggs now rest on the plate.
- Slide the frittata from the plate back onto the pan and brown the underside.
- Cook for another two or three minutes to brown the crumbs and set the bottom.
- Invert the eggs one more time onto a plate for serving.

As with crepes and French omelets, making frittatas requires a well-seasoned pan. A no-stick pan will work *provided* it's ovenproof or you use the stove-top method of cooking.

Note: The following recipes yield two frittatas and four servings, so you must divide all ingredients in half before cooking the eggs. You *can* make one large frittata, but its cooking time will be lengthy, and it will be rather unwieldy.

Spinach Frittata

This is similar to a Swiss chard recipe I picked up at Roger Vergé's school in Provence. If you'd like, you may substitute chard for the spinach.

1 pound spinach
2 cups thinly sliced onions
2 tablespoons olive oil
1 large tomato, seeded and chopped
2 cloves garlic, minced
3 tablespoons minced basil or 2 teaspoons dried basil
1 tablespoon minced thyme or 1 teaspoon dried thyme
¼ cup grated Parmesan cheese
8 eggs
2 tablespoons water
2 tablespoons olive oil

Spinach Frittata—*continued*

Wash the spinach in plenty of cold water, and remove any thick stems. Shred leaves with a knife or scissors.

In a large frying pan or Dutch oven, gently cook the onions in 2 tablespoons of olive oil until they are wilted. Add the spinach and cook until it's wilted. Stir in the tomato and garlic, and cook until the moisture from the spinach and tomato evaporates—about 20 minutes. Do not let the garlic brown. Finally, stir in the basil, thyme and Parmesan.

In a bowl beat 4 eggs and 1 tablespoon of water together with a fork, and stir in half the spinach mixture.

Heat a well-seasoned, ovenproof 9-inch skillet over medium heat until it's quite hot. Add 1 tablespoon of olive oil, and swirl to coat the pan.

Add the eggs. Cook over medium heat, occasionally lifting the sides so that the uncooked portion can flow underneath; cooking time will be about 5 minutes or until the edges are set and the bottom is golden.

Place the skillet about 6 inches from the broiler element and broil until the top is golden and set (about 5 minutes). Slide the frittata onto a large plate. Keep warm.

Repeat with the remaining ingredients.

Serves 4.

Lemon Balm

Lemon balm is a delicate, fragrant herb long revered for its power to calm the nerves and refresh the spirit. The Romans used its leaves to heal wounds, and herbalists still use leaf poultices for sores, tumors and insect bites. Herbals praise lemon balm as an effective remedy for common female complaints, nervous problems, indigestion and lack of sleep. The tea is said to relieve headache and cold symptoms and to soothe a weary body when added to the bath.

Cinnamon Apple Frittata

A lightly sweet frittata for brunch or an interesting dessert.

2 cups finely chopped apples
¼ cup chopped pecans
¼ cup golden raisins
2 tablespoons water
1 tablespoon butter
1 teaspoon ground cinnamon
½ teaspoon grated nutmeg
¼ teaspoon powdered ginger
  pinch of ground cardamom
8 eggs
2 tablespoons water
2 tablespoons butter

In a large frying pan combine the apples, pecans, raisins, 2 tablespoons of water, 1 table-spoon of butter, cinnamon, nutmeg, ginger and cardamom, and cook until the apples are soft and all the liquid has evaporated, about 10 minutes.

In a bowl beat 4 eggs and 1 tablespoon of water together with a fork, and stir in half the apple mixture.

Heat a well-seasoned, ovenproof 9-inch skillet over medium heat until it's quite hot. Add 1 tablespoon of butter, and swirl to coat the pan.

When the foam subsides, add the eggs, and cook over medium heat, occasionally lifting the sides so that the uncooked portion can flow underneath; the cooking time will be about 5 minutes, or until the edges are set and the bottom is golden.

Place the skillet about 6 inches from the broiler element and broil until the top is golden and set (about 5 minutes). Slide the frittata onto a large plate. Keep warm.

Repeat with remaining ingredients.

Serves 4.

Moroccan Carrot Frittata

2 cups of julienne carrots (matchsticks about
  ⅛ by ⅛ by 2 inches)
4 teaspoons butter
1 tablespoon honey
½ teaspoon powdered ginger
¼ teaspoon ground cinnamon
¼ teaspoon ground cumin
⅓ cup grated Parmesan cheese
¼ cup finely chopped almonds
8 eggs
2 tablespoons water
2 tablespoons butter

In a medium saucepan, bring an inch of water to a boil. Put the carrots into a steamer basket and place in the pan, making sure that the water does not come above the level of the steamer. Steam, tightly covered, for about 5 minutes, or until tender.

Remove the steamer from the pan, and discard the water. Add 4 teaspoons of butter, the honey, ginger, cinnamon and cumin to the pan, and stir for 30 seconds. Add the carrots to the mixture, and stir gently for 1 more minute to coat them with the honey and spices. Set aside.

In a bowl beat 4 eggs, 1 tablespoon of water, the Parmesan and almonds together with a fork, and stir in half the carrot mixture.

Heat a well-seasoned, ovenproof 9-inch skillet over medium heat until quite hot. Add 1 tablespoon of butter, and swirl to coat the pan.

When the foam subsides, add the egg mixture, and cook over medium heat, lifting the sides occasionally so that the uncooked portion can flow underneath; cooking time will be about 5 minutes, or until the edges are set and the bottom is golden.

Place the skillet about 6 inches from the broiler element and broil until the top is golden and set (about 5 minutes). Slide the frittata onto a large plate. Keep warm.

Repeat with the remaining ingredients.

Serves 4.

Green Pepper Frittata

½ cup minced onions
½ cup minced green pepper
1 tablespoon butter
½ cup shredded Cheddar cheese
2 tablespoons minced parsley
1 tablespoon minced thyme or 1 teaspoon
    dried thyme
8 eggs
2 tablespoons water
2 tablespoons butter

In a small frying pan cook the onions and peppers in 1 tablespoon of butter until they are soft. Remove from the heat, and cool slightly.

Stir in the Cheddar, parsley and thyme.

In a bowl beat 4 eggs and 1 tablespoon of water together with a fork, and stir in half the pepper mixture.

Heat a well-seasoned, ovenproof 9-inch skillet over medium heat until it's quite hot. Add 1 tablespoon of butter, and swirl to coat the pan.

When the foam subsides, add the eggs, and cook over medium heat, lifting the sides occasionally so that the uncooked portion can flow underneath; cooking time will be about 5 minutes, or until the edges are set and the bottom is golden.

Place the skillet about 6 inches from the broiler element and broil until the top is golden and set (about 5 minutes). Slide the frittata onto a large plate. Keep warm.

Repeat with remaining ingredients.
                                        Serves 4.

Blue Cheese Frittata

The easiest way to crumble blue cheese is to use two forks. If you must buy more than you can use within a reasonable time, freeze the remainder.

⅓ cup crumbled blue cheese
⅓ cup finely chopped walnuts
¼ cup minced parsley
2 tablespoons snipped chives
⅛ teaspoon grated nutmeg
8 eggs
2 tablespoons water
1 tablespoon olive oil
1 tablespoon butter

In a small bowl lightly mix the blue cheese, walnuts, parsley, chives and nutmeg.

In another bowl beat 4 eggs and 1 tablespoon of water together with a fork, and then stir in half of the blue cheese mixture.

Heat a well-seasoned, ovenproof 9-inch skillet over medium heat until it's quite hot. Add 1½ teaspoons of oil and 1½ teaspoons of butter, and swirl them to coat the bottom of the pan.

Add the egg mixture, and cook over medium heat, occasionally lifting the sides so that uncooked portions can flow underneath; cooking time will be about 5 minutes, or until the edges are set and the bottom is golden.

Place the skillet about 6 inches from the broiler element and broil until the top is golden and set (about 5 minutes). Slide the frittata onto a large plate. Keep warm.

Repeat with remaining ingredients.
                                        Serves 4.

Zucchini Frittata

2 tablespoons olive oil
1½ cups thinly sliced zucchini
1 cup thinly sliced mushrooms
⅔ cup minced red pepper
4 scallions, chopped
¼ cup minced parsley
4 teaspoons minced thyme or 1 teaspoon
   dried thyme
½ cup shredded Cheddar cheese
8 eggs
2 tablespoons water
2 tablespoons butter

Heat the oil in a large frying pan over medium-low heat until it's quite hot. Add the zucchini, mushrooms, pepper, scallions, parsley and thyme, and cook until the vegetables are tender, and then cool slightly. Stir in the Cheddar.

In a bowl beat 4 eggs and 1 tablespoon of water together with a fork, and stir in half the zucchini mixture.

Heat a well-seasoned, ovenproof 9-inch skillet over medium heat until it's quite hot. Add 1 tablespoon of butter, and swirl to coat the pan.

When the foam subsides, add the eggs, and cook over medium heat, occasionally lifting the sides so that the uncooked portion can flow underneath; the cooking time will be about 5 minutes, or until the edges are set and the bottom is golden.

Place the skillet about 6 inches from the broiler element and broil until the top is golden and set (about 5 minutes). Slide the frittata onto a large plate. Keep warm.

Repeat with remaining ingredients.

Serves 4.

Spinach Egg Torte

This torte is wonderful for a brunch or light supper, and its several colored layers make for a spectacular presentation. When adding the red-pepper layer, be sure to take it up to the very edge of the dish so it will show after the dish is unmolded.

Although there's a fair amount of work involved here, the ingredients for all the layers can be made ahead and refrigerated until needed. When you're ready to bake the torte, it will only take a few minutes for assembly.

The Yogurt Sauce
2 tablespoons minced dill or 2 teaspoons
   dried dill
2 tablespoons minced parsley
2 tablespoons minced scallion
2 cups yogurt

The Pepper Layer
2 large red peppers

The Spinach Layer
1 pound spinach
½ pound mushrooms
2 shallots, minced
1 tablespoon butter
   few gratings of nutmeg
   dash of cayenne pepper
1 egg white

The Chicken Layer
1½ cups ground cooked chicken
2 tablespoons ground almonds
¼ teaspoon ground black pepper
¼ teaspoon powdered ginger
¼ teaspoon ground cinnamon
½ teaspoon honey
2 tablespoons minced parsley
1 egg

Spinach Egg Torte—*continued*

The Egg Layer
   5 eggs
   1 egg yolk
   ½ cup milk
   1 tablespoon butter
   1 tablespoon lemon juice
   2 tablespoons grated Parmesan cheese
   2 tablespoons shredded Swiss cheese
   3 tablespoons minced dill or 1 tablespoon
      dried dill

The Assembly
   1 tablespoon grated Parmesan cheese
   1 tablespoon shredded Swiss cheese
   roasted red pepper slices (as a garnish)
   toasted sliced almonds (as a garnish)

To make the yogurt sauce: Mix the dill, parsley, scallion and yogurt in a small bowl, and then pour into a strainer lined with several thicknesses of clean cheesecloth. Cover and set the strainer over a bowl in the refrigerator and allow to drain for several hours or overnight.

To make the pepper layer: Place the peppers about 6 inches from the broiler element and broil until they are black on all sides. Use tongs to turn them. Transfer them to a plastic or paper bag, close it tightly, and let the peppers steam for about 10 minutes or until their skins are loosened. When they're cool enough to handle, remove the skin, core and seeds, and pat them dry with paper towels. Cut the peppers into 1-inch slices.

To make the spinach layer: Wash the spinach in plenty of cold water, and cook in a large pot using only the water left clinging to the leaves; cook only until the spinach wilts, and then transfer to a colander or sieve to drain and cool. When the spinach is cool enough to handle, squeeze out *all* the moisture, and chop it finely.

   Mince the mushrooms, and, using a large square of cheesecloth or a clean tea towel,

squeeze out their moisture working with one handful of mushrooms at a time.

   Then, sauté the mushroom pieces with the shallots in butter using a large frying pan over medium-low heat; cook only until the mushrooms are dry, about 10 minutes. Stir frequently.

   Remove the mixture from the heat, and stir in the spinach, nutmeg, cayenne and egg white.

To make the chicken layer: In a medium bowl combine the chicken, almonds, pepper, ginger, cinnamon, honey, parsley and egg.

To make the egg layer: Beat the eggs, yolk and milk together just until they are combined. Melt the butter in a large frying pan, and add the eggs. Cook them over medium-low heat, stirring frequently with a wooden spoon, until they are no longer runny, and then stir in the lemon juice, Parmesan, Swiss and dill.

To assemble: Butter a 5- or 6-cup soufflé dish, and coat it with Parmesan. Spoon the egg layer into the dish, and then cover it with the red pepper slices; be sure that they come right to the edge of the dish; reserve a few slices to use as a garnish.

   Cover the peppers with the chicken layer, and that with the spinach layer. Sprinkle the top with the Swiss.

   Bake the torte at 400°F for 30 minutes, and let it stand for 15 minutes before unmolding it onto a serving plate.

   Garnish the torte with red peppers and almonds, and serve with the cold yogurt sauce.
                                          Serves 4 to 6.

Breakfast Tomatoes

1 red pepper (optional)
4 large firm tomatoes
1 pound spinach or kale
4 mushrooms, thinly sliced
2 tablespoons butter
6 eggs
1 tablespoon minced basil or 1 teaspoon dried basil
1 teaspoon minced marjoram or ¼ teaspoon dried marjoram
2 tablespoons snipped chives
½ teaspoon *Curry Powder* (see *Index*)
1½ ounces cream cheese, cubed

If you're using the pepper, remove the core and seeds, dry it with paper towels and then chop it into small pieces. Set the pieces aside.

Slice stem end tops off the tomatoes, and with a teaspoon, hollow them out, leaving a solid shell about a quarter of an inch thick. Discard the pulp or reserve for another use. Set these tomato shells upside down and allow them to drain.

Wash the spinach or kale in plenty of cold water, and remove any coarse stems. Chop the greens and set them aside.

Place the tomato shells, cut side up, on a lightly buttered and heatproof dish and bake them at 350°F for 10 minutes. Do not overbake to prevent the shells from splitting.

Meanwhile, cook the spinach or kale in a large pot, using only the water left clinging to the leaves; cook only until the greens wilt. Set them aside and keep warm.

In a large frying pan, sauté the mushrooms and red peppers in butter until soft.

In a bowl combine the eggs, basil, marjoram, chives, *Curry Powder* and cream cheese, and beat with a fork. Add to the pan containing the mushrooms and red peppers and cook, stirring frequently, until the eggs scramble.

To serve, place a baked tomato on a nest of greens on each plate, and spoon scrambled eggs into it. Serve hot.

Serves 4.

Spinach Egg Cups with Chive Sauce

The Eggs
1 pound spinach
3 tablespoons minced shallots
1 tablespoon butter
½ cup (packed) sorrel leaves (optional)
¼ cup whole wheat breadcrumbs
¼ cup shredded Cheddar cheese
4 eggs

The Sauce
2 teaspoons herb vinegar or white wine vinegar
1 tablespoon lemon juice
¼ cup cold butter
¼ cup snipped chives

4 slices whole wheat bread or English muffins, lightly toasted

To make the eggs: Wash the spinach in plenty of cold water, and cook in a large pot, using only the water left clinging to the leaves; cook only until the spinach wilts, and then transfer it to a colander or sieve to cool and drain. When the leaves are cool enough to handle, squeeze out the moisture.

Cook the shallots in a small pan with butter until they are tender. Add the sorrel leaves and stir over low heat until they wilt.

Transfer the sorrel and spinach to the bowl of a food processor, and puree or chop finely by hand. Mix in the breadcrumbs.

Spinach Egg Cups with Chive Sauce—*continued*

Heavily butter four ½-cup ramekins or custard cups. Using the back of a spoon or your fingers, pack one-quarter of the spinach mixture into each cup, making an even layer over the bottom and sides.

Sprinkle 1 tablespoon of Cheddar into each cup, and then break an egg over the top of that.

Using a rubber spatula, push the spinach down below the surface of the egg to prevent burning during the baking.

Transfer the cups to a baking sheet, and bake at 350°F for about 20 minutes, or until the whites are set and the yolks are still a little runny (as they are in poached eggs).

To make the sauce: In a small saucepan combine the vinegar and lemon juice, and cook over medium heat until they have reduced in volume to about 1 teaspoon. Remove the mixture from the heat, and whisk in the cold butter, about a teaspoonful at a time, until it is all incorporated. Do *not* stop stirring; the butter must form a creamy emulsion rather than melt. If the pan cools and the butter will not cream into the sauce easily, return the pan to the heat for a few seconds to warm it. When all the butter is incorporated, stir in the chives.

Loosen each spinach and egg cup from its ramekin with a rubber spatula. Turn each cup out onto a slice of lightly toasted bread or English muffin, and spoon about a tablespoon of butter sauce over each. Serve hot.

Serves 4.

Linden

Linden or lime flowers make a delicious soothing tea that is a popular beverage in the cafés of Europe. Herbals describe the tea as having a mild, tranquilizing effect that calms the nerves and alleviates indigestion, trembling or hysteria. They also say it may provide some relief from colds and flu. An infusion of flowers added to the bath is said to refresh and relax the skin.

Bulgur

Bulgur is a wheat product that has been a staple in the Middle East and parts of Asia since biblical times. It is produced by boiling wheat berries (or kernels), drying them and then cracking them under a grinder or stone. Because it has been precooked and dried, bulgur can be stored much longer than other grains.

Since only a small part of its bran has been lost during processing, bulgur is nutritionally almost identical to whole wheat. That means that it contains wheat's fiber, protein, iron, potassium and B vitamins while being low in fat and sodium.

When properly cooked, bulgur fluffs up nicely and can easily substitute for that Moroccan favorite, couscous, which is a refined wheat product. I've found that the best way to cook bulgur is to use equal amounts of liquid and dry grain. Bring the liquid—either stock or water—to a boil in a small saucepan. Stir in the bulgur, remove it from the heat, cover the pan, and let it stand for about 20 minutes while the bulgur absorbs the liquid. Fluff the result with two forks before using.

If you'll be using the bulgur in a salad, add the dressing while the grain is still warm to enhance its absorption.

Wild Basil Bulgur

What's wild about this dish is the wild rice, a good source of riboflavin (vitamin B2). Wild rice is not actually a rice, but rather, it is the grain of a tall grass plant that grows in the northern Minnesota and Wisconsin lake country. It commands a high price, but it is easily extended by combination with brown rice or bulgur. It has a delicate nutty flavor.

¾ cup stock
¾ cup uncooked bulgur
1 carrot, minced
1 stalk celery, minced
½ cup minced scallions
2 tablespoons butter
½ cup uncooked wild rice
1 cup stock
2 tablespoons minced parsley
2 tablespoons minced basil or 2 teaspoons dried basil
1 tablespoon minced oregano or 1 teaspoon dried oregano
2 teaspoons minced marjoram or ½ teaspoon dried marjoram
¼ cup stock
2 cups yogurt

Bring the ¾ cup of stock to a boil in a small saucepan. Stir in the bulgur, cover and remove the pan from the heat, and let it stand for 20 minutes, or until the bulgur is tender and all the liquid has been absorbed.

In a large ovenproof saucepan or flameproof casserole, sauté the carrot, celery and scallions in butter over low heat until the vegetables are soft, about 5 minutes.

Add the rice and 1 cup of stock to the pan. Cover and simmer over low heat for 20 to 30 minutes, or until the rice is tender and most of the liquid has been absorbed.

Then, fold in the bulgur, parsley, basil, oregano, marjoram and ¼ cup of stock. Cover and bake at 350°F for about 15 minutes.

Serve with yogurt.

Serves 4.

South of the Border Bulgur

1½ cups stock
1½ cups uncooked bulgur
  2 large onions, diced
  1 cup thinly sliced celery
  3 cloves garlic, minced
  2 tablespoons butter
  ½ cup stock
1-2 tablespoons *Chili Powder* (see *Index*)
  1 teaspoon ground cumin
    dash of hot pepper sauce or cayenne pepper
  ¼ cup minced parsley
  1 cup shredded Cheddar or Monterey Jack
    cheese
  2 cups yogurt
  1 cup alfalfa sprouts
  1 cup chopped roasted peanuts
  1 pepper, diced
  2 tomatoes, chopped
  ½ cup sliced scallions

Bring the 1½ cups of stock to a boil in a small saucepan. Stir in the bulgur, cover, remove from the heat, and let the mixture stand for 20 minutes.

In a large frying pan combine the onions, celery, garlic, butter and ½ cup stock. Cover and cook over low heat until the onions are very soft, about 20 minutes. Stir in the *Chili Powder*, cumin, hot pepper sauce or cayenne and parsley.

Fluff the bulgur with two forks, and stir it into the onion mixture.

Place the cheese, yogurt, sprouts, peanuts, pepper, tomatoes and scallions into separate bowls and serve as toppings for the bulgur.

Serves 4.

Lovage

The Europeans have cultivated lovage since early times for its aromatic, celery flavor. Lovage's use in herbalism is limited, but some regard it as beneficial for digestive difficulties, flatulence and occasionally for urinary problems and the accumulation of water in the body. Herbals recommend a lovage infusion as a soothing bath for skin problems.

Nutty Broccoli Casserole

A good way to be sure that all the bugs are gone from home-grown broccoli is to soak it for at least 15 minutes in cold water containing a few tablespoons of vinegar.

The Sauce
    2 cups yogurt
    1 egg
    ¼ cup grated Parmesan cheese
    2 tablespoons sesame seeds
      cayenne pepper

The Rice Layer
    ⅔ cup uncooked brown rice
    2 cups stock

The Nut Layer
    1 large onion, thinly sliced
    2 tablespoons olive oil
    1½ cups thinly sliced mushrooms
    1 green pepper, thinly sliced
    1 red pepper, thinly sliced
    4 cloves garlic, minced
    ½ cup minced parsley
    ¼ cup sunflower seeds
    ¼ cup chopped cashews
    1 tablespoon minced dill or 1 teaspoon dried
      dill
    1 tablespoon minced thyme or 1 teaspoon
      dried thyme
    1 tablespoon tamari sauce

The Broccoli Layer
    ½ pound broccoli stalks

To make the sauce: Pour the yogurt into a sieve or colander lined with cheesecloth, and let drain at room temperature for at least an hour.

When you're ready to assemble the casserole, combine the yogurt with the egg and Parmesan, but reserve the sesame seeds and cayenne.

To make the rice layer: Combine the rice and stock in a medium saucepan, and bring to a simmer. Cook, covered, over low heat until the rice is tender and all the liquid has been absorbed (about 50 to 60 minutes).

To make the nut layer: Sauté the onion in oil until it is soft. Add the mushrooms, peppers and garlic, and continue to cook until the peppers are tender and the mushrooms have given up their liquid. If there is more than a thin layer of liquid in the pan, cook until most of it evaporates.

Stir in the parsley, sunflower seeds, cashews, dill, thyme and tamari and set aside.

To make the broccoli layer: Separate the broccoli into florets of approximately the same size.

Then, bring an inch of water to a boil in a medium saucepan. Put the broccoli into a steamer basket and place it in the pan, making sure that the water does not come above the level of the steamer. Steam, tightly covered, for about 8 minutes, or until the broccoli is just tender. Do not overcook.

To assemble: Oil or butter an 8-inch-square baking pan, and spread the rice evenly in it.

Top the rice with the nut layer, and then arrange the broccoli over all.

Spread the yogurt sauce over the broccoli, sprinkle with sesame seeds and dust lightly with cayenne.

Bake at 350°F for 30 minutes.

Serves 4.

Brown Rice Soufflé

This recipe makes a rather dense soufflé because of its brown rice, but it does fluff up a bit in the final step. The eggs, cheese and yogurt add plenty of protein to the brown rice, so this makes a fine main dish, but may also be served as a side dish.

1 onion, minced
1 carrot, minced
2 mushrooms, minced
¼ cup stock
1 teaspoon olive oil
1 teaspoon tamari sauce
2 cups cooked brown rice (see page 205 for cooking instructions)
½ cup minced parsley
⅓ cup shredded cheese
2 teaspoons minced marjoram or 1 teaspoon dried marjoram
3 eggs, separated
2 tablespoons shredded cheese
 yogurt

Combine the onion, carrot, mushrooms, stock, oil and tamari in a saucepan or frying pan. Cook the mixture, covered, until the ingredients are tender. Remove the cover and cook until the excess liquid has evaporated.

Fold the rice, parsley, ⅓ cup cheese, marjoram, egg yolks together with the cooked vegetables.

In a large, clean bowl beat the egg whites until they form stiff peaks, and fold them into the rice mixture.

Transfer to an oiled, 6-cup casserole or soufflé dish. Sprinkle with 2 tablespoons of the shredded cheese.

Bake at 350°F for 25 to 30 minutes, or until the soufflé puffs slightly and browns on top.

Serve with yogurt.

Serves 4.

Onion and Dill Casserole

2 cups diced onions
2 red peppers, diced
¼ cup stock
1 tablespoon butter
1 cup thinly sliced mushrooms
1 clove garlic, minced
2 cups cooked brown rice (see page 205 for cooking instructions)
1 cup cottage cheese
1 egg
⅓ cup grated Parmesan cheese
⅓ cup minced dill or 1 tablespoon dried dill
⅓ cup minced parsley
⅓ cup whole wheat breadcrumbs
1 tablespoon grated Parmesan cheese
1 tablespoon butter, melted

Combine the onions, red peppers, stock and butter in a large frying pan. Cover and cook over medium-low heat until they are limp. Add the mushrooms and garlic, and cook, uncovered, until the mushrooms are limp and all liquid in the pan has evaporated.

In a large bowl fold together the onion mixture, rice, cottage cheese, egg, ⅓ cup Parmesan, dill and parsley, and turn into a buttered 9-inch square baking dish.

Combine the breadcrumbs, 1 tablespoon of Parmesan and the melted butter in a small bowl, and then sprinkle this mixture over the top of the casserole.

Bake at 375°F for 30 minutes.

Serves 4.

Mushroom Tomato Polenta

The Polenta Layer
  1 cup cornmeal
  2 cups stock
  2 eggs
  1 tablespoon butter
  ¼ cup shredded Gruyère or Swiss cheese
  1 tablespoon minced sage or 1 teaspoon dried
    sage

The Mushroom-Tomato Layer
  1 cup finely chopped onions
  1 cup chopped tomatoes
  2 cups thinly sliced mushrooms
  1 red pepper, finely diced
  1 tablespoon butter
  ¼ cup stock

The Sauce
  3 tablespoons butter
  1½ cups milk
  3 tablespoons whole wheat pastry flour
  1 teaspoon dry mustard
  ⅛ teaspoon cayenne pepper
  ¼ cup shredded Gruyère or Swiss cheese
  3 tablespoons minced dill or 2 teaspoons
    dried dill

To make the polenta layer: Combine the cornmeal and stock in a medium saucepan, and cook over medium heat, stirring constantly, until it is very thick. Remove from the heat.

In a small bowl beat the eggs until well blended, and then beat in about ½ cup of hot cornmeal, stirring constantly to keep the eggs from scrambling. Add the rest of the cornmeal, and stir in the butter, cheese and sage.

Pour into a buttered, 9-inch-square baking pan and set aside.

To make the mushroom-tomato layer: Combine the onions, tomatoes, mushrooms, pepper, butter and stock in a large frying pan. Cover and cook over medium heat until the tomatoes are soft and have given up their juices. Uncover and cook, stirring frequently, until all the liquid has evaporated. Be careful that vegetables do not scorch. Set aside.

To make the sauce: Melt the butter in a medium saucepan, and stir in the flour. Cook over medium heat, stirring constantly, for 2 minutes.

In a small saucepan heat the milk, and add to the flour mixture all at once. Beat vigorously with a wire whisk to combine. Cook, stirring constantly, until the sauce thickens and comes to boil. Remove from the heat, and stir in the mustard, cayenne, cheese and dill.

Stir the sauce into the vegetable mixture, and pour it over the cornmeal layer in baking dish.

Bake at 375°F for 30 minutes, or until brown and bubbly. Let stand for about 15 minutes before cutting.

Serves 4.

Deviled Egg Casserole

The Rice Layer
  1 cup uncooked long-grain brown rice
  1 onion, chopped
  1 carrot, diced
  ½ pepper, diced
  3 cups stock
  ¾ cup parsley

The Eggs
  4 hard-cooked eggs
  1 teaspoon minced savory or ¼ teaspoon
    dried savory
  1 tablespoon snipped chives
3-4 tablespoons *Basic Mayonnaise* (see *Index*)

The Sauce
  1½ cups milk
  3 tablespoons butter
  3 tablespoons whole wheat pastry flour
  ⅓ cup grated Parmesan cheese
  1 teaspoon minced savory or ¼ teaspoon
    dried savory

Deviled Egg Casserole—*continued*

The Assembly
    8 asparagus spears, lightly steamed
    2 tablespoons minced parsley
    2 tablespoons grated Parmesan cheese

To make the rice layer: Combine the rice, onion, carrot, pepper and stock in a medium saucepan. Simmer, covered, until the rice is tender and all the liquid has been absorbed, about 50 to 60 minutes. Cool slightly, and then stir in the parsley.

To make the eggs: Cut the hard-cooked eggs in half lengthwise and remove and mash the yolks (or force them through a sieve). Mix them with the savory, chives and enough mayonnaise to hold everything together.

To make the sauce: In a small saucepan heat the milk. Melt the butter in a medium saucepan, and then stir in the flour. Cook, stirring constantly, for 2 minutes over low heat. Pour in the hot milk, and whisk vigorously to combine. Cook this mixture over low heat, stirring constantly, until it thickens and comes to a boil. Remove from the heat and stir in the Parmesan and savory.

To assemble: Butter or oil a 9-inch-square baking dish. Stir about ½ cup of the sauce into the rice, and spoon it into the baking dish.

With the back of a spoon, make eight depressions in the rice, and fill each with an egg.

Cut asparagus spears into bite-size pieces, and arrange them between the eggs.

Pour the remaining sauce overall.

Sprinkle with parsley and more Parmesan.

Bake at 350°F for 30 minutes. If the top has not started to brown at the end of the baking time, place the casserole under the broiler for a minute or two.

Serves 4.

Marigold

Marigold was once regarded as the herb of the sun, probably because of its bright orange blooms. Old herbals describe its power to strengthen the heart and refresh the spirits, but nowadays herbalists employ it mostly in external applications to relieve bruises, muscle pain, sores and insect bites. They say the petals can be mixed with a base such as cold cream to soothe the complexion.

Tarragon Mushroom Stroganoff

I like to serve this rich-tasting stroganoff at dinner parties. Though it retains the traditional taste, it's lower in cholesterol and calories than most stroganoffs because the sour cream is extended with plain yogurt.

3¼ cups stock
1 cup uncooked brown rice
2 cups yogurt
3 large onions, thinly sliced
2 tablespoons butter
1 teaspoon paprika
1 pound mushrooms, thinly sliced
1 red pepper, thinly sliced
3 cloves garlic, minced
1 cup sour cream
2 tablespoons lemon juice
2 teaspoons tamari sauce
1 tablespoon minced tarragon or 1 teaspoon dried tarragon
1 tablespoon minced dill or 1 teaspoon dried dill
½ cup minced parsley
½ cup chopped roasted cashews

In a large saucepan bring 3 cups of the stock to a boil. Stir in the rice, cover the pan and simmer until the rice is tender and the stock has been absorbed, about 50 minutes.

While the rice is cooking, pour the yogurt into a sieve or strainer lined with cheesecloth. Let it drain over a bowl.

In a large pot cook the onions in butter and the remaining ¼ cup of stock over low heat until they are limp. Stir in the paprika, and add the mushrooms, pepper and garlic. Cover and cook until the mushrooms soften and give up their liquid. Then remove the cover and cook, stirring frequently, until the liquid evaporates from the pan. Be sure that the garlic and onions do not scorch.

In a bowl whisk together the sour cream, drained yogurt, lemon juice and tamari. Slowly stir into the mushrooms and cook over low heat until the mixture is just heated through. Then stir in the tarragon, dill and parsley, and sprinkle with cashews. Serve over the cooked brown rice.

Serves 4 to 6.

Tomato Rice Strata

1 tablespoon butter
1 tablespoon oil
1 cup finely chopped onions
1 cup thinly sliced mushrooms
1 cup chopped tomatoes
2 tablespoons minced basil or 2 teaspoons dried basil
2 tablespoons minced parsley
⅛ teaspoon cayenne pepper
1½ cups cooked brown rice (see page 205 for cooking instructions)
1 cup shredded Cheddar cheese
3 eggs
1 cup milk
1 tablespoon butter, melted
½ cup whole wheat breadcrumbs
2 tablespoons grated Parmesan cheese
1 cup yogurt

Over medium-low heat, heat the butter and oil in a large frying pan until foamy. Add the onions and mushrooms, and cook until the onions are tender.

Add the tomatoes, basil, parsley and cayenne, and cook, stirring frequently, over medium heat until the tomatoes have cooked down and most of the excess liquid has evaporated.

Butter an 8- or 9-inch-square baking dish or coat it with equal parts of oil and liquid lecithin.

Spread the cooked rice in the dish. Spread the tomato mixture evenly over the rice, and sprinkle with Cheddar.

Tomato Rice Strata—*continued*

In a small bowl beat the eggs and milk with a fork until they are well combined, and pour over the layer of cheese.

In a small bowl stir the melted butter together with the breadcrumbs and Parmesan, and sprinkle over the top of the casserole.

Bake at 375°F for 35 to 40 minutes, or until the strata is puffed and golden and a knife inserted in the center comes out clean. Serve hot with yogurt.

Serves 4.

Wild Risotto

Here's brown rice made more interesting with saffron, a bit of wild rice and some seeds, beans and carrots. A hearty dinner dish.

1½ cups minced onions
  3 cloves garlic, minced
  1 tablespoon butter
  1 tablespoon olive oil
  ½ cup uncooked long-grain brown rice
  ¼ cup uncooked wild rice
  2 cups stock
  ⅛ teaspoon saffron
  ⅓ cup minced shallots
  1 tablespoon butter
  ¼ cup pumpkin seeds
  ¼ cup sunflower seeds
  2 large carrots, thinly sliced and steamed
      about 5 minutes
  1 cup cooked kidney beans
  ¼ cup minced parsley
  2 tablespoons minced dill or 2 teaspoons
      dried dill
  1 tablespoon minced oregano or 1 teaspoon
      dried oregano
  2 cups yogurt

In a large, ovenproof saucepan, cook the onions and garlic in a tablespoon each of butter and oil until the onions wilt. Then, stir in the brown and wild rice, and sauté a few minutes more.

Add the stock and saffron, cover and cook over low heat until the rice is tender and the liquid has been absorbed, about 50 minutes.

In a small frying pan cook the shallots in a tablespoon of butter until they are limp. Stir in the pumpkin and sunflower seeds, and sauté a few minutes more to lightly toast the seeds.

When the rice is tender, lightly fold the seeds, carrots, beans, parsley, dill and oregano into the rice.

Bake, covered, at 375°F for about 30 minutes, or until the risotto is hot throughout.

Serve with yogurt.

Serves 4.

Openfaced Cheese Sandwiches

Some simple fare for a quick lunch. Alfalfa fights cholesterol, so be generous with the sprouts.

4 slices thinly sliced whole wheat bread
1 cup cottage cheese
1 tablespoon minced basil or 1 teaspoon dried
    basil
1 tomato, thinly sliced
8 slices mild cheese
  alfalfa sprouts

Lightly toast the bread, and spread each slice with about ¼ cup cottage cheese, being careful to spread the cheese out to the edges. Sprinkle with basil.

Top the bread with tomato slices and then pieces of cheese. Broil a few minutes to melt the cheese.

Top the sandwiches with sprouts before serving.

Makes 4 sandwiches.

Eggplant Pesto Bake

The Eggplant Layer
1 large eggplant (about 1½ pounds)
1 egg
2 tablespoons milk
2-3 tablespoons olive oil

The Ricotta Layer
1 cup ricotta cheese
1 egg
1 cup minced parsley
1 clove garlic, minced
¼ cup grated Parmesan cheese

The Pesto Layer
¼ cup (packed) basil leaves
3 tablespoons olive oil
2 tablespoons grated Parmesan cheese
1 clove garlic, minced
1 tablespoon pine nuts

The Assembly
1 cup *Tomato Sauce* (see page 124)
⅓ cup shredded mozzarella or provolone
   cheese

To make the eggplant layer: If you wish, peel the eggplant. Then, cut it into half-inch slices.

In a shallow dish combine the egg and milk, and dip the eggplant slices into the mixture.

Film a large no-stick frying pan with oil, and heat until the oil is hot. Sauté the eggplant until it is browned on both sides. Add more oil as needed.

To make the ricotta layer: With a mixer or food processor blend the ricotta, egg, parsley, garlic and Parmesan until they are smooth.

To make the pesto layer: With a blender or food processor blend the basil, oil, Parmesan, garlic and pine nuts until they are smooth.

To assemble: Spread half the *Tomato Sauce* in a 7-by-11-inch baking dish, and arrange half the eggplant slices on top of the sauce.

Then, spread the ricotta on top of the first eggplant layer, and cover with the remaining slices.

Spread with pesto, pour the remaining sauce over the top, and sprinkle with cheese. Bake at 350°F for about 30 minutes.

Serves 4.

Squash Soufflé

This is a more traditional puffed soufflé, and so it must be served immediately after baking to avoid deflation.

For best results make sure your egg yolks and whites are at room temperature before beating them. (But, by all means, separate them while they are still cold, because the yolks are stronger then and less likely to break.) It is imperative that there be no specks of yolk mixed with the whites as you beat them; impure whites will not inflate properly and will flatten the soufflé.

2 tablespoons grated Parmesan cheese
2 scallions, minced
1 tablespoon butter
1 cup cooked mashed winter squash
1 cup milk
3 tablespoons butter
¼ cup whole wheat pastry flour
1 teaspoon dry mustard
1 teaspoon minced savory or ¼ teaspoon dried
   savory
1 teaspoon minced marjoram or ¼ teaspoon
   dried marjoram
1 teaspoon minced thyme or ¼ teaspoon dried
   thyme
4 egg yolks
6 egg whites
¾ cup shredded Swiss or Cheddar cheese

Generously butter a 5- or 6-cup soufflé dish, and extend it with a wax paper sleeve. Start with a length of paper 4 inches longer than the outside circumference of your dish. Fold it in half lengthwise and butter one side. Now surround the *outside* of the soufflé dish with the paper (keeping its buttered side in), and secure with string.

Squash Soufflé—*continued*

Coat the inside of the dish and paper with Parmesan.

Preheat the oven to 400°F.

In a small frying pan sauté the scallions in 1 tablespoon of butter for 3 minutes. Do not let them brown. Now, add the squash, and cook for 5 minutes over medium heat, stirring frequently, to evaporate the excess moisture from the squash. Do not let the mixture scorch.

In a small saucepan heat the milk.

In a 1-quart saucepan melt 3 tablespoons of butter, stir in the flour, and cook, stirring constantly, for 2 minutes. Now, whisk in the hot milk, and cook over medium heat, stirring constantly, until the sauce is very thick. Remove from the heat. Stir in the mustard, savory, marjoram and thyme, and add the squash.

Beat the egg yolks, one at a time, into the sauce, and then transfer to a very large mixing bowl.

In another large, clean bowl, using clean beaters, beat the egg whites until they are stiff and glossy but not dry.

Gently fold one-third of the whites into the sauce. Sprinkle one-third of the cheese on top, and fold in gently. Repeat the process twice more with the remaining whites and cheese. Do not overmix to avoid deflating the egg whites. It is better for specks of white to remain in the mixture than to overblend the whites.

Gently transfer the mixture to the buttered and papered soufflé dish. Place in the oven and immediately lower the temperature to 375°F.

Bake for about 35 minutes, or until the top is puffed and golden, and a skewer inserted into the center comes out clean.

Cut the string and carefully remove the wax paper collar. Serve the soufflé immediately.

Serves 4.

Marjoram

Sweet marjoram belongs to the same family as oregano and has similar medicinal and culinary uses. Herbalists sometimes recommend a weak marjoram tea for colic in children. Or they apply it externally for relief of rheumatic pain, varicose veins and stiff joints.

Chapter 9
Chicken and Other Poultry

Chicken is high in protein and low in fat and sodium. Since most of the fat is located just under the skin, removing it reduces the chicken's fat content still further. Chicken is also a reliable source of niacin, vitamin B6, iron, potassium and zinc.

Tarragon Chicken

This is a basic way of sautéing chicken breasts, and it involves an herbed white sauce. If the sauce comes out too thick, thin to the desired consistency with more milk. Serve over brown rice.

2 large chicken breasts
2 tablespoons butter
1 tablespoon minced tarragon or 1 teaspoon dried tarragon
1 large onion, minced
3 tablespoons whole wheat pastry flour
½ cup stock
1 cup milk
1 pound whole wheat noodles, cooked

Debone and remove the skin and visible fat from the chicken. Divide each breast in half to produce 4 pieces of meat. Pat dry.

Melt the butter in a large frying pan, and quickly brown the chicken pieces on both sides. Set aside.

Add the tarragon and onion to the pan, and cook over low heat until the onions are limp. Sprinkle flour over the onions and stir to incorporate. Now, add the stock and stir until the mixture thickens. Add the milk and stir as the sauce thickens.

Return the chicken to the pan, cover, and cook over low heat for 20 minutes, or until the chicken is tender and the sauce thickens. Stir occasionally. Serve over cooked noodles.

Serves 4.

Spicy Coconut Chicken

This is my version of a dish I learned from Hella de Beauclair at The Cooking Company in Wescosville, Pennsylvania. The saffron gives a rich color to the chicken, and the hot pepper adds a certain spiciness. Look to the currants, parsley, onions and red pepper for additional vitamins and minerals.

3 tablespoons apple juice
2 tablespoons currants
1 pound boned chicken breasts
1 tablespoon oil
¼ cup grated coconut
¼ cup minced parsley
2 tablespoons butter, melted
2 tablespoons butter
2 cups thinly sliced onions
1 red pepper, cut into ¼-inch slices
1 hot pepper, minced
1 tablespoon lemon juice
⅛ teaspoon saffron

Warm the apple juice, and add the currants. Set aside for 30 minutes.

Place the chicken breasts between two sheets of wax paper, and pound with a mallet until they are about ¼ inch thick. Coat them with oil and set aside for 30 minutes.

In a small bowl combine the coconut, parsley and melted butter, and set aside.

Heat 2 tablespoons of butter in a large skillet, and sauté the chicken pieces in small batches until they are opaque and lightly browned. Transfer them to a 7-by-11-inch baking dish.

Add the onions, red pepper and hot pepper to the frying pan, and sauté until tender. Stir in the lemon juice, saffron, currants and apple juice, and cook over medium heat until the liquid evaporates.

Spread the onions in a thin layer on top of the chicken. Sprinkle with the coconut mixture.

Bake at 350°F for about 15 minutes, or until the coconut is lightly golden.

Serves 4.

Chicken Breasts Vergé

This is adapted from a recipe I learned at Roger Vergé's cooking school in Provence. The sauce is rich and thick, but there's just enough to lightly coat the meat.

2 large chicken breasts
3 tablespoons butter
¾ cup minced shallots
2 tablespoons minced basil or 2 teaspoons dried basil
1 tablespoon minced thyme or 1 teaspoon dried thyme
⅓ cup stock
¼ cup half-and-half
2 egg yolks
½ cup half-and-half
1 tablespoon minced parsley

Debone and remove the skin and visible fat from the chicken. Cut each breast in half to produce four pieces of meat.

In a casserole or frying pan large enough to hold the chicken in a single layer, melt the butter over medium-low heat. Add the shallots, basil and thyme, and place the chicken on top. Cover and cook for 10 minutes. Turn the chicken, re-cover and cook for another 10 minutes. Remove the chicken to a plate and keep warm.

Add the stock to the pan, raise the heat to medium high, and reduce the liquid to 2 or 3 tablespoons. Add ¼ cup of half-and-half, and reduce the liquid to about 3 tablespoons. Remove from heat.

In a cup beat the egg yolks together with ½ cup of half-and-half, and whisk the egg mixture into the sauce. Return to low heat and whisk constantly until the sauce starts to thicken (2 or 3 minutes). Do not let it come to a boil or it will curdle. Stir in the parsley, and serve hot over the chicken.

Serves 4.

Rosy Sweet and Sour Chicken

An unusual version of sweet and sour chicken, this dish gets its color from the tomato paste that is simmered into its sauce, which you can make ahead and keep in the refrigerator. The pineapple adds potassium and vitamins A and C, and the carrots contribute considerable vitamin A. Serve the chicken over brown rice to up the dish's complement of the B vitamins and fiber.

The Sauce
½ cup white vinegar
¼ cup orange juice
¼ cup pineapple juice
¼ cup honey
2 tablespoons tomato paste
1 teaspoon blackstrap molasses
2 tablespoons water
1 tablespoon cornstarch

The Stir-Fry
1 pound boned chicken breasts
2 tablespoons apple juice
4 teaspoons tamari sauce
1 tablespoon oil
1 tablespoon cornstarch
2 large carrots, cut diagonally into ⅜-inch slices
3 tablespoons oil
1 large pepper, cut into ⅜-inch slices
4 scallions, cut into 1-inch sections
1 cup drained pineapple chunks
2 teaspoons grated ginger root
3 cups hot cooked brown rice (see page 205 for cooking instructions)

To make the sauce: In a small saucepan combine the vinegar, orange juice, pineapple juice, honey, tomato paste and molasses. Bring them to a boil, and simmer for 10 minutes.

In a small cup blend the water and cornstarch until smooth, and stir them into the sauce. Cook another 1 to 2 minutes, stirring constantly, until the sauce has thickened. Set aside.

To make the stir-fry: Flatten the chicken with a mallet to an even ⅜-inch thickness, cut it into pieces about 1 by 2 inches, and place the pieces in a large bowl.

In a small cup stir together the apple juice, tamari, 1 tablespoon of oil and the cornstarch until smooth. Pour over the chicken, and toss to combine. Let the chicken marinate for 30 to 60 minutes.

Parboil the carrots in about ½ cup of water for about 10 minutes, or until they are just tender. Do not overcook. Drain and set aside.

In a wok over high heat or in a large, well-seasoned frying pan over medium heat, heat 3 tablespoons of oil until quite hot.

Add the chicken to the pan and stir-fry for 3 to 4 minutes, or until it is opaque throughout. Remove with a slotted spoon and keep warm.

Stir-fry the peppers and scallions for 3 minutes. Add the carrots, pineapple and ginger, and stir-fry for another minute.

Return the chicken to the pan, add the sauce, and heat through.

Serve over hot cooked rice.

Serves 4.

North African Peanut Chicken

Peanuts are a staple in West Africa, where they're known as groundnuts. They're high in protein, potassium and niacin but low in sodium (if they're unsalted, of course). If the sauce comes out too thick to suit you, thin it with tomato sauce or stock.

1 pound boned chicken breasts
¼ cup whole wheat flour
2 tablespoons butter
1 tablespoon oil
3 onions, thinly sliced
1 cup stock
1 cup *Tomato Sauce* (see *Index*)
2 tablespoons peanut butter
¼ cup minced parsley
3 tablespoons minced dill or 1 tablespoon dried dill
2 tablespoons minced basil or 2 teaspoons dried basil
 few coriander sprigs, minced (optional)
3 cups hot cooked brown rice or bulgur (see pages 205 and 144, respectively, for cooking instructions)

Cut the chicken breasts into pieces about ½ by 2 inches.

Put the flour into a plastic or paper bag, add the chicken pieces a few at a time, and shake the bag to coat them.

Heat the butter and oil in a large frying pan until the butter foams. Add the chicken and sauté quickly. When the pieces are lightly colored, remove them with a slotted spoon and keep warm.

Add the onions and stock to the frying pan, cover and cook over low heat until the onions are very tender, about 10 minutes.

Add the *Tomato Sauce* and peanut butter to the pan, and cook for 5 minutes.

Return the chicken to the pan, add the parsley, dill, basil and coriander, and heat through. Serve over hot brown rice or bulgur.

Serves 4.

Mint

According to a rather fanciful legend, the jealous wife of Pluto changed his beloved Menthe into a plant—mint. Throughout more concrete history, peppermint has been considered the strongest of the mints and the one most commonly used by herbalists. They recommend the tea as a soothing remedy for nervousness, poor digestion, headache, cold and flu symptoms. They employ the cooling, slightly numbing leaves for toothaches and itchy skin.

Moroccan Pigeon Pie

This is my version of a classic Moroccan dish I saw Paula Wolfert prepare in her New York classes. I've replaced the traditional phyllo dough made with white flour with whole wheat crepes. This dish is an interesting blend of sweet and spicy flavors and is much easier to make than the original Moroccan dish. The layers can be prepared ahead of time and assembled just before baking.

The Chicken Layer
1 pound chicken breasts
½ cup minced parsley
1 tablespoon minced coriander leaves (optional)
1 large onion, minced
  pinch of saffron (or ⅛ teaspoon turmeric for color)
½ teaspoon ground black pepper
½ teaspoon powdered ginger
2 cinnamon sticks
1 tablespoon butter
1½ cups stock

The Egg Layer
4 eggs
1 tablespoon lemon juice

The Almond Layer
4 ounces whole almonds
½ teaspoon ground cinnamon
1 tablespoon honey
1 tablespoon butter

The Assembly
7 *Whole Wheat Crepes* at least 6½ inches in diameter (see *Index*)
3 tablespoons butter, melted
2 cups yogurt

To make the chicken layer: In a large frying pan combine the chicken, parsley, coriander, onion, saffron or turmeric, pepper, ginger, cinnamon sticks, butter and stock. Cover and simmer until the chicken is very tender.

Remove the chicken, cinnamon sticks and any loose bones from the pan. Remove the chicken from the bones, chop it finely and set aside.

Bring the liquid in the frying pan to a rolling boil over high heat, cook it until it thickens and the contents of the pan measure about ¾ cup. Stir occasionally as the liquid thickens to prevent scorching.

To make the egg layer: Beat the eggs in a small bowl until they are well combined. Beat in the lemon juice.

Lower the heat under the frying pan to a simmer, stir in the eggs, and cook, stirring constantly with a wooden spoon, until they thicken. Do not let them get dry. Transfer the eggs to a small bowl and set aside to cool.

To make the almond layer: Spread the almonds on a cookie sheet, and bake at 325°F for about 15 to 20 minutes, or until the almonds are toasted. Stir frequently to prevent burning. After the toasting, let the almonds cool for a few minutes, and then grind the nuts finely in a blender or food processor. Add the cinnamon, honey and butter, and process until they are combined. Set aside.

To assemble: Brush the spotty side of each crepe with melted butter, and then place one in the center of the cake pan. Now arrange the other five around it so that they overlap and completely cover the bottom and sides of the pan. The tops of the crepes should overlap the top edge of the pan.

Spread the chicken over the crepes, and cover with the eggs, being careful to spread them out to the edges of the pan. Cover all with the almonds.

Moroccan Pigeon Pie—*continued*

Fold the overhanging crepes back on the almonds, and brush them with melted butter. Place the last crepe over the pie, and brush with butter.

Bake at 425°F for 10 minutes.

Remove from the oven and place a pizza pan or a larger cake pan over the baking dish. Now invert so that the pie is sitting on the larger pan. Remove the baking pan.

Return the pie to the oven and bake for 10 more minutes.

Invert once again onto a serving dish, and serve with plain yogurt.

Serves 4.

Chicken and Mushroom Rollups

I first saw this technique demonstrated by Rita Stanton in her Wescosville, Pennsylvania, classes. Serve the chicken hot as a main course, or chill and slice it into half-inch sections for an hors d'oeuvre. The mushrooms add B vitamins and potassium to the dish.

2 large chicken breasts
12 ounces mushrooms
1 medium onion, minced
1 tablespoon butter
1 tablespoon oil
¼ cup whole wheat breadcrumbs
3 tablespoons ricotta cheese
2 tablespoons grated Parmesan cheese
2 tablespoons minced parsley
2 teaspoons minced basil or ½ teaspoon dried basil
1 teaspoon minced rosemary or ¼ teaspoon dried rosemary, crushed
1 egg yolk

Debone and remove the skin and visible fat from the chicken. Cut each breast in half to produce four pieces of meat.

Place each piece between two sheets of wax paper, and pound the meat with a mallet or heavy cleaver until it is about ¼ inch thick, being careful not to tear the flesh. Set aside.

Mince the mushrooms, place them in a clean tea towel or a piece of cheesecloth, and squeeze out as much of the moisture as possible. (This is best done a handful at a time.)

Cook the mushrooms and onions in butter and oil over medium-low heat for at least 10 minutes, or until all the moisture has evaporated. Stir frequently to prevent sticking.

Combine the mushrooms with the breadcrumbs, ricotta, Parmesan, parsley, basil, rosemary and egg yolk.

Divide this filling into four portions, and shape each portion into a log. Place each log lengthwise on a chicken breast, and carefully roll up the breast to enclose the filling.

Place each breast roll on a piece of parchment paper.

Bring an inch of water to a boil in a large pot, and put the rolls and their parchment on a steaming rack and set them in the pot. Make sure that the water does not come above the level of the rack. Cover the pot and steam for 15 to 18 minutes, or until the chicken is cooked through.

Serves 4.

Chicken and Red Pepper Sauté

1 pound boned chicken breasts
¼ cup whole wheat flour
2 tablespoons butter
1 tablespoon oil
2 red peppers, cut into strips ½ by 2 inches
¼ cup minced shallots
½ cup stock
2 large tomatoes, peeled, seeded and chopped
½ cup *Tomato Sauce* (see *Index*)
2 tablespoons lemon juice
1 tablespoon thyme vinegar or white wine
    vinegar
¾ cup half-and-half
2 tablespoons snipped chives
1 tablespoon minced thyme or 1 teaspoon
    dried thyme
1 tablespoon minced oregano or 1 teaspoon
    dried oregano
3 cups hot cooked brown rice or bulgur (see
    pages 205 and 144, respectively, for
    cooking instructions)

Cut the chicken into pieces about ½ by 2 inches. Dredge them in flour.

Heat the butter and oil in a large frying pan until the butter foams, and sauté the chicken until the pieces are lightly browned. Remove them with a slotted spoon and keep warm.

Add the peppers, shallots and stock to the pan, cover and cook over medium heat for 5 minutes, or until the peppers are tender. Remove with a slotted spoon to the chicken dish.

Add the tomatoes, *Tomato Sauce*, lemon juice and vinegar to the frying pan, and cook over medium heat until the mixture is quite thick. Stir frequently to prevent scorching. Remove the pan from the heat.

Slowly whisk the half-and-half into the pan, beating vigorously to prevent curdling. Stir in the chives, thyme and oregano, and return the chicken and peppers to the pan.

Place the dish over medium-low heat until it's just heated through. Do not let the sauce boil. Serve over rice or bulgur.

Serves 4.

Sesame Lemon Chicken

A wonderful stir-fry. If you're out of water chestnuts, you may substitute thinly sliced radishes. Bean thread noodles, which are nearly transparent, are made from mung beans and are available in oriental grocery stores.

1 pound boned chicken breasts
1 tablespoon cornstarch
1 tablespoon water
¼ cup apple juice
¼ cup stock
3 tablespoons lemon juice
3 tablespoons honey
4 teaspoons tamari sauce
3 tablespoons sesame oil or oil
1 cup thinly sliced mushrooms
⅔ cup thinly sliced scallions
1 tablespoon minced ginger
1 clove garlic, minced
1 cup thinly sliced water chestnuts (8 ounces)
¼ cup sesame seeds, lightly toasted
    cooked brown rice or bean thread noodles

Cut the chicken into thin strips about ½ inch wide and 2 inches long. Pat them dry with paper towels.

Dissolve the cornstarch in water, and add the apple juice, stock, lemon juice, honey and tamari.

Heat 2 tablespoons of oil in a wok over high heat or in a Dutch oven over medium heat. Stir-fry the chicken pieces, half at a time, until they are opaque. With a slotted spoon remove them to a plate.

Add an additional tablespoon of oil to the pan, and stir-fry the mushrooms, scallions, ginger and garlic for 2 or 3 minutes. Do not let the garlic brown.

Sesame Lemon Chicken—*continued*

Return the chicken to the pan, stir in the liquid ingredients, add the water chestnuts, and cook for 5 minutes more to thicken the sauce. Sprinkle with sesame seeds.

Serve over brown rice or bean thread noodles.

Serves 4.

Hot Chicken and Peanut Stir-Fry

You can control the spiciness of this dish by adding or subtracting hot pepper.

1 pound boned chicken breasts
1 tablespoon oil
2 tablespoons cornstarch
½ cup apple juice
½ cup stock
4 teaspoons tamari sauce
3 tablespoons peanut oil
⅔ cup sliced scallions
⅔ cup thinly sliced mushrooms
½ cup unsalted roasted peanuts
1 small hot red pepper, minced

Cut the chicken into small pieces about ⅜ inch thick and 1 inch long. Toss in a bowl with 1 tablespoon of oil.

In a small bowl mix the cornstarch and apple juice until smooth; then, stir in the stock and tamari.

In a large frying pan over medium heat or in a wok over high heat, heat the peanut oil until hot. Stir-fry the chicken in batches until it is opaque throughout, and then remove with a slotted spoon to a dish.

Stir-fry the scallions, mushrooms, peanuts and pepper until the vegetables are tender, about 3 minutes.

Return the chicken to the pan. Stir in the cornstarch mixture, cover, and cook 5 minutes, stirring occasionally, or until the sauce thickens.

Serves 4.

Mustard

Mustard is an ancient herb long valued for its hot, heady flavor. Herbals recommend a mustard poultice for its ability to promote blood flow to the skin and to relieve rheumatic pain and other internal inflammations (though they say the application should be brief, since prolonged contact may lead to serious irritation). Some suggest a stimulating mustard footbath to alleviate a cold or fever.

Chicken and Spinach Rollups

The spinach in these rollups adds fiber, magnesium and vitamins A, C and K to the dish. The filling is best made in a food processor.

2 large chicken breasts
½ pound spinach leaves
1 clove garlic, minced
1 shallot, minced
1 tablespoon olive oil
1 tablespoon minced rosemary or 1 teaspoon
      dried rosemary, crushed
¼ cup whole wheat breadcrumbs
¼ cup crumbled feta cheese
1 egg

Debone and remove the skin and visible fat from the chicken breasts. Cut each breast in half to produce four pieces of meat.

Place each piece between two sheets of wax paper, and pound with a mallet or heavy cleaver until the meat is about ¼ inch thick. Be careful not to tear the flesh. Set aside.

Wash the spinach in plenty of cold water, and cook in a large pot using only the water left clinging to the leaves; cook only until the spinach wilts. Transfer to a colander or sieve to cool and drain. When the spinach is cool enough to handle, squeeze out *all* the moisture. Chop finely, either by hand or using a food processor.

Sauté the garlic and shallot in olive oil over medium-low heat for several minutes. Do not let the garlic brown. Add the spinach and sauté briefly to dry it.

In a bowl mix the spinach with the rosemary, breadcrumbs, feta and egg. If the mixture is too soft to form a ball, add more breadcrumbs.

Divide the filling into four portions, shape each into a log, and place lengthwise in the center of a chicken breast. Then, carefully roll up the breasts to enclose the filling.

Place each chicken roll on a piece of parchment paper.

Bring an inch of water to a boil in a large pot. Put the chicken rolls and their parchment on a steaming rack and set them in the pot. Make sure that the water does not come above the level of the rack. Steam, tightly covered, for 15 to 18 minutes, or until the chicken is opaque throughout.

Serves 4.

Rosemary's Thighs

The breading will cling to the chicken better if you dredge it at least an hour ahead and refrigerate it until you are ready to cook.

Be sure to mince or pulverize the rosemary thoroughly before using; this will make for better distribution of this powerful herb.

8 chicken thighs
½ cup minced parsley
1 tablespoon minced rosemary or 1 teaspoon
      dried rosemary, crushed
4 shallots, minced
½ cup sesame seeds
⅓ cup whole wheat flour
1 tablespoon mild Hungarian paprika
1 egg
1 tablespoon yogurt or buttermilk
   whole wheat flour
2 tablespoons olive oil

Remove the skin and visible fat from the chicken. With a sharp knife cut the tendons that hold the meat to the bone at each end of the thigh. Then, remove the meat from the bone by scraping a knife against the bone to loosen it. To keep the piece of meat whole, do not slit it to reach the bone.

In a small bowl combine the parsley, rosemary and shallots, and then place a heaping teaspoon of the mixture along the bone canal inside each thigh.

In a shallow dish or plastic bag, combine the sesame seeds, ⅓ cup of flour, the paprika, and any leftover rosemary mixture.

Rosemary's Thighs—*continued*

In another shallow dish beat the egg and yogurt or buttermilk together with a fork.

Dust each thigh with plain flour, dip it into the egg mixture, and then dredge in the sesame mixture.

Brush a shallow baking dish with 1 teaspoon of olive oil, and arrange the chicken in a single layer. Drizzle with the remaining oil.

Bake at 350°F for 1 hour, basting occasionally with the pan juices.

Serves 4.

Garlic Dill Chicken

The tangy marinade here becomes a creamy sauce for the finished product. Serve it over brown rice or bulgur to add fiber and B vitamins to the meal.

4 cloves garlic, minced
4 large shallots, minced
4 tablespoons chopped dill or 1 tablespoon dried dill
1 tablespoon chopped basil or 1 teaspoon dried basil
1 tablespoon paprika
2 tablespoons olive oil
2 tablespoons oil
6 tablespoons lemon juice
8 chicken thighs (about 1½-2 pounds)
3 tablespoons whole wheat pastry flour
1 cup stock

Combine the garlic, shallots, dill, basil, paprika, olive oil, oil and lemon juice in a shallow baking dish that is large enough to hold the chicken pieces in a single layer. Add the chicken and turn to coat the pieces.

Cover and let the chicken marinate at room temperature for at least 1 hour, turning occasionally.

Bake the chicken skin side up in the same pan at 350°F for about 1 hour, or until it is very tender. Baste with the marinade every 20 minutes.

Remove the chicken to a platter and keep it warm until the sauce is ready.

Sprinkle the pan juices with flour, and stir with a wire whisk to combine. Heat the stock. Transfer the juices to a medium saucepan, and whisk in the hot stock. Cook the sauce over medium heat, stirring constantly, until it comes to a boil and thickens to a medium gravy. If the sauce is too thick, thin it with a little more stock.

Serves 4.

Sesame-Pecan Chicken

⅔ cup buttermilk
1 egg
½ cup whole wheat flour
½ cup sesame seeds
½ cup ground pecans
2 teaspoons paprika
1 teaspoon dried thyme
⅛ teaspoon cayenne pepper
  grated rind of 1 lemon
2 pounds chicken thighs, skin removed
3 tablespoons butter, melted
4 tablespoons stock

Combine the buttermilk and egg in a pie plate or other shallow dish.

Combine the flour, sesame seeds, pecans, paprika, thyme, cayenne and lemon rind in a paper or plastic bag or even a shallow dish.

Dip the chicken pieces, first into the buttermilk mixture, then into the flour mixture. If you are using a bag, shake it gently to coat the pieces.

Combine the butter and stock in a shallow dish.

Dip one side of each chicken piece in the butter mixture, and then arrange the pieces, butter side up, in a buttered baking pan.

Bake at 350°F for about an hour, or until the chicken is tender. Baste occasionally with the remaining butter.

Serves 4.

Savory Turkey Cutlets

Turkey is another star from the poultry family. It's low in fat and high in protein. And yet, it's often overlooked as a dinner dish except at holiday time because of the bird's size. That's why it's good to remember that you don't have to roast a whole turkey to enjoy its flavor and health benefits. Many markets sell whole or half breasts, and others sell sliced breast meat. Breaded and sautéed, these slices are a lower-cost alternative to veal scallops.

 1 pound boned turkey breast
1-2 eggs
1-2 tablespoons milk
 1 cup whole wheat breadcrumbs
½ cup wheat germ
¼ cup grated Parmesan cheese
 2 teaspoons dried savory
 2 teaspoons dried thyme
 whole wheat flour
2-3 tablespoons butter
2-3 tablespoons oil

Cut the turkey breast into slices ⅜ inch thick. Place each slice between two sheets of wax paper, and pound with a mallet. Pound meat until it's about ⅛ inch thick.

In a shallow dish beat 1 egg and 1 tablespoon of milk with a fork until well combined.

In another shallow dish combine the breadcrumbs, wheat germ, Parmesan, savory and thyme.

Dredge the turkey in flour, and then dip it into the egg mixture. (If necessary, add additional eggs and milk.) Finally, dredge the turkey in the crumbs until well coated.

Heat 2 tablespoons of butter and 2 tablespoons of oil in a large frying pan. Fry the turkey, a few pieces at a time, over medium-low heat until it is browned on both sides and cooked through (about 4 to 5 minutes per side). If necessary, add more butter and oil to the pan. Transfer the cooked pieces to a platter and keep warm while the others are cooking.

Serves 4.

Italian Turkey Scallops

 1 pound boned turkey breast
 whole wheat flour
 1 tablespoon butter
 1 tablespoon oil
 1 cup finely chopped onions
 1 pepper, finely chopped
 1 cup sliced mushrooms
 1 clove garlic, minced
1½ cups chopped tomatoes
 2 tablespoons minced basil or 2 teaspoons
 dried basil
 2 tablespoons lemon juice
½ cup stock

Cut the turkey breast into slices ⅜ inch thick. Place each slice between two sheets of wax paper, and pound with a mallet until meat is about ⅛ inch thick.

Dredge the slices in flour.

In a large frying pan heat the butter and oil until it foams. Over medium-low heat fry the turkey until it lightly browns on both sides, about 3 minutes per side. Transfer to a plate.

Add the onions, pepper, mushrooms and garlic to the pan, and stir for a minute. Do not let the garlic burn. Add the tomatoes, basil, lemon juice and stock, and return the turkey to the pan.

Cover and cook over low heat until the vegetables are soft. Remove the lid and cook a few minutes more to evaporate the excess liquid.

Serves 4.

Basil Turkey Scallops

1 pound boned turkey breast
  whole wheat flour
2 tablespoons butter
2 tablespoons oil
⅓ cup minced shallots
1 cup stock
3 tablespoons minced basil or 1½ tablespoons
  dried basil
½ pound whole wheat noodles, cooked
  grated Parmesan cheese

Cut the turkey breast into thin slices about ⅜ inch thick. Place each slice between two sheets of wax paper and pound with a mallet until meat is about ⅛ inch thick. Dredge the slices in flour.

Heat the butter with oil in a large frying pan until it foams. Sauté the turkey, several pieces at a time, until lightly browned on both sides. Remove to a plate.

When all the turkey has been sautéed, add the shallots and stock to the empty pan. Cook for 2 minutes, stirring constantly to get the browned bits off the bottom of the pan.

Return the turkey to the pan, cover and cook for about 10 minutes, or until the turkey is very tender and the sauce has thickened slightly. Stir in the basil and cook for a minute more.

Serve over cooked noodles, and sprinkle with Parmesan.

Serves 4.

Nasturtium

Nasturtium is a delicious, peppery herb native to South America. The leaves are regarded as helpful in breaking up the congestion associated with colds. Nasturtium tea is described in herbals as both a cleansing tonic and an antiseptic wash.

Chicken Kebabs on Rice

The Chicken
  2 large chicken breasts
  2 tablespoons olive oil
  ½ cup whole wheat breadcrumbs
  1 teaspoon dried basil
  ⅛ teaspoon paprika

The Sauce
  2 cups stock
  2 tablespoons butter
  ⅓ cup minced scallions or shallots
  ¼ cup whole wheat pastry flour
  2 teaspoons tamari sauce
  1 teaspoon white wine vinegar
  3 cups hot cooked brown rice (see page 205 for cooking instructions)

To make the chicken: Debone and remove the skin and visible fat from the chicken. Cut it into 1½-inch cubes, and toss with the oil in a large bowl.

In a shallow dish combine the breadcrumbs, basil and paprika.

Pierce the chicken on four 7- or 8-inch metal skewers, and roll them in breadcrumbs until well coated.

Place the kebabs on an oiled cookie sheet, and bake at 375°F for 12 to 15 minutes, or until the chicken is cooked through and the breading is lightly browned.

To make the sauce: In a small saucepan heat the stock.

In a 2-quart saucepan, heat the butter over medium-low heat until it foams. Add the scallions or shallots and cook until soft; do not let them brown.

Stir in the flour, and cook for 2 minutes, stirring frequently.

Add the hot stock to the flour mixture all at once, and beat with a wire whisk to combine well. Add the tamari and vinegar, and cook, stirring frequently, until the sauce comes to a boil and thickens. Cook at a boil for 1 more minute.

Spread the hot rice on a large platter, and arrange the skewers on top.

Serve with the sauce.

Serves 4.

Tandoori Chicken

Traditionally made in a clay oven, this spicy Indian dish can also be made at home in a standard oven. Start the chicken off at a very high temperature, then lower the heat, and bake until tender. The oven will smoke a bit during the first step, but the smoke will soon subside.

  2 pounds chicken thighs
  ¼ teaspoon saffron
  1 tablespoon boiling water
  ½ cup yogurt
  5 cloves garlic, minced
1½ tablespoons grated ginger root
  1 tablespoon lemon juice
1½ teaspoons ground coriander
  1 teaspoon ground cumin
  ¼ teaspoon paprika
  ¼ teaspoon cayenne pepper
  2 tablespoons butter, melted
  3 cups hot cooked brown rice (see page 205 for cooking instructions)

Remove the skin and visible fat from the chicken. Prick it all over with a fork.

In a bowl dissolve the saffron in the boiling water, and then stir in the yogurt, garlic, ginger, lemon juice, coriander, cumin, paprika and cayenne.

Dip the chicken pieces into the yogurt mixture to coat. Arrange the pieces in a baking dish just large enough to hold all pieces in a single layer, and spread any remaining yogurt mixture over the top.

Cover and refrigerate 8 hours or overnight, turning the pieces occasionally.

Tandoori **Chicken**—*continued*

Brush a 7-by-11-inch baking dish with melted butter. Arrange the chicken pieces in the dish. (Do not disturb their yogurt coating, but leave the excess yogurt in the marinating dish.) Drizzle the chicken with the remaining butter.

Bake at 500°F for 10 minutes. (Your oven will probably smoke during this step.) Lower the heat to 350°F and bake for 40 to 45 minutes, or until the chicken is very tender and golden brown.

Serve over hot brown rice.

Serves 4.

Moroccan Chicken and Chick-Peas

The chick-peas in this dish add their protein, B vitamins, potassium and zinc, and the bulgur takes the place of the more traditional, but less nutritious, couscous.

The Chicken
½ cup chick-peas, soaked overnight
1 cup finely chopped onions
2 tablespoons butter
3 cloves garlic, minced
½ cup whole almonds
½ teaspoon powdered ginger
⅛ teaspoon turmeric
⅛ teaspoon saffron
1 cinnamon stick
1 cup sliced onions
1 cup stock
juice of 1 lemon
1 3-pound chicken
paprika

The Bulgur
1½ cups stock
1½ cups uncooked bulgur

To make the chicken: Drain the chick-peas, and transfer them to a large saucepan. Cover with cold water, and cook, tightly covered, over medium heat for 1 hour. Drain.

In a frying pan sauté the onions in butter until they wilt. Add the garlic and almonds, and sauté a few minutes more. Do not let the garlic brown. Stir in the ginger, turmeric, saffron and cinnamon.

Transfer the cooked onions to a 5-quart casserole, add the chick-peas, and cover with the sliced onions. Add the stock and lemon juice, and bring to a simmer on top of stove.

Remove the excess fat from the chicken neck and cavity, and split the chicken in half along the breast and backbone. Lay the pieces over the onions, and sprinkle with paprika.

Cover and bake at 350°F for 1 to 1½ hours, or until the chicken is tender.

To make the bulgur: In a medium saucepan bring the stock to a boil. Stir in the bulgur, cover, remove from heat, and let stand for 20 to 30 minutes, or until soft.

Fluff the bulgur with two forks, and transfer to a large serving platter.

Using a slotted spoon, cover the bulgur with the chick-pea and almond mixture, adding enough liquid to moisten the bulgur. Lay the chicken over the top.

Serves 4.

Spicy Almond Chicken

This spicy dish is similar to one Julie Sahni demonstrates in her Indian cooking classes in New York City. You can control its hotness by adding or subtracting the amount of hot pepper you use. As described here, the dish is quite spicy. You might expect the yogurt to curdle as the chicken cooks, but if it is well whisked into the chopped onions, it won't.

2 pounds chicken thighs with skin and fat
    removed
2 tablespoons oil
4 cups thinly sliced onions
2 tablespoons oil
⅓ cup chopped almonds
1 tablespoon ground coriander
¾ teaspoon ground cardamom
2 red or green hot chili peppers, minced
1 cup water
1 cup yogurt
3 cups hot cooked brown rice (see page 205 for
    cooking instructions)
1 cup yogurt (optional)

Pat the chicken dry with paper towels.

Heat 2 tablespoons of oil over medium heat in a large, heavy frying pan, and add the chicken, a few pieces at a time. Sear the pieces on all sides until they change color. Remove to a plate.

Add the onions and 2 more tablespoons of oil to the frying pan. Cook the onions over low heat for about 10 minutes, or until they are wilted and pale gold. Do not let the onions brown. Add the almonds, coriander, cardamom and peppers to the onions. Cook for another 5 minutes.

Transfer the onions to a blender, add the water, and blend until the onions and almonds are finely chopped, about 30 seconds. Do not blend to a mush.

Return the onions to the frying pan. With a wire whisk stir in the yogurt until the mixture is smooth. Then, add the chicken to the pan, turning to coat the pieces with sauce.

Cover the pan and cook over low heat for about an hour, or until the chicken is very tender when pierced with a fork.

Serve over hot rice and accompany with plain yogurt.

Serves 4.

Shezan's Himalayan Chicken

This popular dish adapted from New York's Shezan Restaurant's menu contains an exotic blend of spices.

1 3-pound chicken, quartered
½ cup oil
¼ cup white vinegar
⅓ cup lemon juice
2 teaspoons tamari sauce
1½ teaspoons paprika
½ teaspoon minced garlic
½ teaspoon grated ginger root
½ teaspoon cumin seeds
½ teaspoon dry mustard

Remove the skin and visible fat from the chicken. With a sharp knife score the fleshy side of the pieces at ¼-inch intervals.

In a shallow baking pan large enough to hold the chicken in a single layer, mix together the oil, vinegar, lemon juice, tamari, paprika, garlic, ginger, cumin and mustard.

Place the chicken in the marinade, and rub each piece with the mixture. Cover and refrigerate for at least 12 hours, turning the chicken frequently.

Remove the chicken from the marinade and place the pieces, skin side up, in a shallow baking dish. Bake at 350°F for 20 minutes. Baste with marinade, and turn the pieces over.

Bake for another 20 minutes, and then baste and turn again. Bake for another 10 to 20 minutes, or until the chicken is tender.

Serves 4.

Chicken with Cherries

A delicious mixture of fruit and fowl. The cherries add pectin, bioflavonoids, potassium and vitamins A and C to the chicken.

2 large onions, finely chopped
2 tablespoons oil
1 cup uncooked long-grain brown rice
1 tablespoon minced thyme or 1 teaspoon dried thyme
2¼ cups stock
2 pounds chicken thighs with skin removed
2 tablespoons oil
2 cups pitted Bing cherries
1 tablespoon honey
3 tablespoons water

In a large frying pan, cook the onions in 2 tablespoons of oil over low heat until they are wilted. Add the rice and continue to cook until it turns golden. Do not let the rice burn. Stir in the thyme.

Transfer the rice to a large (about 5-quart) flameproof casserole, and add the stock. Bring to a simmer on top of the stove.

Pat the chicken pieces dry with paper towels. Heat 2 additional tablespoons of oil in the frying pan, and add the chicken pieces, a few at a time. Brown them on both sides over medium heat, and transfer to the casserole containing the rice. If possible, arrange the chicken in a single layer.

Cover the casserole and bake at 350°F for 45 to 60 minutes, or until the chicken pieces are tender and the rice has absorbed the liquid.

In a small saucepan combine the cherries, honey and water, bring to a boil, and simmer for 2 minutes. Pour the cherries over the chicken, and bake, covered, for 10 more minutes.

Serves 4.

Chicken Paprikas

This old favorite includes a healthy helping of onions in every serving. The traditional complement of sour cream has been lightened with yogurt.

2 pounds chicken with skin and fat removed
2 tablespoons oil
1 tablespoon butter
2 cups chopped onions
2 teaspoons paprika
1 cup stock
½ cup yogurt
½ cup sour cream or *Cottage Cream* (see *Index*)

Pat the chicken dry with paper towels.

In a large frying pan heat the oil and butter until they foam. Brown the chicken pieces, a few at a time, in the oil, and remove to a plate.

Add the onions to the pan, and cook over low heat for several minutes until they are soft. Stir in the paprika.

Add the chicken and stock to the pan, cover and cook over low heat for about an hour, or until the chicken is tender.

Remove the chicken to a plate and keep warm.

Transfer the contents of the pan to a blender and blend for about 10 to 15 seconds until smooth. Return to the pan, and whisk in the yogurt and sour cream or *Cottage Cream.*

Return the chicken to the pan and turn to coat with sauce. Serve immediately.

Serves 4.

Eagle Pie

The name for this dish comes from Gretel Ruppert of The Cooking Company in Wescosville, Pennsylvania, who once made a similar pie for me in one of her classes. She was using an organic chicken from the Rodale farms that was "so big, it could pass for an eagle." The image stuck, and I've been serving eagle pie at home ever since. I generally use chicken, but turkey works equally well in the recipe.

The crust is made with a pâte à choux *(or cream puff) dough that has an interesting twist; whole wheat flour is used instead of white.*

The Filling
- 1 large onion, diced
- 1 cup sliced mushrooms
- 2 cloves garlic, minced
- 1 tablespoon butter
- 1 tablespoon lemon juice
- 2 tablespoons stock
- 2 tablespoons whole wheat flour
- ½ cup stock
- 1½ cups chopped cooked chicken
- 2 tablespoons minced parsley
- 1½ teaspoons thyme leaves or ½ teaspoon dried thyme
- 1 tablespoon minced dill or 1½ teaspoons dried dill
- ¼ cup shredded Swiss cheese

The Crust
- ¾ cup water
- 6 tablespoons butter
- ¾ cup whole wheat flour
- 3 eggs
- ½ teaspoon dry mustard
- ¼ cup shredded Swiss cheese
- 1 tablespoon grated Parmesan cheese (as a topping)

To make the filling: Combine the onion, mushrooms, garlic, butter, lemon juice and 2 tablespoons of stock in a frying pan. Cook all over low heat until the onion is limp and the mushrooms are cooked through. Stir in 2 tablespoons of flour.

Now, stir in the ½ cup of stock and cook until the sauce thickens. Add the chicken, parsley, thyme, dill and the Swiss. Set aside.

To make the crust: Bring the water and butter to a boil in a medium saucepan. Remove from the heat and add the flour to the pan all at once, and stir vigorously with a wooden spoon. Return to the heat and cook for a minute or two, beating hard, until the ingredients are well blended and leave the sides of the pan. Remove again from the heat.

Beat in the eggs, one at a time, making sure that each egg is completely incorporated before adding the next. Stir in the mustard and the Swiss.

Butter a 9-inch pie pan. Using two-thirds of the crust batter, cover the bottom and sides of the pan. Make sure it comes well up the sides of the pan and use the back of a spoon to push it into place.

Add the filling to the crust-lined pan.

With the remaining dough and two spoons or a pastry bag fitted with a large star tube, place teaspoon-size mounds of dough decoratively over the top of the filling, and sprinkle with Parmesan.

Bake at 375°F for 40 to 45 minutes, or until the dough is puffed and the top is golden.

Serves 4.

Chicken Baked in a Crust

The crust with this dish seals in the flavor and juices to keep the chicken moist as it bakes. I first saw this technique demonstrated at Roger Vergé's cooking school in Provence.

    1 4-pound chicken
    6 thyme sprigs or 1 teaspoon dried thyme
    2 rosemary sprigs or ½ teaspoon dried
        rosemary
    1 bay leaf
    2 cloves garlic, halved
    6 cups whole wheat flour
2–2½ cups cold water

Remove the giblets and any excess fat from the neck and cavity of the chicken. Pat it dry with paper towels, and place the thyme, rosemary, bay leaf and garlic into the cavity. If desired, add the liver. Tie up chicken to retain its shape.

In a very large bowl combine the flour with enough water to make a kneadable dough. Knead for a few minutes to produce a smooth dough.

On a lightly floured surface roll out into a rectangle about ¼ inch thick and large enough to envelop the chicken.

Place the chicken breast down in the middle of the dough. Wrap the dough around the chicken, pinch the seams shut and trim off any excess. If the seams will not stay closed, moisten with water to seal. Patch any holes in the crust with trimmings.

Place the chicken in a shallow baking dish, and bake at 350°F for 2 hours. The crust should become very hard and light brown in color.

Remove from the oven, and with a very sharp knife, cut open the crust and remove the chicken. Discard the crust; carve and serve the chicken.

Serves 4.

Nutmeg

Nutmeg is the seed of an evergreen tree growing wild in parts of Indonesia. The seed is protected by a red, fleshy outer layer called mace, which has a flavor similar to nutmeg. In small amounts, herbalists say, nutmeg tends to improve the digestion and relieve flatulence and nausea. Nutmeg oil is sometimes used to flavor medicines.

Chicken with Leeks and Apples

Leeks and apples add extra flavor and a sauce's body to the cooking juice.

3 large leeks, washed and chopped
2 tart apples, cored and sliced
¼ cup chopped dill or 1 tablespoon dried dill
¼ cup chopped parsley
1 lemon
2 bay leaves
1 4-pound roasting chicken with fat removed
1 teaspoon oil
 paprika
1 cup stock
3 cups hot cooked brown rice (see page 205 for cooking instructions)

Spread half of the leeks, apples, dill and parsley in a 5-quart casserole or Dutch oven.

Cut off the top third of a lemon, and reserve. Slice the remaining lemon, and place the slices and the bay leaves in the cavity of the chicken. Truss the bird to retain its shape.

Rub the chicken with the reserved lemon, and then with the oil. Place it breast down in the pot on top of the leeks and apples. Sprinkle the chicken lightly with paprika, and surround with the remaining leeks, apples, dill and parsley. Add the stock.

Cover and bake at 375°F for 1 hour. Then, turn the chicken over, dust it lightly with paprika, cover and bake for another 30 minutes.

Remove the cover and bake 15 more minutes, or until the chicken is lightly browned and the juices run clear.

Remove the chicken to a serving platter and keep warm. Puree the leeks and apples with a food mill or sieve, and skim off any fat.

Serve the chicken with hot brown rice and the leek sauce.

Serves 4.

Linden Chicken

An unusual chicken dish, flavored with the leaves and blossoms of the linden tree. The linden tea required for this recipe is available in many health food stores and gourmet shops.

3 cups thinly sliced onions
1 tablespoon whole wheat flour
1 cup stock
½ ounce dried linden leaves and blossoms or 10 linden tea bags
1 4-pound chicken
3 cloves garlic
1 tablespoon softened butter
 paprika

Spread the onions in the bottom of a casserole large enough to hold the chicken, and sprinkle with flour; pour in the stock.

If you are using loose linden leaves and blossoms, wrap them securely in cheesecloth.

Pat the chicken dry with paper towels and remove the excess fat.

Place the cheesecloth containing the leaves and blossoms or the tea bags in the cavity of the chicken, and add the garlic. Truss the chicken.

Rub the chicken with butter, place it in the casserole, breast side up, on top of the onions. Sprinkle lightly with paprika.

Cover the casserole, and bake at 350°F for 1½ to 2 hours, or until the meat is tender and the juices run clear when a thigh is pierced with a fork.

Remove the chicken from the casserole, untie and remove the linden bags and garlic; discard. Carve the chicken into serving pieces and keep warm.

Strain the pan juices into a large bowl, and skim the fat.

Transfer the onions to a blender or food processor, add about ½ cup of the juices, and blend. If you wish, thin the gravy with more stock.

Serves 4.

Garam Masalla Chicken

An easy meal with an unusual tomato-yogurt sauce. The tomatoes contribute vitamins C and B6, along with potassium, bioflavonoids and pectin. The yogurt adds calcium and extra protein. Serve this chicken with brown rice for its additional fiber.

- 2 pounds chicken thighs with skin and fat removed
- 3 tablespoons butter
- 2 cups chopped onions
- 1 tablespoon *Garam Masalla* (see *Index*)
- 1½ cups chopped tomatoes
- ½ cup stock
- 1 cup yogurt

Pat the chicken dry with paper towels.

Heat the butter in a large frying pan or Dutch oven until it foams. Add the chicken, a few pieces at a time, and brown it lightly on both sides. Remove with a slotted spoon or tongs to a plate.

Add the onions and *Garam Masalla* to the pan, and cook over low heat until the onions are wilted.

Add the tomatoes and stock, cover and simmer for 10 minutes.

Transfer the onion and tomato mixture (along with its liquid) to a blender, and puree for about 15 seconds to chop finely. Return to the pan.

Stir in the yogurt with a whisk until the mixture is smooth. Add the chicken pieces.

Cover and simmer over low heat until the chicken is very tender, or about 1 hour.

Serves 4.

Rosemary Chicken with Bulgur

This is an ideal way to use leftover chicken. The bulgur contributes to a dish that's low in fat and sodium but high in fiber.

- 1½ cups stock
- 1 teaspoon tamari sauce
- 1 teaspoon blackstrap molasses
- 1 tablespoon minced rosemary or 1 teaspoon dried rosemary, crushed
- 1 tablespoon minced thyme or 1 teaspoon dried thyme
- 1½ cups uncooked bulgur
- 1 large onion, minced
- 2 large carrots, minced
- 1 cup stock
- 2 cups finely chopped cooked chicken
  yogurt

Bring the 1½ cups of stock to a boil in a medium saucepan, and stir in the tamari, molasses, rosemary, thyme and bulgur. Remove from the heat, cover and let stand for 20 to 30 minutes while the bulgur softens.

In a large frying pan combine the onion, carrots and 1 cup of stock, cover and cook over low heat until the vegetables are tender. Stir in the chicken and let simmer for a few minutes until the chicken warms through.

When the bulgur is ready, fluff it with a fork, and stir it into the frying pan containing the chicken; toss thoroughly to mix. Serve with plain yogurt.

Serves 4.

Turkey Crepes

Whole wheat crepes with a cheese and turkey filling. Naturally, chicken can also be used.

1 cup milk
2 tablespoons butter
3 tablespoons whole wheat pastry flour
1 egg
¼ cup grated Parmesan cheese
2 tablespoons minced dill or 2 teaspoons dried dill
2 tablespoons minced parsley
2 tablespoons butter
1 cup minced onions
1 red pepper, cut into ½-inch pieces
½ cup thinly sliced mushrooms
1 cup diced cooked turkey
8 large *Whole Wheat Crepes* (see *Index*)
⅓–½ cup milk

In a small saucepan heat the milk.

In a 2-quart saucepan, melt 2 tablespoons of butter, and stir in the flour. Cook the butter and flour together over medium heat, stirring constantly, for 2 minutes.

Then, add the hot milk all at once, and beat with a wire whisk until a smooth sauce forms. Cook over medium heat, stirring constantly, until the sauce thickens and comes to a boil. Remove from heat.

In a small bowl beat the egg until it is well blended, and then gradually whisk in about ½ cup of hot sauce. Beat vigorously to blend; make sure that the egg is warmed through, but do not let it scramble.

Stir the egg mixture into the remaining sauce, and return it to the heat. Cook, stirring constantly, for 1 minute, and remove again from the heat. Stir in the Parmesan, dill and parsley.

In a large frying pan melt 2 tablespoons of butter over medium heat. Add the onions, pepper and mushrooms, and cook, stirring frequently, until the vegetables soften. Then, stir in the turkey and the sauce.

Arrange each crepe, spotty side up, on a plate. Place a heaping spoonful of the filling at one end of the crepes and roll them to enclose the filling.

Butter a 9-by-13-inch baking dish, and transfer the crepes to it, seam side down.

Thin any remaining filling with enough milk to produce a pourable sauce, and spoon it over the crepes.

Bake at 350°F for 30 minutes.

Serves 4.

Nutmeg Chicken

An easy dish lightly spiced with nutmeg.

2 pounds chicken pieces with skin and fat removed
2 tablespoons olive oil
2 tablespoons butter
1 cup finely chopped onions
2 tablespoons whole wheat pastry flour
¼ teaspoon grated nutmeg
 juice of 1 lemon
1 cup stock

Pat the chicken dry with paper towels.

In a large frying pan or Dutch oven, heat the oil and butter over medium heat until they foam. Add the chicken pieces, a few at a time, and brown them on both sides. Remove with a slotted spoon to a dish.

Add the onions to the pan and cook until they are soft but not browned. Sprinkle with flour, and stir to combine. Then, sprinkle with nutmeg, and stir in the lemon juice and stock.

Return the chicken to the pan, cover and cook until it is tender, about 45 to 60 minutes. Skim any excess fat off the surface with paper towels.

Serves 4.

Turkey Rice Casserole

The Rice
- 3 tablespoons butter
- 1 cup minced onions
- 1 cup thinly sliced mushrooms
- 1 cup uncooked long-grain brown rice
- 2 tablespoons minced parsley
- 1½ teaspoons minced thyme or ½ teaspoon dried thyme
- 1 tablespoon snipped chives
- 2½ cups stock

The Sauce
- 1 cup stock
- 1 tablespoon butter
- 2 tablespoons whole wheat pastry flour
- ½ cup ricotta cheese
- 1 egg
- 2 cups chopped cooked turkey
- ⅔ cup shredded mozzarella cheese

To make the rice: In a 3-quart, flameproof casserole heat the butter until it foams. Add the onions, mushrooms, rice, parsley, thyme and chives, and cook over medium-low heat for several minutes, until the onions soften and the rice turns golden. Add the stock and bring to a simmer.

Cover and bake at 350°F for 60 to 70 minutes, or until the rice is tender and has absorbed the liquid. While the rice is baking, make the sauce.

To make the sauce: In a small saucepan heat the stock.

Melt the butter in a medium saucepan, stir in the flour and cook over low heat for 2 minutes. Do not let the flour brown.

Add the stock all at once, and stir with a wire whisk to combine. Cook, stirring constantly, until the sauce thickens and comes to a boil. Remove from heat.

In a cup beat together the ricotta and egg until they are well combined. Whisk them into the sauce, and add the turkey.

When the rice has cooked, fold the sauce into the rice, and sprinkle with mozzarella. Return to the oven and bake at 350°F for 30 minutes, or until the cheese has melted and started to brown.

Serves 4.

Turkey Breast with Dill and Shallots

- 1 pound boned turkey breast (a single piece about ½ inch thick)
- 2 tablespoons butter
- ½ cup minced shallots
- 1 tablespoon butter
- 1 tablespoon white wine vinegar
- ½ cup stock
- 1 tablespoon minced dill or 1 teaspoon dried dill

Pat the turkey dry with paper towels. If the turkey is not of uniform thickness, butterfly the thicker end.

Heat 2 tablespoons of butter in a large frying pan until it foams. Add the turkey and sauté over medium heat until it is browned on both sides (about 8 to 10 minutes per side). Remove to a cutting board, and let it rest a few minutes.

In the same frying pan sauté the shallots in 1 tablespoon of butter over low heat until they are soft. Add the vinegar, stock and dill, and cook over medium heat until the liquid is reduced by about half.

With a sharp knife cut the turkey into ¼-inch slices, cutting diagonally across the large piece. If the meat's pink at the center, return those slices to the pan and cook, covered, for a few more minutes. Then, transfer the turkey to a platter, pour the shallots over the top and sprinkle with dill.

Serves 4.

Chapter 10
Fish

Prime Catch

It's a good idea to include fish in your diet. A major source of protein in many nations of the world, fish sometimes loses out in this country to red meats. That's a shame because fish is low in saturated fat, rich in protein, vitamins and minerals, and downright delicious—especially if very fresh.

Compared to red meat, fish also contains only about a third of the calories per serving. And instead of saturated fat, fish has polyunsaturated fat. That's good, because scientific evidence suggests that polyunsaturated fats lower cholesterol and triglyceride levels in the blood.

What's more, fish is relatively low in sodium. But it's high in other beneficial minerals, particularly iron, iodine and copper. Both iron and copper are necessary for making hemoglobin, a major component of red blood cells. And iodine is needed for the proper functioning of the thyroid gland.

Fish is rich in vitamins, too. A serving of broiled halibut, for example, has almost twice the niacin and 13 times the vitamin A as the same amount of sirloin steak. And it's an excellent source of vitamin D. And as mothers whose children grew up during the Second World War remember, fish-liver oils are very high in vitamins A and D. Ounce for ounce, cod-liver oil has over 30 times more vitamin A than apricots and broccoli, both good sources of the vitamin. And it sports over 200 times more vitamin D than D-supplemented milk. Fish-liver oil also contains a fatty acid, called EPA for brevity's sake, that scientists have found might help prevent blood clots responsible for many heart attacks and strokes.

The only health essential that fish lacks is fiber. But if it's eaten with vegetables and grains, that deficiency is easily remedied.

Of course, you should know that not all fish are equally low in fat. Haddock is the least fatty of all the readily available fish. A little higher on the fat scale are cod, flounder, sole, halibut, ocean perch, red snapper, pike, pollack, skipjack tuna and yellowfin tuna. And considered high in fat are mackerel, herring, albacore and bluefin tuna, salmon, shad, swordfish, sardines, pompano, rockfish and whitefish.

When cooking fish, keep these points in mind:

- Fish cooks quickly. Overcooking toughens it, dries it out and ruins the flavor.
- Allow about 10 minutes of cooking time per inch of thickness. To measure, stand a ruler up against the thickest part.
- If the fish is frozen, double the cooking time.
- To test for doneness, pierce the thickest part of the fish with a fork. If the flesh has lost its translucency and flakes easily, it is done.

Shad Roe *aux Fines Herbes*

Shad roe are the two egg sacs of the female fish. They are generally available only in the spring. Be careful not to toughen them by too much cooking.

This recipe is also suitable for almost any fish fillets as well.

4 pairs shad roe
3 tablespoons butter, melted
3 tablespoons minced parsley
3 tablespoons minced chives
2 tablespoons minced chervil
2 tablespoons minced tarragon
 watercress leaves (as a garnish)

Rinse the roe and remove the center tissue dividing each pair, being careful not to tear the roe.

Brush a baking dish just large enough to hold the roe with melted butter. Sprinkle half the parsley, chives, chervil and tarragon in the pan.

Arrange the roe on top of the herbs, and then sprinkle with remaining herbs. Pour on any remaining butter.

Bake at 400°F for 15 to 20 minutes.

Garnish with watercress leaves.

Serves 4.

Haddock Black Raven

Redolent of garlic and basil, Haddock Black Raven is high in taste, low in calories and quick to make. It is named for a restaurant where I had a similar dish many years ago. It's wonderful served with brown rice.

2 tablespoons butter
2 medium onions, thinly sliced
2 cloves garlic, minced
2 cups chopped tomatoes
1 teaspoon basil vinegar or white wine vinegar
1 tablespoon minced basil or 1 teaspoon dried basil
 pinch of cayenne pepper
1 pound haddock fillets

Heat the butter in a large frying pan over medium-low heat until it foams. Add the onions and garlic, and cook, stirring frequently, until soft, about 5 minutes.

Add the tomatoes, vinegar, basil, cayenne and haddock to the pan, cover and cook until the fish is opaque and flakes easily, about 10 minutes.

Serves 4.

Haddock Provencale

This excellent casserole is almost a complete meal in itself. To complete it, you may serve the fish over brown rice to raise the fiber content. This dish is very similar to one that Rita Stanton of The Cooking Company, Wescosville, Pennsylvania, demonstrates in her classes. Chicken stock may be substituted for the fish stock.

The Tomato Sauce

  5 large shallots, minced
  ½ tablespoon butter
  ¼ cup *Fish Stock* (see *Index*)
  6 large peeled tomatoes
  1 tablespoon minced parsley
  1 tablespoon minced dill or 1 teaspoon dried
     dill
  1 tablespoon snipped chives

The Fish Casserole

  1 cup minced onions
  ½ tablespoon butter
  2 tablespoons *Fish Stock* (see *Index*)
10 spinach leaves
  1 pound haddock fillets
  1 tablespoon lemon juice
  1 tablespoon minced parsley
  1 tablespoon minced dill or 1 teaspoon dried
     dill
  1 tablespoon snipped chives
  4 large mushrooms, thinly sliced
  1 small zucchini, thinly sliced
  1 tablespoon butter, melted

To make the tomato sauce: Combine the shallots, butter and stock in a large saucepan. Cover and cook until the shallots are tender.

To peel the tomatoes, dip the whole tomatoes into boiling water for about 20 seconds. With a sharp knife, remove the stem end. The skin should then peel off easily. Cut the tomatoes in half crosswise, and squeeze each half gently to remove the seeds and excess juice.

Chop into ½-inch pieces. Measure out 1 cup of pulp and reserve for use later.

Chop the remaining tomatoes finely, and add to the saucepan with the shallots. Cook, uncovered, over medium heat until they are very thick. Stir frequently to prevent scorching. Stir in the parsley, dill and chives, and set aside.

To make the fish casserole: Combine the onions, butter and stock in a large frying pan, cover and cook over low heat until the onions are tender. Remove the lid and cook until the liquid has evaporated; stir frequently to prevent scorching. Spread the mixture in a covered casserole just large enough to hold the fish in a single layer.

Spread the 1 cup of tomatoes reserved earlier over the onions.

Cover the tomatoes with spinach leaves, and place the fish over the spinach in a single layer. (Cut the fillets in half, if necessary. Turn under any thin ends so that the fish is uniformly thick.)

Sprinkle all with lemon juice, parsley, dill and chives. Cover with mushroom slices, then with zucchini, and drizzle with melted butter. Cover the mixture with a buttered circle of wax paper, and then put the lid on the casserole.

Bake at 400°F for about 30 minutes or until the fish flakes easily. Do not overbake or the vegetables will become limp and lose their color.

With the casserole lid just slightly askew, pour any accumulated liquid into the tomato sauce, and reheat briefly. Serve the sauce over the fish.

Serves 4.

Moroccan Fish with Dates

This unusual dish is best made with sticky, soft dates. The sweetness of the dates and the spicy almond filling contrast nicely with the bland fish. This is a modified version of a dish Paula Wolfert teaches in her New York City classes.

 2 pounds white fish fillets about ½ inch thick
 ¾ cup cooked brown rice (see page 205 for cooking instructions)
 6 tablespoons chopped almonds
 2 teaspoons honey
 ½ teaspoon ground cinnamon
 ½ teaspoon ground black pepper
 ¼ teaspoon powdered ginger
 ¼ teaspoon ground cumin
32 pitted dates
 4 tablespoons butter, melted
 1 onion, minced
 2 tablespoons chopped almonds
 ½ cup water

Make sure there are no small bones in the fish. Cut or divide the fish into two equal portions, and set aside.

Puree the brown rice in a food mill or food processor, and combine it with 6 tablespoons of chopped almonds, the honey, cinnamon, pepper, ginger and cumin.

Slit one side of each date, and open it flat. Make 16 date sandwiches by placing 1 teaspoon of rice filling between 2 slit-open dates.

Brush the bottom of an ovenproof dish just large enough to hold the fish and dates with 1 tablespoon of melted butter.

Scatter the minced onion in the dish, and cover it with half the fish. Take any filling left over from the dates and spread it on the fish. Cover with the remaining fish.

Surround the fish with the stuffed dates, setting each sandwich on end. Sprinkle the fish with 2 tablespoons of chopped almonds, and pour the remaining butter over the fish. Add water to cover the bottom of the dish.

Bake at 425°F for about 20 minutes, or until the fish is baked through. Baste the fish with pan juices after 10 minutes.

Serves 4.

Simple Salmon

Truly quick and simple. Save any leftovers for Salmon and Avocado Salad (see Index).

 1 pound salmon fillet
 1 stalk celery, cut thinly on diagonal
 1 carrot, cut thinly on diagonal
 1 onion, sliced into thin rounds
 ½ lemon, cut into thin rounds
1¼ cups water
 2 tablespoons tarragon vinegar or lemon juice
 2 large tarragon sprigs or 1 teaspoon dried tarragon
 2 large oregano sprigs or 1 teaspoon dried oregano
 1 bay leaf
 4 parsley sprigs

Place the salmon, celery, carrot, onion, lemon, water, vinegar or lemon juice, tarragon, oregano, bay leaf and parsley in a large frying pan. (If you are using dried herbs, tie them in a square of cheesecloth.)

Cover and simmer gently for 15 to 20 minutes or until salmon turns opaque and the vegetables are tender-crisp.

Remove the herbs.

Serves 4.

Garlic Monkfish

Long appreciated abroad, monkfish is just gaining popularity in this country. Its firm texture and sweet taste have earned it the name "the poor man's lobster." When baking or broiling this lean fish, frequent basting is necessary to prevent drying and toughening the meat.

This is a slimmed-down version of a recipe I picked up at Roger Vergé's cooking school in Provence.

10 cloves unpeeled garlic
¼ cup softened butter
  several thyme sprigs or 1 teaspoon dried thyme
2 pounds thick (1½–2 inches) monkfish fillets
9 tablespoons thyme vinegar or white wine vinegar

Parboil the garlic for 5 minutes in 1 cup of water. The skins will then slip off easily. Coarsely chop the garlic.

Use half the butter to coat a shallow baking dish just large enough to hold the fish in a single layer, and sprinkle with the garlic and thyme. Lay the fish on the herbs and dot with the remaining butter.

Bake at 400°F for 5 minutes, and then add 3 tablespoons of vinegar. Now bake and baste twice more until all the vinegar is used. Then bake for another 5 to 15 minutes, basting every 5 minutes, until the fish is opaque. (Cut through the thickest part to test. Do *not* let the fish become flaky or it will lose its lobsterlike texture.)

Strain the sauce through a sieve, using a wooden spoon to push the garlic through the screening.

Serves 4.

Sautéed Swordfish

Swordfish steaks are firm fleshed. This recipe asks you to cut them into thin scallops, like veal, and then to sauté the pieces quickly so that they retain their shape and texture. The julienned vegetables add a touch of nouvelle cuisine, as well as vitamins and fiber.

3 carrots
2 leeks (white parts only)
1 teaspoon butter
2 tablespoons stock
1 pound swordfish steaks
2 tablespoons butter
  juice of 1 lemon
3 tablespoons minced parsley
1 tablespoon snipped chives
1 teaspoon minced oregano or ½ teaspoon dried oregano

Cut the carrots and leeks into julienne pieces (matchsticks about ⅛ by ⅛ by 2 inches).

Combine the carrots, leeks, 1 teaspoon of butter and stock in a frying pan; cover and cook over low heat until the vegetables are tender. Remove the cover and allow the remaining liquid to cook away. Do not let the vegetables scorch. Set aside and keep warm.

Remove any bones from the swordfish, separating each steak into two pieces. Now, slice each piece through the center to make two thin pieces. Pound lightly with a mallet until the pieces are about ¼ inch thick.

Sauté the pieces in butter a few minutes on each side or until they are lightly browned. Squeeze lemon juice over them, and sprinkle with parsley, chives and oregano.

Transfer to a serving plate, and surround with the cooked carrots and leeks.

Serves 4.

Shad with Tarragon Butter

Shad is a seasonal delicacy found along the East Coast in the spring, but it's slowly becoming available in other parts of the country. If shad is not available, you can substitute another oily fish. Adjust the baking time according to the thickness of the fish.

When making the beurre blanc *sauce, be very careful not to let the butter melt rapidly. Using very low heat, raise the temperature of the sauce just enough to allow the butter to cream into it. Make the sauce just before serving, and do not reheat.*

Although the sauce in almost pure butter (that is, calories!), this recipe makes just enough of it to lightly coat each serving of fish.

     1 tablespoon butter, melted
 1½ pounds boned shad
     2 tablespoons tarragon vinegar
     1 tablespoon lemon juice
     4 tablespoons softened butter
     1 tablespoon minced tarragon or 1½ teaspoons
        dried tarragon

Brush a large baking dish with melted butter. Place the fish, skin side down, in the dish. Brush the top with butter.

Bake at 400°F for 15 to 20 minutes or until the fish flakes easily.

To make the *beurre blanc* sauce, combine the vinegar and lemon juice in a small saucepan, and cook over high heat until the liquid is reduced to about 1 tablespoon.

Remove from heat, and whisk in the softened butter, ½ tablespoon at a time, until it is well incorporated. Do not stop stirring. Stir in the tarragon.

Spoon the butter over the baked shad.

Serves 4.

Onion

The ancient Egyptians appreciated onions and employed them as both food and medicine. Herbalists often use onion juice for removing excess water from the body, for strengthening the heart and for relieving stomach disorders. Onion juice also serves as an antiseptic wash for wounds.

Shrimp Frittata

½ cup minced shallots
½ cup thinly sliced mushrooms
¼ cup minced peppers
2 tablespoons butter
½ cup shredded Swiss cheese
1 cup chopped cooked shrimp
2 teaspoons minced dill or ½ teaspoon dried dill
8 eggs
2 tablespoons water
2 tablespoons butter

Cook the shallots, mushrooms and peppers in 2 tablespoons of butter until soft. Cool slightly, and then stir in the Swiss, shrimp and dill.

In a bowl beat 4 eggs and 1 tablespoon of water with a fork until well combined. Stir in half the shrimp mixture.

Heat a well-seasoned, 9-inch, ovenproof skillet over medium heat until it is quite hot. Add 1 tablespoon of butter, and swirl to coat the bottom.

When the butter foam subsides, add the egg mixture, and cook over medium heat for about 5 minutes, frequently lifting the sides so that the uncooked portion can flow underneath. The omelet is done when the edges are set and the bottom is golden.

Place the omelet in the broiler about 6 inches from the element until the top is golden and set (about 5 minutes). Slide the frittata onto a large plate, and keep warm.

Repeat with the remaining ingredients to make a second frittata.

Serves 4.

Tuna Frittata

Frittatas are Italian-style omelets. They're quick to prepare and can be served hot or at room temperature. This simple recipe makes two nine-inch frittatas or, if you have a large enough skillet, one big one. Cooking time will, of course, be longer with a larger pan. For best results, use a well-seasoned pan. There's nothing worse than a frittata that sticks.

7 ounces waterpack tuna
4 scallions, chopped
4 teaspoons minced basil or 1 teaspoon dried basil
2 tablespoons grated Parmesan cheese
8 eggs
2 tablespoons water
2 tablespoons butter

Drain the tuna well, and flake the fish into a small bowl. Stir in the scallions, basil and Parmesan.

In another bowl beat 4 eggs and 1 tablespoon of water with a fork until all is well combined. Stir in half of the tuna mixture.

Heat a well-seasoned, 9-inch, ovenproof skillet over medium heat until it is quite hot. Add 1 tablespoon of butter, and swirl to coat the bottom.

When the butter foam subsides, add the egg mixture. Cook over medium heat for about 5 minutes, frequently lifting the sides so that the uncooked portion can flow underneath. The omelet is done when the edges are set and the bottom is golden.

Place the omelet in the broiler about 6 inches from the element until the top is golden and set (about 5 minutes). Slide onto a large plate and keep warm.

Repeat with the remaining ingredients to make the second frittata.

Serves 4.

Tuna Macaroni and Cheese

Plain old macaroni and cheese gets a boost in taste and appeal from tuna and tomatoes. To lower the fat content here, use tuna packed in water.

  1   cup minced onions
  ½   cup minced celery
  1   pepper, minced
  1   tablespoon oil
  2   cups chopped tomatoes
  3   tablespoons butter
  3   tablespoons whole wheat pastry flour
  2   teaspoons dry mustard
  2   cups milk
  7   ounces waterpack tuna, drained and
        flaked
  8   ounces uncooked whole wheat macaroni
        (elbows, shells or twists)
1½   cups shredded Cheddar cheese

In a large frying pan cook the onions, celery and pepper in oil over medium-low heat until the onions wilt. Add the tomatoes and cook until thick.

To make the sauce: In a small saucepan heat the milk.

Heat the butter in a 2-quart saucepan until it foams. Then, stir in the flour and the mustard, and cook over medium heat, stirring constantly, for 2 minutes. Add the hot milk all at once, and beat with a wire whisk until the mixture is smooth. Cook, stirring constantly, until the sauce comes to a boil and thickens.

Blend the sauce into the tomato mixture, and add the drained tuna.

Boil the macaroni in a large pot of water for about 6 minutes or until it is tender, but not mushy, that is, *al dente*. Drain and fold it into the sauce mixture.

Butter a 3-quart casserole. Layer half of the macaroni in it, and top with half of the Cheddar. Now, repeat the process.

Bake at 325°F for 40 minutes.

Serves 4.

Oregano

The ancient Greeks wore garlands of oregano during wedding ceremonies to ensure continuing happiness. Herbalists recommend the tea as a tonic for upset stomach, headache, coughs and nervousness. It is also said to ease menstrual cramps. They describe it as an effective remedy for morning sickness or motion sickness and employ a poultice of the leaves for rheumatic pain and aching joints.

Shrimp Fried Rice

Here's an oriental stir-fry dish that goes much lighter on the tamari sauce (and hence sodium) than most traditional recipes. For best results use long-grain rice and cook a day ahead. The combination of rice, vegetables, eggs and shrimp makes this a one-dish dinner. Preparing the egg squares ahead also makes it a quick dinner.

The Rice
⅔ cup uncooked long-grain brown rice
1⅔ cups stock

The Egg Squares
  2 eggs
  2 tablespoons minced parsley
  1 clove garlic, minced
  1 teaspoon sesame oil

The Stir-Fry
½ pound shrimp, shelled and deveined
  3 tablespoons sesame oil
¼ cup whole almonds
  1 cup thinly sliced mushrooms
  1 red pepper, cut into ½-inch slices
  8 scallions, cut into ½-inch sections
  1 cup peas
  1 tablespoon grated ginger root
  2 tablespoons apple juice
  1 tablespoon tamari sauce

To make the rice: Make the rice a day ahead. Cook it in stock over medium-low heat until all the liquid has been absorbed, about 50 minutes. Do not stir while the rice is cooking.

To keep the rice from sticking: Remove from the heat, and lift the lid. Place two layers of paper toweling across the top of the pan, and replace the lid. Let sit about 20 minutes until the towels absorb the excess moisture from the rice. Fluff the rice lightly with a fork, and refrigerate overnight. Before using, fluff it again to separate the grains.

To make the egg squares: Lightly beat the eggs, parsley and garlic together. Heat the oil in a large, no-stick frying pan over medium-low heat, and add the eggs. Do not stir. Let the mixture cook gently for about 10 minutes or until the top is dry. Remove it from the pan and allow to cool. Cut into ½-inch squares.

To make the stir-fry: Cut each shrimp in half lengthwise, and then in half crosswise; that is, make four pieces from each shrimp. Pat the pieces dry with paper towels.

Heat the oil in a wok (over high heat) or in a large well-seasoned frying pan (over medium heat) until it is quite hot. Add the shrimp and almonds, and stir-fry until the shrimp turn opaque. Remove with a slotted spoon and keep warm.

Add the mushrooms, red pepper strips and scallions to the wok, and stir-fry for 3 minutes, or until they are soft.

Add the rice, and stir-fry about 4 minutes. Add the peas, ginger, egg squares, shrimp and almonds, and stir-fry another 2 minutes.

Mix the apple juice and tamari in a small cup, and add to the wok. Toss the rice to coat.

Serves 4.

Curried Shrimp

  1 pound shrimp, shelled and deveined
  1 tablespoon sesame oil
  1 cup thinly sliced celery
  2 yellow or red peppers, cut into ⅛-inch slices
  1 cup sliced scallions
  2 teaspoons *Curry Powder* (see *Index*)
  2 tablespoons sesame oil
¼ cup apple juice
  1 tablespoon cornstarch

Cut each shrimp in half lengthwise. If the shrimp are very large, also cut them in half crosswise. Set aside.

Heat 1 tablespoon of oil in a wok (over high heat) or in a large frying pan (over medium heat). Add the celery, peppers, scallions and

Curried Shrimp—*continued*

Curry Powder, and stir-fry them for 3 minutes or until tender. Remove with a slotted spoon and keep warm.

Add 2 tablespoons of oil to the wok, and stir-fry the shrimp until they are opaque. Return the vegetables to the wok.

In a small cup combine the apple juice and cornstarch, stir into the wok, and cook 1 minute to thicken.

Serves 4.

Shad with Cheese Soufflé

This soufflé technique will work beautifully with any fish fillets or even most shellfish including lobster or crab.

1½ pounds boned shad
¼ cup minced shallots
 3 tablespoons stock
 1 tablespoon minced dill or ¾ teaspoon dried dill
 1 tablespoon minced parsley
 2 tablespoons butter
 2 tablespoons whole wheat pastry flour
¾ cup milk
   few gratings of nutmeg
 3 egg yolks
 3 egg whites
¼ cup grated Parmesan cheese
   minced parsley and dill (as a garnish)

Butter an ovenproof platter large enough to hold the shad with plenty of room to spare.

Arrange the fish, skin side down, on the platter and set aside.

In a medium saucepan cook the shallots in the stock until tender. Continue to cook until the liquid evaporates, stirring all the time to keep the shallots from browning.

Sprinkle the shallots, dill and parsley over the fish.

Melt 2 tablespoons of butter in the same saucepan. Stir in the flour until well combined. Cook over medium heat, stirring constantly, for 2 minutes.

In a small saucepan heat the milk. Remove the butter and flour mixture from the heat, and pour in the hot milk all at once. Beat vigorously with a wire whisk until thoroughly blended. Return to the heat and cook, stirring constantly, until the mixture bubbles and is very thick.

Remove from heat. Whisk in the egg yolks, one at a time. Add the nutmeg.

In a large, clean bowl and with clean beaters, beat the egg whites until they are stiff and shiny. Do not overbeat.

Stir about one-quarter of the whites into the yolk mixture, and then carefully fold about half of the new mixture back into the rest of the whites. Sprinkle half of the Parmesan on top, and then continue to fold. Now add the remaining yolk mixture and cheese. Do not overmix. It's better to leave some streaks of white than to deflate the beaten whites by overblending.

Spoon the soufflé mixture over the shad, covering the fish completely.

Bake at 375°F for 20 minutes or until the soufflé is puffed and golden. Garnish with parsley and dill. Serve immediately.

Serves 4.

Crab Roulade

This is a soufflé with a difference. Baked like a jelly roll, this soufflé can't fall, because it never rises more than an inch. This basic soufflé can be filled with any meat, poultry, seafood or vegetable sauce.

For best results, line your jelly-roll pan with wax paper that is well buttered and floured; if you don't, the soufflé may stick. Also work quickly after removing the soufflé from the oven. Invert it, peel off the paper, fill and roll it as fast as possible. For easier rolling, work on a double sheet of wax paper or parchment.

The Filling
- 3 tablespoons butter
- ½ cup minced onions
- ¼ cup whole wheat pastry flour
- 1½ cups milk
- 2 egg yolks
- ⅛ teaspoon grated nutmeg
- dash of cayenne pepper
- 1 cup flaked crab meat
- 1 cup chopped cooked broccoli
- ⅓ cup shredded Swiss cheese
- 1 tablespoon minced dill or ½ teaspoon dried dill

The Soufflé
- 3 tablespoons butter
- ⅓ cup whole wheat pastry flour
- 1½ cups milk
- 4 egg yolks
- 6 egg whites
- ½ cup shredded Swiss cheese

To make the filling: Melt the butter in a 2-quart saucepan. Add the onions and cook over low heat until they are soft. Stir in the flour, and cook together for 2 minutes, stirring constantly.

In a small saucepan heat the milk.

Remove the onion and flour mixture from the heat, and pour in the hot milk all at once. Beat vigorously with a wire whisk until thoroughly blended, return to the heat and cook, stirring constantly, until the mixture bubbles and is very thick.

Again, remove from the heat, stir in the egg yolks, the nutmeg and cayenne, and then fold in the crab, broccoli, Swiss and dill. Set aside.

To make the soufflé: Oil or butter a 10-by-15-inch jelly-roll pan. Line with wax paper, and butter the paper generously, taking special care with the sides and corners. Flour the pan well, and set aside.

In a 2-quart saucepan melt the butter, stir in the flour, and blend thoroughly. Cook over low heat, stirring constantly, for 2 minutes.

In a small saucepan heat the milk.

Remove the flour mixture from the heat, and pour in the hot milk all at once. Beat vigorously with a wire whisk to blend, and return to the heat and cook, stirring constantly, until the mixture bubbles and is very thick.

Again, remove from the heat, and stir in the egg yolks.

In a large clean bowl, using clean beaters, beat the egg whites until they are stiff and shiny. Do not overbeat.

Stir about one-quarter of the whites into the yolk mixture, and then carefully fold about one-half of the yolk mixture back into the rest of the whites. Sprinkle one-half of the Swiss on top, and then continue to fold. Repeat with the remaining yolk mixture and cheese, but do *not* overmix. It's better to leave some streaks of white than to deflate the beaten whites by overblending.

Spread the soufflé mixture in the prepared pan, smoothing it into the corners with a spatula.

Bake at 425°F for 15 minutes or until the soufflé puffs and is golden on top.

Remove from the oven, and cover the pan with two large sheets of parchment or wax paper. Then top with a large cookie sheet, and invert so that the soufflé rests on the sheet. Remove the soufflé pan, and very carefully peel the wax paper from the bottom of the soufflé.

Spread the soufflé with the filling. Starting with one short end and using the paper underneath to help you, roll up the soufflé. Now use the paper to transfer the soufflé to a serving dish.

Serves 4.

Maryland Crab Cakes

Delicious patties from the Eastern Shore of Maryland where crabs abound. There are cheaper kinds of crab meat than lump or backfin, but you'll have to pick them over carefully to remove the pieces of shell that are invariably mixed in with the budget versions.

1 pound lump crab meat, lightly flaked
½ cup whole wheat breadcrumbs
2 tablespoons minced onion
1 tablespoon minced thyme or 1 teaspoon
   dried thyme
¼ cup *Basic Mayonnaise* (see *Index*)
1 egg
2 teaspoons Dijon-style mustard
1 cup whole wheat breadcrumbs
2 tablespoons butter

In a large bowl lightly toss the crab, ½ cup of breadcrumbs, onion and thyme together.

In a small bowl combine the mayonnaise, egg and mustard and then stir them into the crab mixture.

Form into eight patties, and coat with the breadcrumbs.

Heat the butter in a large frying pan over medium heat until it melts and the foam subsides. Sauté the patties until they are golden on both sides.

Serves 4.

Parsley

Parsley is a highly nutritious garden herb that, paradoxically, was used by the ancient Greeks as a symbol of death. Nowadays herbalists recommend parsley tea as a general tonic that is also beneficial for anemia. They credit parsley with stimulating the digestive system and kidneys and helping to relieve breathing difficulties and menstrual pain. They use the crushed leaves as a soothing poultice for bruises, sprains and insect bites and make a cleansing wash for the skin from parsley. Chewing the leaves will freshen the breath.

Chapter 11
Meats

Stir-Fried Beef with Snow Peas

1-pound flank steak
2 tablespoons cornstarch
2 tablespoons apple juice
1 tablespoon oil
1 tablespoon grated ginger root
4 teaspoons tamari sauce
2 cloves garlic, minced
1 tablespoon oil
½ pound snow peas
8 scallions, cut into ½-inch pieces
3 tablespoons oil
¼ cup apple juice

If you wish, partially freeze the beef (about 1 hour) to make the cutting easier. Then, cut it lengthwise into 2-inch strips, then across the grain into ¼-inch strips.

In a large bowl combine the cornstarch, 2 tablespoons of apple juice, 1 tablespoon of oil, ginger, tamari and garlic; add the beef, and toss to combine. Marinate 1 hour, turning the meat occasionally. Drain the beef, and reserve the marinade.

Heat 1 tablespoon of oil in a wok over high heat or in a large frying pan over medium heat. Add the snow peas and scallions, and stir-fry 1 minute. Remove with a slotted spoon and set aside.

Add 3 tablespoons of oil to the pan, and stir-fry the beef in small batches for about 5 minutes each, or until the beef is tender and cooked through.

Return all the beef, the snow peas and the leftover marinade to the wok. Add the rest of the apple juice, cover and cook 5 minutes longer.

Serves 4.

Veal and Carrot *Blanquette*

Here's another French classic slimmed down to healthy proportions. The carrots give the sauce a lovely color plus lots of vitamin A.

Tɪᴘ: *You can prepare this casserole ahead of time. But stop after you remove the veal from the oven. At mealtime, gently reheat the casserole on top of the stove, puree the vegetables and then whisk in the sour cream and yogurt. If you must reheat the dish after the yogurt and sour cream have been added, do it over* very low *heat and stir frequently to prevent curdling.*

1½ pounds boned veal, cut into 1-inch cubes
    whole wheat flour
 2 tablespoons butter
 2 tablespoons oil
¾ pound carrots, halved or quartered and cut
    into 2-inch pieces
 1 stalk celery, minced
 2 cups minced onions
 1 bouquet garni (1 bay leaf, small handful
    parsley, few sprigs of thyme or ½ teaspoon
    dried thyme, few sprigs oregano or
    ½ teaspoon dried oregano tied in a piece
    of cheesecloth)
 2 cups stock
½ pound button mushrooms
⅓ cup sour cream or *Cottage Cream* (see *Index*)
⅓ cup yogurt
 3 cups hot cooked brown rice (see page 205
    for cooking instructions)

Dredge the veal pieces in the flour.

In a large, flameproof casserole or Dutch oven, heat the butter and oil until they foam, and brown the veal in several batches. Return them all to the pan.

Add the carrots, celery, onions, bouquet garni and stock. Bring all to a simmer on top of the stove.

Then cover and bake at 350°F for 1 hour.

Add the mushrooms to the pan, cover and bake for 30 minutes more, or until the veal is very tender. Remove the bouquet garni.

With a fork or slotted spoon transfer the veal pieces, mushrooms and carrots to a platter, leaving as many onions behind as possible. Remove about ½ cup of carrots to use in the sauce. Cover the platter and keep warm.

Strain the liquid from the casserole into a bowl and reserve.

Place the strained vegetables, the remaining ½ cup of carrots and 1 cup of the reserved liquid into a blender. Blend at high speed for 10 seconds.

Pour the blended liquid into the empty casserole, and whisk in the sour cream or *Cottage Cream* and yogurt.

Drain any accumulated liquid from the veal platter into a bowl, and return the veal and vegetables to the casserole. Stir gently to coat the veal with the sauce.

Serve over hot brown rice.

Serves 4.

Shezan's Curried Lamb

This curried lamb is from the menu of the Shezan Restaurant on 58th Street in New York City. Although the recipe looks imposing, it's quite easy once you assemble the spices. I've adapted the traditional recipe for home use.

    6 cloves
    4 green cardamom pods
    2 black cardamom pods
    1 teaspoon cumin seeds
    2 teaspoons poppy seeds
    ½ cup oil
    1 cup thinly sliced onions
    1 cup water
    1 cinnamon stick
    1 bay leaf
    2 teaspoons paprika
    1 teaspoon turmeric
    ½ teaspoon ground coriander
    1 tablespoon grated ginger root
    1 tablespoon minced garlic
    1 cup chopped tomatoes
    1 cup yogurt
    1½ pounds boned leg of lamb, cut into 1-inch
       cubes
    ⅛ teaspoon powdered mace
    ⅛ teaspoon grated nutmeg

With a spice mill or mortar and pestle, grind the cloves, cardamom, cumin and poppy seeds, and set aside.

In a Dutch oven or 5-quart casserole, heat the oil over medium heat, add the onions and stir until they are wilted and golden. Add the water, ground spices, cinnamon, bay leaf, paprika, turmeric, coriander, ginger and garlic, and cook, stirring occasionally, for 5 minutes.

Add the chopped tomatoes and cook, stirring constantly, until the tomatoes soften and their juices evaporate. Now, whisk in the yogurt. The mixture may look curdled, but do not despair.

Add the lamb and cook, stirring constantly, until the cubes are browned.

Cover the pan and cook over medium-low heat for 1 to 1½ hours, or until the meat is very tender. Stir occasionally. Remove the cinnamon stick and bay leaf, and stir in the mace and nutmeg.

Serves 4.

West Indian Lamb Chops

This is my variation of a pork recipe I learned at Roger Vergé's cooking school in Provence. Even people who don't like lamb should love this casserole. The tomatoes, bananas and brown rice add B vitamins, fiber and potassium to this low-sodium dish.

    2 pounds lamb chops with fat trimmed
       whole wheat flour
    3 tablespoons olive oil
    2 large onions, thinly sliced
    2 cloves garlic, minced
    1 bouquet garni (a few sprigs of thyme or
       ½ teaspoon dried thyme, 1 bay leaf, a few
       sprigs of parsley and a piece of celery tied
       together with string or in a piece of
       cheesecloth)
    1 cinnamon stick
       few gratings of nutmeg
    3 large tomatoes, peeled, seeded and chopped
    ½ cup stock
    2 large bananas
    1 tablespoon butter
    3 cups hot cooked brown rice (see page 205 for
       cooking instructions)

Dredge the lamb lightly in the flour.

Heat the oil in an ovenproof skillet or flameproof casserole large enough to hold the meat in a single layer. Quickly brown the meat on both sides, and remove to a plate.

Add the onions and garlic to the pan and sauté until golden, make sure that the garlic doesn't burn. Return the chops to the pan, add

West Indian Lamb Chops—*continued*

the bouquet garni, and bury the cinnamon stick among the chops. Then, sprinkle lightly with nutmeg, and cover with the tomatoes; add the stock.

Cover and bake at 300°F for 1¼ hours, or until the chops are tender.

Cut the bananas in half lengthwise and then in half crosswise. Heat the butter in a small frying pan, add the bananas and sauté a few minutes on each side.

Serve the chops and their vegetables with the rice, and top with the sautéed bananas.

Serves 4.

Braised Beef Roast

Here's a classic French pot roast that has been stripped of its calorie-laden wine and flour sauce. The nouvelle cuisine practice of pureeing the vegetables to make a rich, flavorful sauce also conserves their vitamins and fiber.

When there are guests for dinner, I like to make this beef a day ahead and reheat just before the company is due. In fact, I think the flavors improve if they have a chance to meld overnight.

3-pound piece of beef rump roast
1 tablespoon butter
2 tablespoons olive oil
1 cup chopped carrots
1 cup chopped celery
1 cup chopped onions
1 cup chopped parsley
  handful of thyme sprigs or 1 tablespoon dried
    thyme
2 bay leaves
2 allspice berries
3 cloves garlic, chopped
3 cups stock
1 tablespoon tomato paste

Tie the roast securely with string to retain its shape and for easier handling. Broil until it is browned on all sides, or about 15 minutes.

Heat the butter and oil in a 4-quart casserole or Dutch oven. Add the carrots, celery, onions and parsley, and cook over low heat until the vegetables are wilted, about 10 minutes.

If you are using fresh thyme sprigs, tie them with string for easier removal.

When the beef has browned, add it to the casserole, and surround it with the vegetables. Add the thyme, bay leaves, allspice, garlic and enough stock to nearly cover the roast. Stir in the tomato paste.

Bring the liquid to a simmer on top of the stove, and then cover and bake at 350°F for 3 to 3½ hours, or until a long-tined fork can easily be inserted into the meat.

Remove the meat from the casserole to a carving board.

Set the casserole on medium-high heat and rapidly reduce the braising liquid by half. Remove the thyme bundle and bay leaves.

Run the liquid and vegetables through a food mill or a sieve to puree. (Do *not* use a blender or food processor.) Skim any fat from the sauce.

Remove the string from the beef, and slice it thinly across the grain. Serve with the sauce.

Serves 4 to 6.

Pasta Shells Stuffed with Veal

A delicious Italian dish that can be assembled ahead and baked whenever you're ready. The whole wheat breadcrumbs not only extend the veal, but they also add B vitamins and fiber. As a variation, use ground breast of chicken.

The Stuffing
1 pound ground veal
1 egg
¾ cup whole wheat breadcrumbs
2 tablespoons minced parsley
2 teaspoons minced basil or ¾ teaspoon dried basil
1 teaspoon minced marjoram or ¼ teaspoon dried marjoram

The Sauce
3 tablespoons butter
6 tablespoons whole wheat pastry flour
2 cups milk
1 cup shredded mozzarella cheese

The Assembly
20 jumbo pasta shells (about ½ pound)
¼ cup grated Parmesan cheese

To make the stuffing: Mix the veal, egg, breadcrumbs, parsley, basil and marjoram together until they are well blended.

To make the sauce: In a medium saucepan melt the butter, stir in the flour, and cook over medium heat for 2 minutes, being careful not to brown the flour.

In a small saucepan, heat the milk, and add all at once to the flour mixture. Cook, whisking constantly, until the sauce comes to a boil and thickens. Remove from the heat, and stir in the mozzarella.

To assemble: Cook the shells in a very large pot of boiling water according to package directions (10 to 20 minutes for *al dente*). Drain them on paper towels.

When the shells are cool enough to handle, stuff them with the filling.

Lightly butter a 7-by-11-inch baking dish, and pour about 1 cup of the sauce into it. Arrange the shells filling side up, in rows, to fill the pan. Pour the remaining sauce over all, and sprinkle with Parmesan.

Cover the pan and bake at 350°F for 30 minutes. Remove the cover and bake for another 20 minutes, or until lightly golden.

Serves 4 or 5.

Tofu Burgers

Tofu, a soybean product, is an excellent extender for ground beef. High in protein, low in fat and calories, and free of cholesterol, tofu also makes burgers juicier. These patties mix about two parts of beef to one part tofu, but you may want to lower the calorie, fat and sodium content even further by using a half-and-half mixture; that is, ¾ of a pound of beef to 1½ cups of mashed tofu.

1 pound lean ground beef
1 cup mashed tofu
1 onion, minced
½ pepper, minced
2 cloves garlic, minced
2 tablespoons minced parsley
2 tablespoons minced basil or 2 teaspoons dried basil
2 tablespoons minced dill or 2 teaspoons dried dill
½ cup whole wheat breadcrumbs
1 egg
⅓ cup *Tomato Sauce* (see *Index*)

In a large bowl or in a food processor, thoroughly mix the beef, tofu, onion, pepper, garlic, parsley, basil, dill, breadcrumbs and egg with enough *Tomato Sauce* to hold all the ingredients together.

Form the mixture into eight patties, and then broil them until cooked through.

Serves 4.

Beef and Onion Stew

Long, slow cooking mellows the onions and tenderizes the beef.

4 cups thinly sliced onions
2 tablespoons olive oil
¼ cup whole wheat flour
1 pound beef, cut into 1-inch cubes
1 pound carrots
4 cloves garlic, minced
1 tablespoon minced savory or 1 teaspoon dried savory
1 tablespoon thyme leaves or 1 teaspoon dried thyme
2 tablespoons thyme vinegar or white wine vinegar
2 cups stock
¼ cup chopped parsley
3 cups hot cooked brown rice (see page 205 for cooking instructions)

In a 4-quart, ovenproof pot, slowly cook the onions in olive oil until they are limp, about 20 minutes. Stir the flour into the cooked onions, and then add the beef to the pot.

Cut the carrots into thin, 2-inch pieces, and add them to the pot, along with the garlic, savory, thyme, vinegar and stock.

Cover and bake at 375°F for about 2 hours, or until the beef is very tender. Now, stir in the parsley and serve the stew over hot brown rice.

Serves 4.

Rose

Rose, the queen of flowers, has long been esteemed by poet and herbalist alike for its beauty, which combines a perfect blossom of softness with the sharp thorns of pain. It has also been regarded through the centuries as a symbol of silence and trust. The red rose is the most useful medicinally. Rose tea is described in herbals as a nerve and stomach tonic. Honey of roses is an ancient remedy for sore throat. Herbals recommend crushed blossoms in a tea or a cooling compress to relieve headaches.

Butternut and Bulgur Beef

Based on a Moroccan recipe, this slightly sweet dish combines the health bonuses of onions with the vitamin A in carrots and butternut squash and the B vitamins and zinc in chick-peas. The bulgur is a more nutritious substitute for the more traditional couscous. It is high in fiber, B vitamins and potassium, and low in fat and sodium.

¼ cup chick-peas, soaked overnight
½ pound beef, cut into ⅜-inch cubes
  whole wheat flour
2 tablespoons oil
2 cups thinly sliced onions
2 cups stock
½ teaspoon powdered ginger
⅛ teaspoon turmeric
  pinch of saffron
½ pound carrots
1 pound butternut squash
1 tablespoon honey
⅓ cup raisins
1 cup stock
1 cup uncooked bulgur

Drain the soaked chick-peas, cover with fresh water and cook for 1 hour. Drain again.

Dredge the beef in the flour.

In a large frying pan or casserole, heat the oil, and brown the beef over medium heat. Now, stir in the onions, and continue to cook until they are wilted.

Add the chick-peas, 2 cups of stock, the ginger, turmeric and saffron to the beef; cover and simmer over low heat for 1 hour.

Cut the carrots into thin strips, each about 2 inches long.

Peel and seed the squash, and cut it into 1-inch chunks.

Add the carrots, squash and honey to the pan, and simmer another 30 minutes. Add the raisins, and simmer 15 minutes more, or until the carrots, chick-peas and beef are tender.

Bring 1 cup of stock to a boil in a small saucepan, and stir in the bulgur. Cover, remove from heat, and let stand about 20 to 30 minutes, or until all the liquid is absorbed and the bulgur is tender.

Fluff the bulgur with two forks, transfer to a large serving platter, and spoon the vegetables and beef over the top.

Serves 4.

The Spiral Meatloaf

A new twist for plain old meatloaf. The spinach spiral contributes vitamins A and C, fiber and magnesium to the beef, and the mashed potatoes extend the beef while adding their own store of nutrients.

The Filling
½ pound spinach leaves
½ cup whole wheat breadcumbs
⅓ cup shredded Swiss cheese
¼ cup ricotta cheese
1 egg

The Beef
1 pound lean ground beef
½ cup mashed potatoes
1 large onion, minced
1 clove garlic, minced
2 teaspoons minced oregano or ½ teaspoon
  dried oregano
2 teaspoons minced basil or ½ teaspoon dried
  basil
2 teaspoons minced thyme or ½ teaspoon
  dried thyme
1 egg
  whole wheat breadcrumbs

To make the filling: Wash the spinach in plenty of cold water, and cook it in a large pot using only the water left clinging to the leaves; cook only until the spinach wilts. Transfer to a colander or sieve to cool and drain. When the spinach is cool enough to handle, squeeze the

The Spiral Meatloaf—*continued*

moisture out, and chop finely. (If you are using a food processor for the next step, omit the chopping.) With a mixer or food processor cream the spinach, breadcrumbs, Swiss, ricotta and egg together until they are smooth. Set aside.

To make the beef: With a mixer or food processor blend the beef, potatoes, onion, garlic, oregano, basil, thyme and egg.

Sprinkle a large piece of wax paper with breadcrumbs, and then pat the meat mixture into a rectangular shape about 8 by 11 inches on top of the crumbs.

Spread the filling on top of the rectangle being careful to leave a 1-inch border all around. Now, roll up the rectangle, starting with an 8-inch end.

Transfer the roll, seam side down, to an oiled or buttered 8½-by-4½-inch loaf pan, and bake at 350°F for about 1 hour.

Serves 4.

Spaghetti Squash and Meatballs

High in fiber and mildly crunchy when it's not overcooked, spaghetti squash is a delicious, low-calorie substitute for fattening noodles.

1 large spaghetti squash (2½–3 pounds)
1 pound lean ground beef
1 egg
⅔ cup minced onions
1 cup rolled oats
¼ cup *Tomato Sauce* (see *Index*)
2 tablespoons minced parsley
1½ teaspoons minced basil or ½ teaspoon dried basil
1½ teaspoons minced oregano or ½ teaspoon dried oregano
4 cups *Tomato Sauce*
¼ cup *Pesto Sauce* (see *Index*)
½ cup grated Parmesan cheese

Puncture the squash once or twice with a skewer, and place it in a large pot. Add hot water to nearly cover the squash, cover the pot and bring to a boil. Now, lower the heat and cook for 1 to 1½ hours, or until the squash is easily pierced with a skewer.

While the squash is cooking, make the meatballs. In a large bowl or food processor mix the beef, egg, onion, oats, ¼ cup of *Tomato Sauce,* the parsley, basil and oregano until they are thoroughly combined.

Form the meat into balls about 1½ inches in diameter (this recipe will yield about 24). Broil them about 6 inches from the element for 5 minutes, turn, and broil for another 5 minutes.

Place 4 cups of *Tomato Sauce* in a large pot, and add the meatballs. Simmer over low heat for 30 minutes.

When the squash is cooked, remove from the pot and run it under cold water until it's cool enough to handle. Cut in half *crosswise*, and carefully scoop out the seeds and darker pulp with a spoon, and discard.

With a fork flake the flesh of the squash. It will come away from the rind in strands that resemble spaghetti. Taste the strands; if they are too crisp to suit you, transfer to a large frying pan and add ¼ cup of water. Cover and cook over medium heat until the squash softens, but do not let it turn mushy.

Toss the cooked squash with the *Pesto Sauce,* and serve with the meatballs and tomato sauce. Top with grated Parmesan.

Serves 4.

Savory Stuffed Peppers

A terrific way to use up the small peppers that remain on your plants in late September. Oats extend the beef while contributing their own fiber and protein.

1 pound lean ground beef
1 cup rolled oats
¾ cup *Tomato Juice* (see *Index*)
1 large onion, minced
½ cup minced celery
⅓ cup grated Parmesan cheese
3 tablespoons minced parsley
1 tablespoon minced savory or 1 teaspoon dried savory
2 cloves garlic, minced
1 egg
¼ teaspoon cayenne pepper
4 very large bell peppers or 8 small ones
1-1½ cups *Tomato Juice*

In a bowl thoroughly mix the beef, oats, ¾ cup of *Tomato Juice,* onion, celery, Parmesan, parsley, savory, garlic, egg and cayenne.

Cut large peppers in half lengthwise, remove the seeds and core. If you are using small peppers, cut off the tops, and scoop out the seeds and core.

Fill the peppers with the beef mixture, using all the filling. Arrange the peppers in a shallow baking dish just large enough to hold them all in one layer. Pour in enough *Tomato Juice* to fill the pan with about ½ inch of juice.

Cover the pan, and bake at 350°F for 45 minutes. Remove the cover, and bake for another 30 minutes, or until browned on top.

Serves 4.

Moussaka with Zucchini

A moussaka that substitutes zucchini for the traditional eggplant. Cinnamon in the meat lends a definite Middle Eastern zest to this dish. For best results, use very thin zucchini.

The Zucchini Layer
4 thin (1½-inch diameter) zucchini (about 1 pound)
1 tablespoon softened butter
1 tablespoon olive oil

The Meat Layer
¾ pound lean ground beef
2 cups finely chopped onions
3 cloves garlic, minced
2 tablespoons whole wheat flour
½ teaspoon ground cinnamon
¼ teaspoon grated nutmeg
1½ tablespoons minced oregano or 1½ teaspoons dried oregano
1½ cups pureed tomatoes
½ cup stock
¼ cup minced parsley

The Cheese Sauce
3 tablespoons butter
5 tablespoons whole wheat pastry flour
1½ cups milk
⅛ teaspoon grated nutmeg
3 eggs
¼ cup grated Parmesan cheese

To make the zucchini layer: Cut the zucchini into four lengthwise pieces. (If the zucchini are thicker than 1½ inches, cut them into 8 pieces.) Divide each piece in half.

Spread the butter and oil in a shallow baking dish, add the zucchini and toss to coat with oil. Bake at 400°F for about 30 minutes, turning occasionally, until the zucchini are soft and have browned slightly.

Drain on paper towels and set aside.

To make the meat layer: Crumble the meat into a large frying pan, and cook over medium

Moussaka with Zucchini—*continued*

heat until browned. Add the onions and garlic, and stir for a few minutes to soften the onions. Do not let the garlic brown. Spoon off any excess fat.

Sprinkle the meat with flour, add the cinnamon, nutmeg, oregano, tomatoes, stock and parsley; cover and cook over medium heat for 10 minutes. Uncover and cook, stirring frequently to prevent scorching, until the mixture is very dry and all the liquid has evaporated. As the mixture thickens, lower the heat to medium low to prevent sticking.

To make the cheese sauce: Melt the butter in a medium saucepan, stir in the flour, and cook over low heat, stirring constantly for 2 minutes.

In a small saucepan heat the milk.

Add the hot milk to the flour mixture all at once, and beat with a wire whisk until a smooth sauce forms. Cook over medium heat, stirring constantly, until the sauce thickens and comes to a boil. Stir in the nutmeg, and remove from the heat.

In a small bowl beat the eggs until well blended. Then, gradually beat in about ½ cup of the hot sauce. Beat vigorously to blend and to prevent the eggs from scrambling.

Stir the eggs into the rest of the sauce, and return to the heat. Cook, stirring constantly, for 1 minute, and then remove from the heat. Stir in the Parmesan.

To assemble: Place a layer of zucchini in a 9-inch-square baking pan. If there is too much for a single layer, save the excess for another layer.

Stir about half of the cheese sauce into the meat, and spoon the meat on top of the zucchini. Cover with any remaining zucchini.

Spread the remaining sauce smoothly over the top.

Bake at 350°F for 40 minutes, or until the top is golden. Let stand about 15 minutes before cutting.

Serves 4.

Rosemary

Rosemary has been the herb of remembrance since Greek students wore garlands of rosemary to strengthen their memories. Generally, herbalists apply the herb externally to treat rheumatism, eczema, bruises and wounds. Rosemary tea is suggested by one herbalist as a mouthwash. It is also said to be an excellent hair rinse that stimulates the roots, improves the condition of the hair and helps prevent dandruff.

Million Dollar Casserole

My version of a dish my friend Marjorie Compton served the first time my husband and I dined at her house. I thought it tasted like a million dollars then, and I still do. The dish can be prepared ahead and baked at mealtime.

TIP: *Use an egg slicer to slice the mushrooms thinly.*

    4 ounces small whole wheat shells
    4 ounces Cheddar cheese, shredded
    1 pound lean ground beef
    2 large onions, diced
    4 ounces mushrooms, thinly sliced
 1½ cups milk
    2 tablespoons butter
 2½ tablespoons whole wheat pastry flour
    ¼ cup minced parsley
    2 tablespoons minced dill or 2 teaspoons dried
        dill
    1 tablespoon tamari sauce
    2 tablespoons chopped pecans
    2 tablespoons sunflower seeds
    2 tablespoons pumpkin seeds
      yogurt (optional)

Cook the shells in boiling water until they are just tender, about 8 minutes. Do not overcook. Drain and pour them into an oiled, 9-inch-square baking pan. Sprinkle with half of the Cheddar and set aside.

In a large frying pan, brown the beef. When the beef is thoroughly browned, spread the onions and mushrooms on top, cover the pan and cook over medium heat for about 5 minutes, or until the onions and mushrooms are tender.

In a small saucepan heat the milk.

Melt the butter in a medium saucepan, stir in the flour, and cook over low heat, stirring constantly, for 2 minutes. Pour in the hot milk, and beat with a wire whisk to combine. Cook over medium heat, stirring constantly, until the sauce comes to a boil and thickens. Then stir in the parsley, dill and tamari.

Drain off any fat from the beef, and stir the sauce into the beef. Pour it over the shells in their baking dish, and sprinkle with the remaining Cheddar.

Bake at 350°F for about 15 minutes, or until the cheese melts.

Top with pecans, sunflower seeds and pumpkin seeds, and bake for another 10 minutes. Serve with plain yogurt.

Serves 4.

Stuffed Zucchini Parmesan

    4 small zucchini (about 6 inches long and
        ½ pound each)
    1 pound lean ground beef
    1 cup chopped tomatoes
    ½ cup rolled oats
    ½ cup grated Parmesan cheese
    ⅓ cup minced onions
    2 tablespoons minced parsley
    1 tablespoon minced basil or 1 teaspoon
        dried basil
    1 teaspoon minced rosemary or ¼ teaspoon
        dried rosemary, crushed
    1 egg
    ¼ cup shredded Cheddar cheese or grated
        Parmesan cheese
 1½ cups *Tomato Sauce* (see *Index*)

Cut the zucchini in half lengthwise, and scoop out and discard the seeds and pulp; leave a shell ⅜ of an inch thick.

To a large bowl or food processor add the beef, tomatoes, oats, the ½ cup of Parmesan, the onions, parsley, basil, rosemary and egg, and mix until thoroughly combined.

Fill the zucchini halves with the meat mixture. Place the zucchini in a lightly oiled, 9-by-13-inch baking dish, and cover with foil.

Bake at 350°F for 1 hour. Then remove the foil, sprinkle the zucchini with Cheddar or Parmesan, and bake for another 15 minutes.

Serve with hot *Tomato Sauce*.

Serves 4.

Hot Kebabs

My version of a dish I learned from Indian cook Julie Sahni in her New York City classes. Mildly spicy, these wurst-shaped kebabs are delightful on a summer day, because the yogurt and tomatoes tame the hot taste.

  1 pound lean ground beef
  ½ cup whole wheat breadcrumbs
  3 tablespoons minced parsley
  3 tablespoons minced mint or 1 tablespoon dried mint
  2 hot chili peppers, minced
  1 tablespoon ground cumin
  1 tablespoon grated ginger root
  3 cloves garlic, minced
  1 tablespoon lemon juice
  1 egg
1-2 tablespoons oil
4-8 whole wheat pita breads, warmed
  1 cup yogurt
  2 tomatoes, chopped

Place the beef, breadcrumbs, parsley, mint, chili peppers, cumin, ginger, garlic, lemon juice and egg in a large bowl. Work the ingredients with your hands or a heavy-duty mixer until they are well combined.

Form the mixture into small logs about 4 inches long and ½ inch thick. The recipe will yield about 16 kebabs.

Film the bottom of a large frying pan with oil, and place over medium heat until the pan is hot. Add the kebabs, leaving a little space between them, and brown. Shake the pan to keep the kebabs from sticking or overbrowning.

Continue until the kebabs are browned on all sides and cooked through, about 10 minutes.

To serve, cut the pitas in half. Open each pocket, fill with one or two kebabs, spoon on a little yogurt, and top with chopped tomatoes.

Serves 4.

Saffron

Saffron is the dried orange stigmata of a crocus flower—prized through the ages for its color, scent and flavor. It is also rather costly since 60,000 flowers are needed to provide one pound of saffron. Herbals describe saffron tea as a warming drink useful in small amounts for coughs, colic and sleeplessness. In the past, saffron was regarded as a medicine for women's diseases and is still occasionally recommended by herbalists as a menstrual aid.

Italian Meat-Filled Crepes

I frequently add shredded carrots to meat sauces, because they add fiber, vitamin A and a pleasant sweetness to the sauce. You can fill these crepes ahead and bake them whenever you're ready.

½ pound lean ground beef
1 tablespoon oil
1 tablespoon whole wheat flour
¼ cup shredded carrots
½ cup minced onions
½ cup diced tomatoes
1 clove garlic, minced
1 tablespoon minced basil or 1 teaspoon dried basil
1 tablespoon minced fennel
8 *Whole Wheat Crepes* (see *Index*)
1 cup *Tomato Sauce* (see *Index*)
½ cup grated Parmesan cheese

In a large frying pan brown the beef in oil. Sprinkle it with flour and stir to combine. Now, add the carrots, onions, tomatoes, garlic, basil and fennel.

Cover and cook over medium-low heat until the vegetables are tender and the sauce is thick.

Butter a 9-by-13-inch baking dish.

Arrange each crepe, spotty side up, on a plate. Place about 3 tablespoons of the meat sauce at one end, and roll the crepe to enclose the filling.

Transfer to the baking dish and place seam side down. When all the crepes have been arranged, spread any leftover filling over the top of them.

Cover with *Tomato Sauce*, and sprinkle with cheese.

Bake at 350°F for 30 minutes.

Serves 4.

Mexican Pasta

Corn noodles are available in many health food stores. They're a nice change of taste from wheat-based pastas, and they add a lovely color to most dishes. One word of caution: Be careful not to overcook them! They are thin and delicate and can turn to mush easily. Begin testing the noodles after only three minutes of boiling.

You can control the spiciness of this dish by varying the amount of hot peppers used. The coriander leaves are not essential, but they do lend an authentic Mexican flavor to the sauce.

1 tablespoon olive oil
½ pound lean ground beef
2 cups thinly sliced onions
1-2 hot peppers, minced
1 red pepper, finely chopped
2 tablespoons minced coriander leaves
1 teaspoon *Chili Powder* (see *Index*)
2½ cups *Tomato Sauce* (see *Index*)
8 ounces corn noodles
1 tablespoon oil
¾ cup shredded Cheddar cheese

Heat the oil in a large frying pan over medium heat. Add the beef and stir until it browns evenly. Lower the heat to medium low, and add the onions, hot pepper, red pepper, coriander and *Chili Powder*. Cook until the onions are tender, stirring frequently to prevent sticking.

Stir in the *Tomato Sauce*, and simmer until the sauce thickens, about 20 minutes.

Cook the corn noodles in a large amount of boiling water to which a tablespoon of oil has been added. Cook until they are just tender, about 4 minutes. Test them frequently to prevent overcooking. Gently strain the delicate noodles in a colander.

Transfer the noodles to a serving dish, and ladle on the sauce. Sprinkle with Cheddar.

Serves 4.

Beef Tacos

Prepare the filling and shredded cheese ahead, and be ready for last-minute meals. While the tortillas are crisping in the oven, quickly chop the tomatoes and shred the lettuce. Then when the tortillas are set, you will be too!

The Filling
1 pound lean ground beef
1 tablespoon oil
2 tablespoons whole wheat flour
1 cup minced onions
½ cup minced celery
2 tablespoons *Chili Powder* (see *Index*)
2 tablespoons minced basil or 2 teaspoons
    dried basil
1 teaspoon ground cumin
2 tablespoons chopped chili peppers
2 cups chopped tomatoes
1 cup *Tomato Sauce* (see *Index*)

The Assembly
8 corn tortillas
  shredded cheese
  chopped tomatoes
  shredded lettuce

To make the filling: Brown the beef in oil in a large frying pan over medium heat. Stir in the flour.

Add the onions, celery, *Chili Powder*, basil, cumin, chili peppers, tomatoes and *Tomato Sauce.*

Cover and cook the mixture over medium-low heat until the tomatoes have cooked down. Uncover and cook, stirring occasionally, until the filling thickens.

To assemble: Heat the tortillas in the oven at 350°F for 5 to 8 minutes, or until crisp. Fill the tortillas, and top with cheese, tomatoes and lettuce.

Serves 4.

Sage

Sage brings to mind wisdom, strength and long life. Sage tea made with lemon is a refreshing, cooling drink noted for reducing fever and perspiration. Herbals describe the tea as an effective remedy for nervous conditions, trembling and depression. They suggest an infusion as a healing gargle for sore throats or as a skin wash. Fresh leaves rubbed on the teeth are said to help cleanse them and strengthen the gums.

Tamale Pie

A favorite in the Southwest on both sides of the U.S.-Mexico border. The corn, cheese and cornmeal add to the beef's protein so half a pound of meat can easily feed four. This casserole can be assembled ahead and baked whenever you're ready.

Adjust the amount of cayenne to suit your taste; as the recipe stands, the pie is medium hot.

The Filling
½ pound lean ground beef
1 tablespoon oil
1 cup diced onions
3 cloves garlic, minced
¼ cup stock
2 tablespoons whole wheat flour
2 tablespoons *Chili Powder* (see *Index*)
1½ teaspoons cumin, crushed
¼ teaspoon cayenne pepper
1 cup peeled, seeded and chopped tomatoes
1 cup corn
½ green pepper, diced
½ cup *Tomato Sauce* (see *Index*)
½ cup chopped parsley
1 tablespoon minced sage or ¼ teaspoon
   dried sage

The Crust
1 cup cornmeal
1 cup cold water
2 cups stock
¼ cup grated Parmesan cheese

½ cup shredded Cheddar cheese (as a topping)
½ green pepper, cut into thin strips (as a
   topping)

To make the filling: In a 3- or 4-quart saucepan brown the ground beef in oil, crumbling the beef as it browns. Add the onions, garlic and stock, cover, and cook over low heat for 5 minutes until the onions soften. Stir in the flour and mix well.

Add the *Chili Powder*, cumin, cayenne, tomatoes, corn, diced pepper, *Tomato Sauce*, parsley and sage. Cover and cook over low heat until the tomatoes are soft, and the mixture is thick. Stir frequently to prevent scorching or sticking.

To make the crust: With a wire whisk combine the cornmeal and water in a 2-quart saucepan until smooth. Gradually stir in the stock, and cook over medium heat, stirring constantly, until the mixture bubbles and becomes very thick, about 15 minutes. Stir in the Parmesan.

Pour the cornmeal into a buttered 9-by-13-inch baking dish, and let sit several minutes to firm up.

Spread the filling over the cornmeal layer.

Set the dish on a counter with one 13-inch side directly in front of you. Make four even rows of Cheddar across the top of the filling with the rows running parallel to the 9-inch sides. Fill in the space between the cheese rows with green pepper strips.

Bake at 350°F for 30 minutes.

Serves 4.

Medium-Hot Chili

Lots of spices and slow simmering give this chili its extra zing. Adzuki beans look like miniature kidney beans, but they cook much faster.

1 tablespoon oil
1 pound lean ground beef
1 cup finely chopped onions
½ cup finely chopped celery
2 cloves garlic, minced
3 cups coarsely pureed tomatoes
1 cup stock
3 cups cooked kidney or adzuki beans, about
   1 cup dried (see page 109 for cooking
   instructions)
1 tablespoon *Chili Powder* (see *Index*)
1 tablespoon minced marjoram or 1 teaspoon
   dried marjoram
1 tablespoon minced oregano or 1 teaspoon
   dried oregano
1 tablespoon minced thyme or 1 teaspoon
   dried thyme
1 tablespoon minced sage or ¼ teaspoon dried
   sage
½ teaspoon paprika
¼ teaspoon ground cumin
¼ teaspoon cayenne pepper
⅛ teaspoon ground coriander seeds
⅛ teaspoon powdered ginger
  pinch of ground allspice
1 bay leaf
2 small jalapeño peppers, chopped (remove
   the seeds, if desired)

Heat the oil in a Dutch oven, crumble in the beef and cook until browned. Add the onions, celery and garlic, and cook over low heat until the onions are soft.

Add the tomatoes, stock, beans, *Chili Powder*, marjoram, oregano, thyme, sage, paprika, cumin, cayenne, coriander, ginger, allspice, bay leaf and jalapeño peppers. Cover and cook over low heat for about 1 hour, or until the chili has thickened. Stir frequently to prevent sticking.

Remove the bay leaf before serving.

Serves 4 to 6.

Chapter 12
Vegetables

Brown Rice

Brown rice is nice. Nice and low in calories, sodium and fat. Nice and high in protein, fiber and other nutrients. It's also a filling food whose complex carbohydrates satisfy hunger and are easily digested. It's so nice that it's the undeniable champ of your supermarket's rice section. And that's important to know, because with brown, white, converted, instant and dozens of flavored rice mixes to choose from, you're often left scratching your head in confusion. Well, scratch no more. Just remember that brown is the best rice and you'll never go wrong.

Of course, *all* rice starts out brown. When rice comes in from the fields, it's stripped of its tough, inedible outer hull and right there becomes brown rice, because of the brownish color imparted by the kernel's bran layers. It's a natural, whole food packed with fiber, B vitamins and minerals.

Unfortunately, commercial rice millers generally don't stop there. They feed the rice into machines that scrape away those bran layers (now called the "polish") and the nutrient-rich rice germ. Fiber, B vitamins and other nutrients are allowed to go right down the drain. To compensate, some processors put back just three of these pilfered nutrients in a process they have the nerve to call "enrichment." But even this sleight of hand leaves the newly white rice with less fiber, riboflavin, B6, folate, pantothenate, magnesium, zinc and potassium than the original brown rice had. The only benefit that comes of this processing is that it produces a faster cooking rice, one that is fluffier and lighter in color than natural brown rice. What you should do is leave the stuff on your grocer's shelf.

Here is a more graphic illustration of the nutritional differences between brown and white. The figures are for one cup of cooked rice.

Nutrient	Brown Rice	White Rice
protein (grams)	4.9	4.1
fiber (grams)	1.25	0.38
thiamine (milligrams)	0.18	0.04
riboflavin (milligrams)	0.04	0.02
niacin (milligrams)	2.7	0.8
iron (milligrams)	1.0	0.4
potassium (milligrams)	137	57
magnesium (milligrams)	60.3	15.28
zinc (milligrams)	1.25	0.76
energy (calories)	232	223

There *is* a rice that lies halfway between the brown and white varieties for those times when you want a fluffy texture without totally sacrificing nutrition. It's called converted (or parboiled) rice. Although it is a processed rice, it retains some of its natural nutrients thanks to a special pressure and steam process that drives them out of the bran and into the starchy center of each kernel before the damage of milling. But be smart and reserve converted rice for special occasions.

Rice has a high-quality protein which contains a fairly good balance of the essential amino acids and yet it is slightly deficient in two of them: lysine and isoleucine. To compensate for those weaknesses, serve rice with legume vegetables (such as peas, kidney beans or lentils) or with sesame seeds, dairy products or spinach. All of these foods contain the amino acids that rice lacks.

When buying brown rice, you'll probably notice that it comes in three forms: long grain, medium grain and short grain. Long-grain rice cooks up light and fluffy, with each kernel remaining separate from the others. It's great for rice pilafs, paella and other rice side dishes. Most of the rice sold in supermarkets is long grain. Medium grain is stubbier and becomes slightly moist and sticky when it's cooked. Use it for puddings or to extend the meat in meatloaf or croquettes. Short-grain rice is even stickier and so is excellent in puddings.

Whichever variety you are using, the cooking directions are the same. One cup of raw rice cooks up into 3 cups of prepared rice. To make basic brown rice, bring 2½ to 3 cups of water or stock to a boil in a saucepan, and then stir in 1 cup of rice. To prevent boilovers, also add a tablespoon of oil or butter to the pan. Cover the pan with a tight-fitting lid and simmer the rice for about 50 minutes, or until all the liquid has been absorbed, and the rice is tender. To prevent long-grain rice from sticking together, do not stir it while it is cooking.

Baked Saffron Rice

A nice accompaniment to chicken or spicy Indian foods.

1 onion, minced
1 tablespoon butter
3 cups stock
1 cup uncooked long-grain brown rice
⅓ cup raisins
¼ teaspoon saffron

In a large, flameproof casserole, sauté the onion in butter until limp. Add the stock, rice, raisins and saffron, and bring to a simmer.

Cover and bake at 350°F for 1 hour, or until the rice is tender and the liquid has been absorbed.

Serves 4.

Tomato Rice

- 1 onion, minced
- 1 stalk celery, minced
- 1 tablespoon olive oil
- 1 clove garlic, minced
- 1 cup uncooked long-grain brown rice
- 1 teaspoon minced thyme or ½ teaspoon dried thyme
- 1 teaspoon minced oregano or ½ teaspoon dried oregano
- 1 teaspoon minced savory or ½ teaspoon dried savory
- ½ teaspoon minced marjoram or pinch of dried marjoram
- 1 bay leaf
- 1½ cups stock
- 1½ cups peeled and chopped tomatoes

Over low heat, sauté the onion and celery in oil until the onion is soft. Add the garlic, rice, thyme, oregano, savory and marjoram, and cook, stirring constantly, for a few minutes more.

Add the bay leaf, stock and tomatoes; cover and bring to a boil. Now, lower the heat and simmer for about 50 minutes, or until the rice is tender and all the liquid has been absorbed. Remove the bay leaf.

Serves 4.

Curried Rice

- 1 tablespoon oil
- ⅔ cup uncooked long-grain brown rice
- 2 cups stock
- 1 cup minced onions
- 2 cloves garlic, minced
- 2 tablespoons oil
- 1 tablespoon *Curry Powder* (see *Index*)
- ¼ cup raisins
- 3 tablespoons stock
- 2 tablespoons grated coconut

In a medium saucepan heat 1 tablespoon of oil until it is quite hot. Add the rice and cook, stirring constantly, for a few minutes or until the rice begins to turn golden. Now add the stock, cover and simmer until the rice is tender and all the liquid has been absorbed, about 50 minutes.

In a large frying pan sauté the onions and garlic in 2 tablespoons of oil until the onions wilt, and then stir in the *Curry Powder*. Add the raisins, stock and coconut; cover and cook over low heat for about 10 minutes or until the raisins plump and the flavors blend.

When the rice is cooked, fluff it lightly with two forks, and add to the frying pan. Gently toss or fold with a rubber spatula to combine.

Serves 4.

Festive Rice Pilaf

An easy and attractive side dish. The sunflower seeds will soften during cooking, so if you prefer them crunchy, add them near the end of the cooking time.

- 1 large onion, minced
- 1 stalk celery, minced
- 1 carrot, minced
- 1 tablespoon oil
- ¾ cup uncooked long-grain brown rice
- ½ cup sunflower seeds
- ½ red pepper, diced
- 1 clove garlic, minced
- 1 tablespoon minced thyme or 1 teaspoon dried thyme
- 2½ cups stock
- 1 bay leaf

In a large saucepan over low heat, sauté the onion, celery and carrot in oil until the onion is soft.

Add the rice, sunflower seeds, pepper, garlic and thyme, and sauté a few minutes more.

Festive Rice Pilaf—*continued*

Add the stock and bay leaf, and bring to a simmer. Now, cover and cook for 45 to 50 minutes, or until the liquid has been absorbed and the rice is tender. Remove the bay leaf.

Serves 4.

Rice Pilaf with Oranges

An easy rice pilaf that's baked in the oven. Serve it with chicken.

2 navel oranges
2 tablespoons butter
1 cup minced onions
1 cup minced celery
1 cup uncooked long-grain brown rice
½ cup chopped or slivered almonds
2 cups orange juice
1 cup stock

Grate the rind from one orange and reserve. Peel and section both oranges, and remove the membranes from each segment. Chop the pulp coarsely.

In a 2-quart, flameproof casserole, heat the butter until it foams and add the onions and celery. Cook over low heat until the onions are transparent.

Add the rice, almonds and the reserved orange rind. Cook, stirring constantly, for several minutes, or until the rice has turned light gold.

Add the orange juice and stock, bring to a simmer, and stir in the orange pieces.

Cover and bake at 350°F for 1 hour, or until the rice is tender and the liquid has been absorbed. Fluff with two forks.

Serves 4.

Savory

Savory is valued more for its aromatic, peppery flavor than for its medicinal properties, but herbalists use both winter and summer savory tea as a remedy for stomach and intestinal disorders. Freshly pressed leaves are reputed to provide immediate relief from wasp or bee stings.

Asparagus Amandine

A triple dose of B vitamins comes from the asparagus, almonds and mushrooms in this dish, which is also high in fiber and low in sodium.

1 pound asparagus
1 tablespoon butter
1 cup sliced mushrooms
⅓ cup sliced or slivered almonds
¼ cup minced parsley
2 teaspoons grated lemon rind

Break off the tough ends of the asparagus, and tie the spears into small bundles about 2 to 3 inches in diameter; use two lengths of kitchen string per bundle. Make sure the spears in each bundle are nearly the same thickness to ensure uniform cooking.

Melt the butter in a large frying pan, and add the mushrooms and almonds. Cook over low heat, stirring frequently, until the almonds are golden, the mushrooms are tender, and their liquid has evaporated. Stir in the parsley and lemon rind.

Bring a large pot of water to a boil, and carefully lower the asparagus bundles into the water. Cook at a boil until the asparagus is *just* tender, about 5 minutes. To test, pierce with the point of a sharp knife.

Remove the bundles, snip the string and place the spears on a serving platter. Cover with the mushrooms and almonds.

Serves 4.

Sage Grits

Grits are a favorite in the South, where they're served with just about everything. This cheese and sage side dish is delicious straight from the oven.

½ cup minced onions
2 tablespoons butter
2 cups stock
1 cup corn grits
2 eggs
1 cup shredded Cheddar cheese
2 tablespoons minced sage or 1 teaspoon dried sage
1 tablespoon butter

Sauté the onions in butter in a 2-quart saucepan over medium-low heat until the onions are tender. Add the stock and bring to a boil.

Slowly whisk in the grits so that the stock does not stop boiling, and then cook, stirring constantly, until they thicken. Remove from the heat.

In a small bowl beat the eggs with a fork until they are well combined. Beat in ½ cup of hot grits to heat the eggs, and then add the egg mixture to the pan containing the grits. Stir well to incorporate, and then add the cheese and sage.

Butter a 1½-quart casserole or coat it with equal parts of oil and liquid lecithin.

Pour the grits into the casserole, and dot with butter. Bake at 375°F for 45 minutes, or until golden. Serve immediately.

Serves 4.

Marjoram Cabbage au Gratin

This wonderful side dish is best served piping hot from the oven; it does not reheat well. Bake only until the cabbage is just heated through and remains a little crisp.

Cabbage is low in sodium, and high in fiber and vitamins C and K.

1 large onion, minced
1 tablespoon butter
2 tablespoons water
1½ pounds green cabbage, finely sliced or shredded
3 tablespoons butter
4 tablespoons whole wheat pastry flour
1½ cups milk
2 teaspoons minced marjoram or ½ teaspoon dried marjoram
⅛ teaspoon cayenne pepper
1 tablespoon butter, melted
½ cup whole wheat breadcrumbs
2 tablespoons grated Parmesan cheese

Cook the onion in 1 tablespoon of butter and water over low heat until it is tender and the liquid has evaporated.

In a very large bowl combine the cabbage and onion, and set aside.

In a medium saucepan melt 3 tablespoons of butter, stir in the flour and cook, stirring constantly, for 2 minutes.

In a small saucepan heat the milk.

Remove the flour mixture from the heat, and pour in the hot milk. With a wire whisk beat the milk and flour together until they are smooth. Return to the stove and cook over medium heat, stirring constantly, until the mixture bubbles and becomes very thick. Stir in the marjoram and cayenne.

Pour the sauce over the cabbage and stir well to blend.

Spread the mixture in a well-buttered, 9-inch-square baking dish.

In a small bowl combine the melted butter, breadcrumbs and cheese, and then sprinkle over the cabbage.

Bake at 400°F for 20 minutes, or until the cabbage is just heated through. Do not overcook. Serve immediately.

Serves 4.

Curried Cabbage and Apples

1 large onion, thinly sliced
1 tablespoon butter
1 teaspoon *Curry Powder* (see *Index*)
½ pound cabbage, thinly sliced
1 tart apple, thinly sliced
1 tablespoon raisins
½ cup stock
2 tablespoons minced parsley

In a large frying pan cook the onion in butter over low heat for a minute or two. Add the *Curry Powder* and cook another minute, stirring frequently to distribute the curry.

Add the cabbage, apple, raisins and stock; cover and cook over low heat until the cabbage is tender, about 10 minutes.

Remove the lid, raise the heat and allow most of the liquid to evaporate; stir to prevent sticking.

Sprinkle on the parsley.

Serves 4.

Fennel Carrots

I first had carrots with fennel at my favorite restaurant, the Landis Store Hotel near Boyertown, Pennsylvania, and I loved the slight anise taste of fennel with the sweetness of carrots. Only fresh fennel will do, and don't use the seeds.

1 pound carrots
1 tablespoon butter
¼ cup stock
2 tablespoons minced fennel

Cut the carrots into julienne pieces (matchsticks about ⅛ by ⅛ by 2 inches).

In a large frying pan combine the carrots, butter, stock and fennel; cover and simmer over low heat until the carrots are tender. Remove the lid and cook for a few minutes more to evaporate the remaining liquid.

Serves 4.

Apple-Carrot Curry

Here's a sweet and spicy side dish for fish or other bland entrees. The carrots and apples are an ideal combination.

1 large onion, thinly sliced
1 tablespoon olive oil
1 tablespoon butter
1 tablespoon *Curry Powder* (see *Index*)
4 large carrots, thinly sliced on diagonal
¼ cup stock or water
2 tart apples, peeled, cored and thinly sliced
1 teaspoon grated lemon rind
1 tablespoon minced oregano or 1 teaspoon dried oregano
1 tablespoon minced parsley

Cook the onion in oil and butter for several minutes until the onion softens. Add the *Curry Powder* and stir to disperse it.

Add the carrots and stock or water, and cook, covered, for about 10 minutes, or until the carrots are tender.

Add the apple slices and lemon rind, and cook, stirring frequently, for a few minutes more, or until the apples just begin to soften. Do not overcook.

Stir in the oregano and parsley. Cook 1 minute.

Serves 4.

Gold and Platinum

Carrots and parsnips complement each other well because they require the same amount of cooking time and taste great together.

3 carrots
3 parsnips
2 large shallots, minced
1 tablespoon butter
2 tablespoons stock
1 tablespoon minced basil or 1 teaspoon dried basil
1 tablespoon minced chervil or 1 teaspoon dried chervil

Cut the carrots and parsnips into julienne pieces (matchsticks about ⅛ by ⅛ by 2 inches).

Bring an inch of water to a boil in a medium saucepan. Put the carrots and parsnips into a steamer basket and place it in the pan, making sure that the water level does not rise above the steamer. Steam, tightly covered, for 10 minutes, or until the vegetables are tender.

Cook the shallots in the butter and stock in a large frying pan over low heat until tender. Cook a few minutes more to evaporate the remaining liquid.

Stir in the cooked vegetables, basil and chervil.

Serves 4.

Curried Gold and Platinum

3 carrots
3 parsnips
1 tablespoon olive oil
3 tablespoons stock
1 tablespoon *Curry Powder* (see *Index*)
1 large onion, thinly sliced

Cut the carrots and parsnips into julienne pieces (matchsticks about ⅛ by ⅛ by 2 inches).

Bring an inch of water to a boil in a medium saucepan. Put the carrots and parsnips into a steamer basket and place in the pan, making sure that the water level does not rise above the steamer. Steam, tightly covered, for 10 minutes, or until the vegetables are very tender.

Combine the oil, stock, *Curry Powder* and onion in a large frying pan, and cook, covered, until the onion is very tender. Remove the lid and cook for several minutes more, until most of the liquid has evaporated. Stir in the steamed vegetables.

Serves 4.

Carrots and Parsnips with Basil

Another pairing of carrots and parsnips.

½ pound carrots
½ pound parsnips
1 tablespoon butter
1 tablespoon minced basil or 1 teaspoon dried
    basil
1 tablespoon lemon juice

Cut the carrots and parsnips into strips or slices. Cook in about ½ inch of water until they are tender. Pour off the water.

Toss with butter, basil and lemon juice.

Serves 4.

Sorrel

Sorrel is a refreshing salad herb recommended in herbals as a cooling, cleansing tea for fevers and urinary complaints. They say an infusion of the leaves and flowers may provide relief from mouth ulcers and sore throat, and they also suggest using a sorrel wash or poultice for skin problems.

Curried Carrots and Bananas

I've enjoyed curried bananas ever since I first had them at a Scandinavian restaurant in Toronto, where they were served with a simple sautéed fish. This variation combines bananas with carrots, mushrooms and green peppers and will stand up to the heartiest main dish.

1 large onion, thinly sliced
½ cup sliced mushrooms
1 tablespoon olive oil
1 tablespoon butter
2 teaspoons *Curry Powder* (see *Index*)
4 large carrots, thinly sliced on diagonal
1 green pepper, thinly sliced into strips
½ cup stock
2 ripe bananas, cut into ⅜-inch slices
1 tablespoon minced thyme or 1 teaspoon
    dried thyme

Sauté the onion and mushrooms in oil and butter in a large frying pan for several minutes. Add the *Curry Powder* and stir to disperse it.

Add the carrots, pepper and stock; cover and simmer for about 10 minutes, or until the carrots are almost tender. Then, add the bananas, and cook a few minutes longer, stirring frequently; be careful not to mash the bananas. Add the thyme. If there is any liquid left in the pan, cook rapidly until it evaporates.

Serves 4.

Minted Julienne of Carrots

The fresh taste of mint is a surprisingly good accent for cooked carrots.

1 pound carrots
1 tablespoon butter
¼ cup stock
1 tablespoon chopped mint or 1 teaspoon
    dried mint
2 tablespoons snipped chives
1 teaspoon lemon juice
  chive flowers (as a garnish)

Cut the carrots into julienne pieces (matchsticks about ⅛ by ⅛ by 2 inches).

Combine the carrots, butter and stock in a large frying pan; cover and cook over low heat until the carrots are tender. Remove the lid and simmer a few minutes more to cook off the remaining liquid.

Toss with mint, chives and lemon juice.

Garnish with the chive flowers.

Serves 4.

Dilled Carrots

1 pound carrots
1 tablespoon butter
2 tablespoons minced dill or 2 teaspoons dried
    dill

Cut the carrots into julienne pieces (matchsticks about ⅛ by ⅛ by 2 inches).

Bring an inch of water to a boil in a medium saucepan, put the carrots into a steamer basket, and place it in the pan. Make sure that the water does not rise above the level of the steamer. Steam, tightly covered, for 10 minutes, or until the carrots are very tender.

Transfer to a large serving bowl, and toss gently with butter and dill.

Serves 4.

Dilled Cauliflower

Steamed cauliflower adorned with chopped herbs is low in sodium and high in vitamin C, fiber and bioflavonoids.

1 head of cauliflower
1 tablespoon butter
1 tablespoon minced dill or 1 teaspoon dried dill
1 tablespoon minced parsley
1 teaspoon snipped chives

Bring an inch of water to a boil in a large saucepan. Break the cauliflower into florets, and put them into a steamer basket and place it in the pan, making sure that the water level does not rise above the steamer. Steam, tightly covered, for 10 minutes, or until the cauliflower is tender.

Toss lightly with butter, dill, parsley and chives.

Serves 4.

Buttered Cauliflower and Crumbs

2 cloves garlic, minced
1 tablespoon butter
1 tablespoon olive oil
½ cup whole wheat breadcrumbs
1 tablespoon lemon juice
2 tablespoons minced parsley
½ teaspoon minced marjoram or ¼ teaspoon dried marjoram
1 head of cauliflower

Gently cook the garlic in butter and oil over low heat for 2 minutes, stirring constantly. Add the breadcrumbs, lemon juice, parsley and marjoram.

Separate the cauliflower into florets. Bring an inch of water to a boil in a medium saucepan. Put the cauliflower into a steamer basket and place it in the pan, making sure that the water level does not rise above the steamer. Steam, tightly covered, for 10 minutes, or until the cauliflower is tender. Do not overcook.

Transfer to a serving dish and sprinkle with the breadcrumbs.

Serves 4.

Basiled Beet Greens

Beet greens are good sources of potassium and vitamin A, and they also contain calcium, iron and vitamin C. What's more, they are low in fat and contain a reasonable amount of protein.

4 large shallots, minced
¼ cup stock
1 tablespoon butter
1 pound beet greens
3 tablespoons minced basil or 1 teaspoon dried basil
1 tablespoon toasted sesame seeds

In a large frying pan over low heat, cook the shallots in stock and butter until they are soft.

Wash the beet greens well and remove the thick stems. Shred or leave them whole, add to the pan along with the basil, and cook, using only the water left clinging to the greens; cook only until they wilt. Stir over medium heat to evaporate the excess liquid. Sprinkle with sesame seeds.

Serves 4.

Savory Green Beans

1 pound green beans
1 tablespoon butter
2 teaspoons minced savory or ¾ teaspoon dried savory

Bring an inch of water to a boil in a large saucepan. Put the beans into a steamer basket and place it in the pan, making sure that the water level does not rise above the steamer. Steam the beans, tightly covered, for 5 minutes or until they are just tender. Do not overcook.

Toss with butter and savory.

Serves 4.

Parsnips au Gratin

One of my favorite ways to enjoy parsnips. Pretty with the tomatoes and melted cheese.

1 pound parsnips
1 large onion, thinly sliced
1 tablespoon butter
¼ cup stock
1 large tomato
2 ounces thinly sliced Swiss or Gruyère cheese

Cut the parsnips into julienne pieces (matchsticks about ⅛ by ⅛ by 2 inches).

In a large frying pan cook the onion in the butter over medium-low heat for 5 minutes. Add the stock and parsnips, cover and cook until tender, about 10 minutes.

Lightly butter a 9-inch pie plate, and transfer the parsnips to it.

Slice off the stem end of the tomato, and cut it in half crosswise. Gently squeeze each half to remove the seeds and juice, and then cut into very thin slices.

Arrange the tomato slices over the parsnips, and cover with cheese. Broil until the cheese is melted and bubbly.

Serves 4.

Eggplant Medley

In this spicy mixture similar to ratatouille, the eggplant is low in calories, fat and sodium, but high in potassium. Enjoy this dish hot or cold. It can be made ahead, because the flavors improve in the refrigerator. You might want to adjust the amount of fiery cayenne pepper to your taste.

¼ cup olive oil
1½ cups thinly sliced onions
1 clove garlic, minced
1 small eggplant (about 1 pound)
1 small zucchini, thinly sliced
1 pepper, sliced
1 cup thinly sliced mushrooms
2 cups chopped tomatoes
2 tablespoons minced parsley
2 tablespoons minced basil or 2 teaspoons dried basil
1 tablespoon minced oregano or 1 teaspoon dried oregano
1 teaspoon minced thyme or ½ teaspoon dried thyme
¼ teaspoon cayenne pepper (or to taste)
½ cup grated Parmesan cheese

Heat the oil in a Dutch oven or 5-quart, flameproof casserole. Add the onions and cook over medium heat until soft, stirring frequently.

Add the garlic and stir for another minute. Do not let the garlic burn.

Cut the eggplant into ½-inch cubes. Add it and the zucchini, pepper, mushrooms, tomatoes, parsley, basil, oregano, thyme and cayenne to the pot. Cover and cook over medium-low heat for 10 minutes, or until the vegetables have released their juices.

Now, raise the heat to medium and continue to cook, covered, for another 20 to 30 minutes, or until the vegetables are soft. Stir occasionally. If the vegetables become too dry, add some stock or water to the pan.

Sprinkle with cheese and serve hot or cold.

Serves 4.

Thyme for Baked Onions

Slow baking turns the onions sweet and mild.

2 large red onions
4 teaspoons olive oil
1 tablespoon thyme leaves or 1 teaspoon dried thyme

Peel the onions, cut off the root end and slice in half lengthwise.

In a small cup combine the olive oil and thyme, and brush it on the cut side of the onions. Arrange the onions, cut side down, in a shallow baking dish, and brush with more oil.

Bake at 350°F for 45 to 60 minutes, or until tender. Baste occasionally with oil.

Serves 4.

Mint Peas

Peas are low in fat and sodium but high in potassium, protein and fiber. They also contain iron and calcium.

1 pound shelled peas
1 tablespoon butter
1 tablespoon minced spearmint or 1 teaspoon dried mint
1 teaspoon grated lemon rind

Bring a small amount of water to a boil in a large saucepan or frying pan. Add the peas and cook, covered, for just a few minutes, or until the peas are tender. Do not overcook.

Drain off any remaining liquid, and toss the peas with butter, mint and lemon rind.

Serves 4.

Tarragon

Tarragon derives its name from the Latin word for "little dragon." According to herbal lore, this herb was able to cure the bites and stings of venomous beasts. The leaves, say herbalists, may help to revive the appetite and improve digestion, but are seldom used medicinally.

Garlic and New Potatoes

This is a technique I learned from Judith Olney at her classes in North Carolina. The slow cooking softens both the flavor and the texture of the garlic, and it's wonderful with French bread.

12 small new potatoes, all about same size
1-2 tablespoons olive oil
12 large unpeeled cloves garlic
 2 bay leaves
 2 tablespoons minced parsley

Scrub the potatoes carefully so as not to damage the skins. Dry thoroughly.

Pour the olive oil into a shallow baking dish just large enough to hold the potatoes in a single layer. Add the potatoes and garlic, and toss in the oil to completely coat them. If necessary, add a bit more oil.

Break the bay leaves in half, and bury among the potatoes.

Bake at 350°F for 45 to 60 minutes, or until the potatoes are tender. Remove the bay leaves.

Sprinkle the potatoes and garlic with parsley. As you eat, peel the garlic cloves, mash with fork, and spread on the potatoes.

Serves 4.

Golden Mashed Potatoes

These are very pretty potatoes with a vitamin A bonus—squash.

1 pound baking potatoes
1 pound butternut squash
5 cloves unpeeled garlic
1 tablespoon butter
¼-½ cup milk
 ¼ cup minced parsley

Peel the potatoes, and cut them into ½-inch cubes. Cover with water in a covered pan and cook until tender. Drain off the liquid and return the potatoes to the heat. Stir over medium heat for about 1 minute to remove any excess moisture.

Peel the squash. Cut it in half, remove the seeds and then cut it into 1-inch cubes. Bring an inch of water to a boil in a medium saucepan. Put the squash into a steamer basket and place it in the pan, making sure that the water level does not rise above the steamer. Steam, tightly covered, for 5 to 10 minutes, or until the squash is tender. Pour off the water, and then return the squash to the heat. Stir over medium heat for about 1 minute to remove any excess moisture.

Cook the garlic in boiling water for 2 minutes. The skins will then slip off easily and the garlic will be reduced in strength. Mince it, then mash to a paste.

In a small saucepan heat the milk.

Using a food mill, potato ricer, electric mixer or old-fashioned potato masher, blend the squash and potatoes together until smooth. Beat in the garlic, butter and enough hot milk to make a creamy mixture. Beat in the parsley.

Serves 4.

Radical Radishes

What makes these radishes sort of radical is that they're cooked, which tames their bite.

1 pound small red radishes
¾ cup stock
2 teaspoons minced thyme or ½ teaspoon dried thyme
1 tablespoon butter

Trim the radishes, and cut the large ones in half to speed the cooking.

Add the radishes and stock to a large saucepan or medium frying pan, cover and cook until they are easily pierced with a fork.

Add the thyme and butter and cook, uncovered, until most of the liquid evaporates.

Serves 4.

Minted Acorn Squash

2 medium acorn squash
4 teaspoons butter, melted
2 teaspoons honey
2 teaspoons chopped mint or ½ teaspoon dried
    mint
 grated nutmeg

Cut the squash in half lengthwise, and scoop out and discard the seeds. Place in a large pan with about an inch of water, cover and cook until it is easily pierced with a fork. Be careful that the water does not boil away.

Drain any water from the squash cavities, and transfer to an ovenproof dish.

In a small bowl combine the butter, honey and mint, and then drizzle it into the cavities of the squash; sprinkle with a little grated nutmeg.

Broil about 6 inches from the element for about 5 minutes.

Serves 4.

Dilled Squash

1 large butternut squash (about 2 pounds)
1 tablespoon butter
½ teaspoon honey
1 tablespoon minced dill or 1 teaspoon dried
    dill
1 tablespoon snipped chives

Peel the squash, cut it in half, and remove the seeds. Cut the flesh into 1-inch cubes.

Bring an inch of water to a boil in a large saucepan. Put the squash into a steamer basket and place it in the pan, making sure that the water level does not rise above the steamer. Steam the squash, tightly covered, for about 5 minutes, or until it is tender.

Transfer to a serving dish, and toss with butter, honey, dill and chives.

Serves 4.

Butternut Squash *aux Fines Herbes*

Easy squash with a French touch — this is best when made with fresh herbs.

1 large butternut squash (about 2 pounds)
1 tablespoon olive oil
1 large onion, thinly sliced
2-3 large mushrooms, thinly sliced
¼ cup stock
1½ teaspoons minced chervil or ½ teaspoon
    dried chervil
½ teaspoon minced tarragon or ¼ teaspoon
    dried tarragon
1 tablespoon minced parsley
1½ teaspoons snipped chives

Peel the squash, remove the seeds, and cut into ¾-inch cubes.

Heat the oil in a large frying pan over medium-low heat, and add the onion and mushrooms. Sauté for about 5 minutes, or until the onion softens.

Add the squash and stock, cover tightly, and cook until it is tender, about 20 minutes. (If you are using dried chervil and tarragon, add after 15 minutes of cooking.)

Remove the cover and cook a minute or two longer to evaporate most of the remaining liquid. Sprinkle on the parsley, chives, fresh chervil and tarragon.

Serves 4.

Thymed Butternut Squash

Fluffy mashed squash with just a hint of the herbs.

1 large butternut squash
1 tablespoon butter
1 tablespoon milk
1 teaspoon honey
  dash of ground cinnamon or grated nutmeg
1 tablespoon thyme leaves or 1 teaspoon dried
  thyme

Cut the squash in half lengthwise, scoop out and discard the seeds.

Place the squash in a large frying pan with about an inch of water, cover and cook until it is easily pierced with a fork. Be careful that the water does not boil away.

With a spoon remove the pulp from the skin, and mash it well. Beat in the butter, milk, honey, cinnamon or nutmeg and thyme, and whip until fluffy.

Serves 4.

Apple-Stuffed Acorn Squash

TIP: *Use a serrated grapefruit spoon to clean out the squash. The sharp edges remove the tough fibers while the bowl scoops out the seeds.*

2 medium acorn squash
1 apple, diced
2 tablespoons orange juice
1 tablespoon minced dill or 1 teaspoon dried
  dill
1 tablespoon raisins
1 tablespoon butter, melted
2 teaspoons honey
½ teaspoon grated lemon rind

Cut the squash in half lengthwise, and scoop out and discard the seeds.

In a small bowl combine the apple, orange juice, dill, raisins, butter, honey and lemon rind. Fill the squash halves with the mixture.

Place the filled squash in a baking dish, and add an inch of water. Cover with foil.

Bake at 350°F for 45 minutes. Uncover and bake for 15 minutes more, or until the squash is thoroughly tender.

Serves 4.

Stewed Tomatoes and Peppers

5 medium tomatoes (about 1½ pounds)
1 large onion, thinly sliced
1 tablespoon oil
2 cloves garlic, minced
2 peppers, thinly sliced
1 tablespoon minced marjoram or 1 teaspoon
  dried marjoram
1 tablespoon minced oregano or 1 teaspoon
  dried oregano
1 tablespoon minced basil or 1 teaspoon dried
  basil
¼ teaspoon sweet Hungarian paprika

Dip the whole tomatoes into boiling water for about 20 seconds, and then remove the stem end with a sharp knife. The skin should peel off easily. Cut the tomatoes in half crosswise, and squeeze each half to remove the seeds and excess juice. Chop coarsely.

Sauté the onion in oil until limp. Add the garlic, peppers, tomatoes, marjoram, oregano, basil and paprika.

Now, cover and cook over medium heat until the vegetables are tender and the tomatoes have cooked down. Remove the cover and cook over medium heat, stirring frequently, until most of the liquid has evaporated.

Serves 4.

Tomatoes Provencale

Simple baked tomatoes with a basil and breadcrumb topping.

4 large tomatoes
1 tablespoon butter
1 tablespoon olive oil
2 cloves garlic, minced
2 tablespoons minced parsley
2 teaspoons minced basil or ½ teaspoon dried basil
1 tablespoon lemon juice
⅓ cup whole wheat breadcrumbs
¼ cup grated Parmesan cheese

Carefully cut the stem end from the tomatoes, removing as little flesh as possible. Cut the tomatoes in half crosswise, and squeeze the pieces gently to remove the seeds and excess juice. Drain the pieces upside down for 5 minutes.

In a small frying pan heat the butter and oil until they foam. Add the garlic and cook over low heat for several minutes, stirring frequently; do not let the garlic brown.

Remove from the heat and stir in the parsley, basil, lemon juice, breadcrumbs and Parmesan.

Now, arrange the tomatoes, cut side up, on a buttered baking dish. Bake at 350°F for 10 minutes.

Then, top each tomato with the crumb mixture, and return to the oven for 15 minutes.

Serves 4.

Thyme

The Romans used thyme to purify and freshen the air. They also believed it could instill courage through its invigorating qualities. Today herbals chiefly regard thyme as an effective antiseptic useful in treating mouth ulcers, wounds and scalp disorders. And they recommend the tea for colds, bronchial problems and indigestion.

Julienne Turnips and Carrots

2 large carrots
4 large turnips
½ cup sliced mushrooms
4 large shallots, minced
1 tablespoon butter
3 tablespoons minced dill or 2 teaspoons dried dill
1 tablespoon minced parsley
2 tablespoons grated Parmesan cheese

Cut the carrots and turnips into julienne pieces (matchsticks about ⅛ by ⅛ by 2 inches).

Bring an inch of water to a boil in a medium saucepan. Put the carrots and turnips into a steamer basket and place it in the pan, making sure that the water level does not rise above the steamer. Steam, tightly covered, for 8 to 10 minutes, or until the vegetables are tender.

In a large frying pan, sauté the mushrooms and shallots in butter until they are soft. Add the carrots and turnips and then the dill, parsley and Parmesan. Toss gently to mix.

Serves 4.

Tomatoes Stuffed with Potato-Turnip Puree

A unique dish that can be adapted to any other vegetable puree.

4 large tomatoes
¾ pound baking potatoes
¾ pound turnips
¼ cup grated Parmesan cheese
1 tablespoon butter
1 tablespoon minced dill or ½ teaspoon dried dill

Cut the top quarter off each tomato, and scoop out the seeds and pulp; leaving a shell ¼ inch thick. Allow the tomatoes to drain upside down until you are ready to fill them.

Peel the potatoes and turnips, and cut them into ½-inch cubes. In separate pots, cover them with water and cook until tender. Drain both vegetables and return them to their respective pots. Cook over medium heat, stirring constantly, for about 2 minutes to evaporate any remaining moisture.

Puree the potatoes and turnips together. Add the cheese, butter and dill to produce a thick mixture. If it is not, place in a large frying pan and cook over medium heat, stirring constantly, until it thickens.

Using a spoon or pastry bag fitted with a large star tip, fill the tomato shells with puree.

Bake on a buttered platter for 10 minutes at 350°F. Do not overbake to keep the shells from splitting.

Serves 4.

Zucchini *al Pesto*

¼ cup (packed) basil leaves
3 tablespoons olive oil
2 tablespoons grated Parmesan cheese
1 tablespoon pine nuts
1 clove garlic, minced
3 small zucchini (about 1 pound)
1 tablespoon butter

In a blender or food processor blend the basil, oil, Parmesan, pine nuts and garlic into a paste.

Cut the zucchini into julienne pieces (matchsticks about ⅛ by ⅛ by 2 inches).

Heat the butter in a large frying pan until it foams, and add the zucchini. Stir-fry about 3 minutes, or until tender-crisp. Add the basil mixture and toss to coat.

Serves 4.

Zucchini au Gratin

2 tablespoons butter
¾ cup minced onions
1 clove garlic, minced
1 pound zucchini, shredded and squeezed dry
2 tablespoons sour cream or yogurt
2 tablespoons grated Parmesan cheese

Melt the butter in a large frying pan over low heat. And the onions and garlic, and cook until the onions are wilted. Add the zucchini and cook, stirring constantly, until it is tender and any remaining liquid has evaporated.

Stir in the sour cream or yogurt and the Parmesan.

Serves 4.

Zucchini Provencale

1 large onion, minced
½ pepper, minced
½ cup sliced mushrooms
2 cloves garlic, minced
2 tablespoons olive oil
1 small zucchini, thinly sliced
1 tomato, diced
¼ cup *Tomato Sauce* (see *Index*)
1 tablespoon minced oregano or 1 teaspoon dried oregano
1 tablespoon minced basil or 1 teaspoon dried basil

In a large frying pan over medium-low heat, sauté the onion, pepper, mushrooms and garlic in oil until the vegetables are limp.

Stir in the zucchini, tomato, *Tomato Sauce*, oregano, and basil; cover and simmer for about 5 minutes or until the tomato has softened.

Uncover and continue to cook, stirring constantly, until the zucchini is tender and the sauce is thick.

Serves 4.

Broccoli Custards

Individual baked custards brimming with broccoli. Do not overcook the broccoli before adding it to the other ingredients or both its color and its nutrients will turn sickly. Broccoli is a good source of vitamin A, potassium and vitamin C.

1 large onion, minced
1 tablespoon butter
3 eggs
2 cups chopped, lightly steamed broccoli
½ cup half-and-half
½ cup shredded Cheddar cheese
  few gratings of nutmeg

Butter or coat with equal parts of oil and liquid lecithin six ¾-cup custard cups. Fit a square of wax paper into the bottom of each and butter or grease it.

Cook the onion in butter over low heat until it is tender.

Place the onion, eggs, broccoli, half-and-half, Cheddar and nutmeg in a blender or food processor and process until they are smooth.

Pour the mixture into the prepared cups, filling them about two-thirds full. Cover each with a buttered square of foil, and transfer to a large pan or baking dish big enough to hold them all. Add hot water to the pan until the level reaches about halfway up the sides of the cups.

Bake at 350°F for about 30 minutes, or until a knife inserted in the center of a custard comes out clean. Remove the cups from the pan, and let cool for 5 minutes. Then, run a knife around the edge of each cup, and unmold the custard onto a plate. Peel the wax paper off the bottom.

Serves 6.

Peach Chutney

A spicy, sweet condiment perfect with almost any meat.

2 cups chopped peaches
1 cup chopped mango flesh
½ cup chopped dates
¼ cup water
¼ cup white vinegar
2 tablespoons honey
1 tablespoon lemon juice
1 clove garlic, minced
¾ teaspoon mustard seeds
¼ teaspoon powdered ginger
⅛ teaspoon cayenne pepper
⅛ teaspoon ground allspice

Combine the peaches, mango, dates, water, vinegar, honey, lemon juice, garlic, mustard seeds, ginger, cayenne and allspice in a large saucepan.

Cover and simmer over medium heat for 45 minutes, stirring frequently to prevent sticking.

Remove the lid and simmer for another 15 to 30 minutes, or until very thick. Stir frequently.

Store in refrigerator or freezer.

Makes about 1 pint.

Banana Raita

This is a refreshing side dish for spicy foods.

2 tablespoons honey
¼ teaspoon nutmeg
1 cup yogurt
2 small bananas, thinly sliced
2 tablespoons sunflower seeds

In a bowl, whisk the honey, nutmeg and yogurt together. Fold in the bananas and sunflower seeds, and chill for 1 hour.

Serves 4.

Shezan Cucumber Raita

A sweet and spicy side dish adapted from the menu of the Shezan Restaurant on 58th Street in New York City.

1 medium cucumber
1 pint yogurt
2 tablespoons honey
¼ cup golden raisins
¼ cup black currants
½ teaspoon *Garam Masalla* (see *Index*)
¼ teaspoon cumin seeds
2 tablespoons minced parsley
  paprika

Peel and seed the cucumber, and then grate or shred it finely. Mix with the yogurt and honey.

Place the raisins and currants in four small serving dishes, and spoon the yogurt mixture over them.

Sprinkle all with *Garam Masalla*, cumin, parsley and paprika.

Refrigerate for about an hour before serving.

Serves 4.

Carrot and Chive Timbales

½ pound carrots, diced
1 medium onion, minced
1 tablespoon butter
½ cup half-and-half
3 eggs
1 tablespoon snipped chives
1 tablespoon minced dill or 1 teaspoon dried dill
¼ cup grated Parmesan cheese

Butter or coat with equal parts of oil and liquid lecithin six ¾-cup custard cups or ramekins. Fit a square of wax paper into the bottom of each and butter it.

Bring an inch of water to a boil in a large saucepan. Put the carrots into a steamer basket and place it in the pan, making sure that the water level does not rise above the steamer. Steam, tightly covered, for 15 minutes, or until the carrots are very tender.

In a small frying pan sauté the onion in butter until tender but not browned.

Combine the carrots and onions in a blender or food processor. Add the half-and-half and process until smooth. Now, add the eggs, chives, dill and Parmesan, and process until smooth and light.

Pour into the prepared cups, and cover each with a buttered square of foil. Transfer to a large baking dish, and add enough hot water to the dish until the level reaches about halfway up the sides of the cups.

Bake at 350°F for about 30 minutes, or until a knife inserted in the center of a custard comes out clean. Remove from the baking pan, and let cool for 5 minutes. Run a knife around the edges of each cup, and unmold onto a plate. Peel the wax paper off the bottom.

Serves 6.

Sweet Cardamom Boats

2 large sweet potatoes (about 1½ pounds)
2 tablespoons milk
1 tablespoon honey
1 tablespoon butter, melted
1 teaspoon *Vanilla Extract* (see *Index*)
¼ teaspoon grated nutmeg
⅛ teaspoon ground cardamom

Pierce the sweet potatoes in one or two places to allow moisture to escape and bake them at 375°F for an hour or more; a skewer will pierce the flesh easily when they are done.

Allow the potatoes to cool. When they are cool enough to handle, cut them in half lengthwise, and scoop out the pulp, leaving a shell about ¼ inch thick.

Transfer the pulp to a small bowl, mash it, and then beat in the milk, honey, butter, vanilla, nutmeg and cardamom. Spoon the mixture back into the shells.

Bake at 350°F for about 10 minutes.

Serves 4.

Chapter 13
Desserts

An Apple a Day

It's no wonder that old wives said that an apple a day can keep the doctor away. Apples are low in sodium and high in fiber, potassium and pectin. You already know that pectin is what makes jellies gel, but did you know that it has valuable health benefits too? Studies have shown that pectin can reduce cholesterol levels in the bloodstream, apparently by blocking the absorption of those fats. In addition, pectin may help fight diabetes by combating the rise in blood sugar associated with the disease. And it may also help protect us against certain environmental poisons (like lead and strontium 90) by blocking their absorption into the body.

The best way to get pectin into your diet is by eating apples—preferably with their skins on. Other good sources of pectin include avocados, bananas, carob, cherries, grapes, peaches, pineapple, raisins, raspberries, sunflower seeds and tomatoes.

Because apples are so beneficial to health, I've featured them in a number of dessert recipes. You'll notice that some of these recipes specify "baking" apples, while others call for "cooking" apples. The difference is that baking apples hold their shape better under heat, and are thus better for pies and tarts. Cooking apples, on the other hand, soften faster and are perfect for applesauce. Here are lists of the readily available baking and cooking apples:

Baking Apples

Cortland	Rhode Island Greening
Golden Delicious	Rome Beauty
Granny Smith	Stayman
Jonathan	Winesap
Northern Spy	York Imperial

Cooking Apples

Cortland	McIntosh
Gravenstein	Rome Beauty
Jonathan	Stayman

Ruby Crowned Apples

Choose firm baking apples that won't lose their shape during the steaming. Top these apples with raspberries and use them for dessert or as a side dish to meats.

4 baking apples (such as Golden Delicious or
  Granny Smith)
2 tablespoons lemon juice
1 tablespoon honey
1 cup apple juice
1 cinnamon stick
4 pieces lemon rind
2 teaspoons *Vanilla Extract* (see page 247)
1 cup raspberries

Starting at the bottom of each apple, remove half the peel and reserve. Rub the peeled sections with lemon juice to prevent discoloration, place the apples in a steamer rack and drizzle with honey.

In a saucepan large enough to hold the steamer, combine the peel, apple juice, cinnamon stick, lemon rind, vanilla and any remaining lemon juice, and bring to a boil.

Now, lower the heat, and place the rack in the pan. Cover it tightly and steam until the apples are tender, about 20 minutes. Do not overcook. Remove steamer rack from the pan, and transfer the apples to a serving dish.

Reduce the liquid until it is syrupy, and then strain it over the apples.

Serve with raspberries.

Serves 4.

Stewed Fruit Compote

This easy compote is loaded with the fiber and iron of the dried fruits, and the applesauce kicks in its pectin, too. Serve the compote warm or cold, as a dessert — when it's great with the Creamy Custard Sauce *(see page 246) — or as a side dish with meats.*

1 cup applesauce or *Lemon Apple Delight* (see
  page 226)
1 cup apple juice or water
 juice and grated rind of 1 lemon
2 tablespoons honey
1 tablespoon *Vanilla Extract* (see page 247)
½ teaspoon ground cinnamon
¼ teaspoon powdered ginger
¼ teaspoon grated nutmeg
½ cup dried apricot halves
½ cup dried prunes, pitted
 5 dried figs, halved
¼ cup currants
¼ cup golden raisins
 1 pear, thinly sliced

In a 2-quart casserole combine the applesauce or *Lemon Apple Delight,* the apple juice or water, the lemon juice and rind, the honey, vanilla, cinnamon, ginger and nutmeg.

Stir in the apricots, prunes, figs, currants, raisins and pear.

Cover and bake at 300°F for 1½ hours.

Serve warm or cold.

Serves 4.

Apple Custard Pudding

An unusual dessert that's halfway between apple-sauce and a thick custard. Baking it in a bain-marie (water bath) helps it bake slowly to maintain creaminess.

1 cup applesauce
3 eggs
½ cup half-and-half
2 tablespoons honey
   juice and grated rind of ½ lemon
1 tablespoon *Vanilla Extract* (see page 247)
¼ teaspoon grated nutmeg
¼ cup whole wheat breadcrumbs
2 tablespoons currants or raisins

Beat together the applesauce, eggs, half-and-half, honey, lemon juice and rind, vanilla, nutmeg, breadcrumbs and currants or raisins.

Pour the mixture into a buttered, 1½-quart casserole dish, and place the casserole in a large, shallow baking dish. Add hot water until the level rises about halfway up the side of the casserole.

Place in the oven, and bake at 350°F for about 50 minutes, or until a knife inserted in the center comes out clean.

Chill before serving.

Serves 4.

Panned Apples

A wonderful breakfast side dish that I first enjoyed on a trip to Virginia. For maximum fiber and pectin, don't peel the apples.

3 baking apples (such as Granny Smith)
2 tablespoons butter
2 tablespoons honey
1 teaspoon lemon juice
1 teaspoon *Vanilla Extract* (see page 247)
½ teaspoon ground cinnamon
   few gratings of nutmeg
2 tablespoons water

If desired, peel the apples. Core, and then cut them into thin slices about ⅜ inch thick.

Melt the butter in a large frying pan, add the honey, lemon juice, vanilla, cinnamon and nutmeg, and stir to combine.

Add the apples to the frying pan, and cook over medium heat, stirring frequently, until they are fork tender, but still retain their shape, about 10 minutes.

Reduce the heat to low, add the water, cover and cook for 5 more minutes.

Serves 4.

Lemon Apple Delight

3 cooking apples (such as McIntosh)
3 baking apples (such as Granny Smith)
1 teaspoon honey
1 teaspoon *Vanilla Extract* (see page 247)
2 tablespoons raisins
½ teaspoon ground cinnamon
⅛ teaspoon cardamom seeds, crushed
2 tablespoons water
2 tablespoons lemon juice
   grated rind of 1 lemon
¼ cup water
1 tablespoon cornstarch

Peel the apples, if desired. Then, quarter them, remove the cores and slice thinly. Combine the apples, honey, vanilla, raisins, cinnamon, cardamom, 2 tablespoons water, lemon juice and rind in a large frying pan or pot.

Cover and cook until the cooking apples have turned to mush and the baking apples are tender. Do not overcook; the baking apples should retain some texture.

In a small cup mix ¼ cup water and the cornstarch, stir into the apples and cook over low heat for a minute or two or until the sauce thickens.

Serve warm or cold.

Serves 4.

Pecan Bananas

A wonderfully simple dessert or side dish with fish with lots of fiber, potassium and pectin plus some protein too. Don't overbake the bananas or they'll collapse on you.

2 tablespoons butter
¼ teaspoon ground cardamom
⅛ teaspoon powdered ginger
2 tablespoons honey
   juice of 2 small oranges (about ½ cup)
4 small firm bananas
¼ cup chopped pecans

Melt the butter in a small saucepan, and stir in the cardamom and ginger. Add the honey and orange juice.

Peel the bananas and cut them in half lengthwise. Arrange them, cut side down, in a shallow baking dish, and sprinkle with the pecans. Pour the flavored juice over the top.

Bake at 375°F for about 10 minutes, or until the bananas are softened and warmed through.
Serves 4.

Nice 'n' Easy Peaches

The name says it all: These peaches are nice, and they are easy. Serve the peaches as is, or use them to top your favorite sponge cake or French toast.

2 tablespoons butter
1 tablespoon honey
½ teaspoon lemon juice
4 large peaches, thinly sliced
⅛ teaspoon grated nutmeg

In a large frying pan heat the butter until it foams. Stir in the honey and lemon juice, and add the peaches and nutmeg. Sauté over medium heat for several minutes, or until the peaches are soft and lightly glazed.

Serves 4.

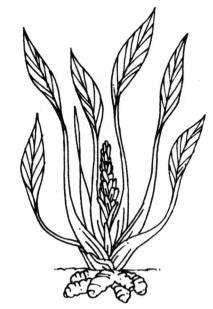

Turmeric

Turmeric is related to ginger and is chiefly used as a curry ingredient because of its pungent, warming flavor and rich color. Turmeric is rarely used in herbalism except as a mild digestive.

Pear Custard

Pears are low in sodium and high in fiber, and the nut topping contributes protein, vitamins, minerals and a rich buttery flavor. This custard is best when made with maple syrup.

The Pears
 2 large pears
 1 tablespoon butter
 1 teaspoon honey
 ¼ teaspoon ground cinnamon
 ¼ teaspoon grated nutmeg
 2 tablespoons water

The Custard
 3 eggs
 2 tablespoons honey
 2 teaspoons *Vanilla Extract* (see page 247)
 2 cups milk

The Topping
 ½ cup chopped pecans
 2 tablespoons butter, melted
 2 tablespoons maple syrup or honey
 3 tablespoons milk or cream

To make the pears: Cut the pears into lengthwise quarters, remove the cores and slice them into ½-inch slices. In a large frying pan combine the pears, butter, honey, cinnamon, nutmeg and water; cover and cook until the pears are tender but not mushy, about 5 minutes over medium heat. Remove the cover and cook, stirring frequently, until all the liquid has evaporated, and the pears have started to caramelize in the butter and honey — just a few minutes.

To make the custard: In a blender or with a wire whisk, combine the eggs, honey, vanilla and milk until smooth.

Fill four 1½-cup or eight ¾-cup custard cups with the pears, and pour the custard over them.

Arrange the cups in a large, shallow baking pan, and transfer to the oven. Add hot water to the pan until the level reaches about halfway up each cup.

Bake at 350°F for about 30 minutes, or until the custard is set and a knife inserted into the center comes out clean.

Remove the cups from the water and cool on a wire rack. Then, refrigerate until they are cold.

To make the topping: Sprinkle the cold custards with chopped nuts.

In a small bowl combine the melted butter, maple syrup or honey and the milk or cream, and pour over the custards.

Broil about 6 inches from the element for a few minutes, or until the topping bubbles. Watch carefully so that the topping does not burn.

Serve the custards immediately.

Makes 4 to 8 servings.

Mincemeat

There's no meat in this masquerading fruit mixture. Use it alone as a side dish for meats, or bake it into a pie. It is also wonderful atop the Ginger Roll *on page 234.*

2½ cups finely chopped apples
 ½ cup currants
 ¼ cup golden raisins
 ¼ cup honey
 ¼ cup chopped pecans
   grated rind of 1 lemon
   juice and grated rind of 1 orange
 ½ cup apple cider or apple juice
 ½ teaspoon ground cinnamon
 ½ teaspoon grated nutmeg
 ⅛ teaspoon ground cloves
   dash of ground allspice
   dash of ground mace

Mincemeat—*continued*

Combine the apples, currants, raisins, honey, pecans, lemon rind, the orange juice and rind, cider or apple juice, cinnamon, nutmeg, cloves, allspice and mace in a saucepan. Bring all to a boil over medium heat, then lower the heat to medium low, and simmer for 20 minutes, or until thick. Stir occasionally to prevent sticking.

Makes 2 cups.

Perfect Poached Pears

4 large firm pears
¾ cup apple or pear juice
1 teaspoon honey
1 teaspoon *Vanilla Extract* (see page 247)
1 cinnamon stick
  several strips of lemon rind
3 tablespoons ground pecans
2 tablespoons currants
½ teaspoon grated lemon rind
  Creamy Custard Sauce (see page 246)

Using a melon baller, core and seed each pear through the bottom.

Combine the juice, honey, vanilla, cinnamon and lemon rind in a saucepan just large enough to hold the pears upright. Add the pears.

Cover and simmer until the pears are easily pierced with a knife (about 30 to 40 minutes, depending on the size and ripeness of the pears). Do not overcook.

In a small bowl combine the pecans, currants and grated lemon rind. Add 1 or 2 tablespoons of the cooking liquid to moisten the mixture, and fill the pears with it.

If desired, serve with the custard sauce.

Serves 4.

Violet

Violets have been known throughout history not only for their sweet scent and rich color, but also for their calming quality. Herbals describe violets as a remedy for nervousness, respiratory problems and mild constipation and say the leaves make a soothing tea for headache.

Plum Pudding

You may wonder where the plums went but don't worry. "Plum Pudding" is simply a traditional name for all steamed puddings made of dried or candied fruits and served during the Thanksgiving and Christmas holidays. What's decidedly untraditional about this recipe are its honey and whole wheat. They've been added in place of the suet and candied fruit that usually start plum puddings off on the road to lots of calories and fat.

If you'd like to increase the pudding's iron content (dried fruits are a good beginning), add some blackstrap molasses.

Tip: *You can make* Plum Pudding *well ahead and store it, tightly wrapped, in the refrigerator. To serve, return the pudding to its original container, cover tightly with foil and steam it for an hour.*

¾ cup whole wheat pastry flour
½ teaspoon baking soda
½ teaspoon ground cinnamon
¼ teaspoon grated nutmeg
6 tablespoons cold butter
¾ cup whole wheat breadcrumbs
½ cup golden raisins
½ cup currants
½ cup chopped walnuts
   grated rind of 1 lemon
   grated rind of 1 orange
2 eggs
2 tablespoons honey
2 tablespoons molasses
⅓ cup milk
   Soft Sauce (see page 246)

Sift the flour, baking soda, cinnamon and nutmeg into a large bowl. Using two knives or a pastry blender, cut in the butter until it forms pieces about the size of small peas. Then, stir in the breadcrumbs, raisins, currants, walnuts, lemon and orange rinds.

In a small bowl combine the eggs, honey, molasses and milk until they are well blended.

Pour the liquid ingredients into the dry ones, and stir well to combine.

Butter a 1½-quart, ovenproof bowl or a plum pudding mold, or coat well with equal parts of oil and liquid lecithin. Fit a piece of wax paper or parchment into the bottom and grease it thoroughly.

Pour the batter into the bowl, and cover tightly with aluminum foil or the lid. (If you are using foil, tie a string around the bowl to ensure a waterproof seal.)

Place a small metal trivet in a pot large enough to hold the pudding. Add 2 inches of water to the pot and bring it to a boil. Now place the pudding on the trivet, cover the pot and lower the heat to simmer.

Cook for 1½ hours.

To unmold, run a thin knife around the sides of the pudding, and unmold onto a plate; carefully remove the paper from the bottom.

Serve warm with the *Soft Sauce.*

Serves 8.

Fancy Figs

It's the anise seeds that "fancify" these figs.

1 pound dried figs
1½ cups water
2 tablespoons honey
¾ teaspoon anise seeds, crushed
1 teaspoon *Vanilla Extract* (see page 247)

In a 2-quart saucepan combine the figs, water, honey, anise and vanilla; cover and simmer over low heat for 45 minutes.

Serve warm or cold.

Serves 4.

Swedish Spice Cake

This dessert is dark in color but surprisingly light in texture, especially when served warm from the oven. The blackstrap molasses is rich in calcium, iron and potassium.

The Cake
1½ cups sifted whole wheat pastry flour
  1 teaspoon *Baking Powder* (see *Index*)
½ teaspoon baking soda
1½ teaspoons ground cinnamon
1½ teaspoons powdered ginger
½ teaspoon ground cloves
¼ teaspoon cardamom seeds, crushed
¼ cup butter, melted
¼ cup honey
¼ cup blackstrap molasses
  2 eggs
½ cup sour cream or *Cottage Cream* (see *Index*)
⅓ cup milk

The Glaze
¼ cup water
  2 tablespoons orange juice
  1 tablespoon honey
  1 teaspoon butter

To make the cake: Generously butter an 8- or 12-cup, fluted tube pan, or coat it with equal parts of oil and liquid lecithin. Dust with wheat germ or whole wheat breadcrumbs, and set aside.

Resift the flour with the *Baking Powder*, baking soda, cinnamon, ginger, cloves and cardamom.

In a large bowl combine the butter, honey, molasses, eggs and the sour cream or *Cottage Cream* and beat until smooth.

Add the milk and flour to the batter by alternating small portions of each so that the mixture does not get too dry. Begin and end with the flour.

Pour the batter into the prepared pan, and smooth the top with a spatula.

Bake at 350°F for 30 to 40 minutes, or until the cake pulls away from the sides of the pan and a toothpick inserted into the cake comes out clean.

Turn out onto a wire rack to cool.

To make the glaze: In a small saucepan, bring the water, orange juice, honey and butter to a boil. Simmer for 5 minutes, and then pour over the warm cake.

Makes 1 cake.

Applesauce Bran Cake

This supercake is loaded with the fiber of a whole cup of bran, the applesauce's potassium and the currants' vitamin C.

2½ cups whole wheat pastry flour
  1 teaspoon *Baking Powder* (see *Index*)
  1 teaspoon baking soda
  2 teaspoons ground cinnamon
½ teaspoon grated nutmeg
¼ teaspoon ground cloves
  1 cup bran
1¼ cups applesauce
½ cup oil
½ cup honey
⅔ cup milk
  2 eggs
  1 cup currants

Butter a 12-cup, fluted tube pan, or coat it with equal parts of oil and liquid lecithin.

Sift the flour, *Baking Powder*, baking soda, cinnamon, nutmeg and cloves into a large bowl, and stir in the bran.

In another bowl combine the applesauce, oil, honey, milk and eggs.

Then, stir the wet ingredients into the dry ones, and add the currants.

Pour the batter into the prepared pan, and bake at 325°F for about 40 minutes, or until a skewer inserted in the center comes out clean.

Makes 1 cake.

Sunflower Apple Cake

Perfect with an afternoon cup of herb tea.

The Cake
2 cups sifted whole wheat pastry flour
2 teaspoons *Baking Powder* (see *Index*)
½ teaspoon baking soda
1 teaspoon ground cinnamon
¾ teaspoon ground cardamom
3 eggs
¼ cup oil
½ cup honey
¼ cup milk
1 teaspoon *Vanilla Extract* (see page 247)
2 cups finely chopped apples
½ cup sunflower seeds

The Glaze
¼ cup water
1 tablespoon honey
1 tablespoon butter
1 teaspoon *Vanilla Extract* (see page 247)

To make the cake: Generously butter a 12-cup, fluted tube pan, or coat it with equal parts of oil and liquid lecithin. Then dust it with wheat germ or whole wheat breadcrumbs, and set aside.

Resift the flour with the *Baking Powder*, baking soda, cinnamon and cardamom, and combine in a large bowl.

In a medium bowl, beat the eggs, oil, honey, milk and vanilla together until they are smooth. Then, pour into the flour mixture and stir to combine. Stir in the apples and sunflower seeds.

Pour the batter into the prepared pan.

Bake at 325°F for about 45 minutes, or until a skewer inserted in the center comes out clean.

Allow the cake to cool in the pan for 15 minutes, and then turn it out onto a wire rack to cool completely.

To make the glaze: Combine the water, honey and butter in a small saucepan, bring to a boil and continue boiling for 2 minutes. Stir in the vanilla.

Place the cake and its rack on a dish, and slowly spoon the glaze over it allowing it to soak in.

Transfer to a clean dish before serving.

Makes 1 cake.

Molasses Cake

2 cups sifted whole wheat pastry flour
1 teaspoon baking soda
1 teaspoon ground cinnamon
¼ teaspoon ground cloves
1 egg
½ cup molasses
2 tablespoons oil
1 cup buttermilk
Creamy Custard Sauce (see page 246)
blueberries, sliced peaches or halved
   strawberries

Butter an 8-inch-square baking pan, or coat it with equal parts of oil and liquid lecithin.

Resift the flour and the baking soda, cinnamon and cloves into a large bowl.

In a small bowl beat the egg, molasses, oil and buttermilk together until they are smooth.

Pour the liquid ingredients into the dry ones, and beat with a wire whisk until well blended, about 15 seconds.

Pour the batter into the prepared pan, and bake at 350°F for 30 minutes, or until a toothpick inserted in the center comes out clean.

Cool the cake in its pan. Then, cut into squares and serve with the custard sauce and blueberries, sliced peaches or strawberries.

Makes 9 to 12 servings.

Pineapple Apple Cake

The Cake

1½ cups whole wheat pastry flour
 1 teaspoon baking soda
 1 teaspoon ground cinnamon
 ¾ teaspoon grated nutmeg
 ¼ cup wheat germ
 ¼ cup softened butter
 ½ cup honey
 2 eggs
 2 teaspoons *Vanilla Extract* (see page 247)
 8 ounces crushed pineapple, undrained
 1 cup finely chopped apples
 ½ cup golden raisins

The Frosting

 6 ounces softened cream cheese
 ¼ cup honey
 1 teaspoon *Vanilla Extract* (see page 247)

To make the cake: Butter a 7-by-11-inch baking pan, or coat it with equal parts of oil and liquid lecithin.

Sift the flour, baking soda, cinnamon and nutmeg into a large bowl, and stir in the wheat germ.

In a smaller bowl beat the butter, honey, eggs and vanilla together until they are well blended. Stir in the pineapple and its juice.

Stir the pineapple mixture into the flour, but do not overbeat. Fold in the apples and raisins.

Pour the batter into the prepared pan, and bake at 350°F for 30 minutes, or until a toothpick inserted in the center comes out clean.

Cool on a wire rack before frosting.

To make the frosting: In a small bowl beat together the cream cheese, honey and vanilla until they are well blended. Spread over the cake.

Makes 12 to 15 servings.

Watercress

Watercress, peppery in taste and rich in vitamin C and iron, has long been used as a salad ingredient. One herbalist suggests watercress for clearing the sinuses and for anemia. The bruised leaves applied to the skin are said to help remove spots and blemishes.

Ginger Roll

For best results the eggs should be at room temperature before beating. If you haven't removed them from the refrigerator beforehand, place them in a pan of warm water for 10 minutes to remove the chill.

Be sure to butter the pan's paper lining and to dust it with flour before adding the batter; it will help prevent sticking later. Even so, be very careful when removing the paper from the hot cake. And to prevent cracking, trim off the crisp edges and roll up the cake immediately.

The Cake
¾ cup whole wheat pastry flour
1 teaspoon powdered ginger
¾ teaspoon ground cinnamon
½ teaspoon grated nutmeg
5 egg whites
5 egg yolks
⅓ cup honey
1 teaspoon *Vanilla Extract* (see page 247)

The Filling
1 teaspoon unflavored gelatin
½ cup milk
2 tablespoons cornstarch
¼ cup milk
2 tablespoons honey
2 egg yolks
1 teaspoon *Vanilla Extract* (see page 247)
½ cup heavy cream

The Topping
hot *Panned Apples* or *Mincemeat* (see pages 226 and 228, respectively)

To make the cake: Oil a 10-by-15-inch jelly-roll pan, line it with wax paper and butter the paper generously. Dust with flour, and set aside.

Sift the flour, ginger, cinnamon and nutmeg together. Set aside.

In a large bowl using clean beaters, beat the egg whites until they form stiff peaks. Set aside.

In another bowl, beat the yolks, honey and vanilla together until they are very thick and lemon colored.

Gently fold one-third of the whites into the yolk mixture. Then sift in one-third of the flour, and gently fold together. Repeat the process twice more with the remaining egg whites and flour. Do not overmix. It is better to leave a few streaks of white than to deflate the egg whites with overbeating.

Spread the mixture evenly in the prepared pan, bake at 375°F for 12 to 15 minutes, or until the cake is puffed and golden.

Remove from the oven, and immediately cover the cake with a sheet of parchment or two sheets of wax paper. Cover all with a cookie sheet, and invert the pan so that the cake is resting upside down on the cookie sheet. Now, remove the pan, and carefully peel off the wax paper.

Starting at one 10-inch side, and using the paper under the cake to help you, roll it into a jelly roll. Set the roll on a wire rack to cool.

To make the filling: Sprinkle the gelatin into the ½ cup of milk. Let it soften for 2 minutes.

In a 1-quart saucepan, mix the cornstarch with the ¼ cup milk and blend until smooth. Stir in the gelatin mixture and honey. Cook over medium heat, stirring constantly with a wooden spoon, until it is thick enough to coat the back of the spoon. Remove from the heat.

In a small cup beat the egg yolks, and then gradually stir in a few tablespoons of hot sauce to warm the eggs. Now add the yolks to the pan and stir well.

Return to the heat and cook, *stirring constantly,* for 1 minute. Again, remove from the heat, and stir in the vanilla.

Whip the heavy cream.

Place the saucepan in a large bowl containing ice cubes and cold water. Stir the sauce constantly until it is cool to the touch; do not let it jell. Then, fold in the whipped cream.

Unroll the cooled cake, being careful not to crack it. Spread it with the filling, and reroll.

To serve, cut into slices, and top them with hot *Panned Apples* or *Mincemeat.*

Serves 6 to 8.

Mammy's Nut Roll

This is a whole wheat version of the nut roll my grandmother makes each Christmas. As it bakes, the top often splits, but that won't hurt the wonderful taste. This delicate dough needs careful handling, so roll it between sheets of wax paper, and gently transfer it to the baking sheet. After the baking, handle the roll carefully until it has cooled, when it will be a little less fragile. Cut the roll with a serrated knife, and, for the best flavor, warm the slices before serving them.

The Pastry
    ½ cup milk
    1 tablespoon dry yeast
    1 tablespoon honey
    6 tablespoons butter, melted
    1 egg yolk
    ½ teaspoon *Vanilla Extract* (see page 247)
1½-2 cups whole wheat pastry flour

The Filling
    ½ pound walnuts, ground
    ½ teaspoon ground cinnamon
    ¼ teaspoon grated nutmeg
    ¼ cup honey
    ¼ cup milk
    ½ teaspoon *Vanilla Extract* (see page 247)
      grated rind of 2 oranges
    1 egg yolk beaten with 1 teaspoon milk (as
      a glaze)

To make the pastry: Heat the milk to lukewarm and then combine it with the yeast and honey in a cup. Set aside until the yeast forms.

Beat in the butter, egg yolk and vanilla. Now, add the flour, ½ cup at a time, and beat to form a soft, kneadable dough. Turn the dough out onto a lightly floured surface, and knead until it is smooth; add enough additional flour only when necessary to prevent sticking.

Transfer the dough to an oiled bowl and turn to coat it. Cover and let rise in a warm place until it has doubled in bulk, about 30 to 60 minutes.

Punch down the dough, and divide it in half. On a lightly floured surface, roll out each half into a rectangle about 8 to 10 inches.

To make the filling: Combine the walnuts, cinnamon, nutmeg, honey, milk, vanilla and orange rind. Spread half of this filling on each piece of dough, leaving a ½-inch border on all sides.

Now, roll up the dough lengthwise, and pinch the bottom and side seams shut. Carefully place the roll on a cookie sheet, seam side down, cover lightly, and let it rise until doubled in bulk, about 30 minutes.

When the dough has risen, brush it with the egg glaze, and bake at 350°F for 30 to 35 minutes, or until golden on top.

Serve warm.

Makes 2 rolls.

Linzertorte

A classic holiday dessert with a rich almond crust. You can make this filling during cherry season and freeze it for later use. Cook the cherries until they are quite thick, but do not let them scorch.

The crust with this tart is a fragile dough, so handle it carefully. If the butter becomes too soft, the dough will be unmanageable. If that happens, refrigerate the dough until the butter congeals again. If the lattice strips forming the crust break while you're arranging them, don't be too concerned. Just press them lightly together again.

Date sugar is simply the result of grinding dried dates. It is available in health food stores. It is useful because it adds sweetness without moisture (as honey does) and produces a flakier pastry.

The Filling

  5 cups pitted Bing cherries, coarsely chopped
 ⅓ cup honey
  2 tablespoons water
  1 tablespoon lemon juice

The Crust

1⅓ cups whole wheat pastry flour
  1 teaspoon ground cinnamon
 ¼ teaspoon ground cloves
  1 cup ground pecans
 ⅓ cup date sugar
  2 teaspoons grated lemon rind
 ½ cup cold butter
  2 egg yolks
  1 tablespoon *Vanilla Extract* (see page 247)
  1 egg yolk or white beaten with 1 teaspoon
     water (as a glaze)

To make the filling: Combine the cherries, honey, water and lemon juice in a 3-quart saucepan. Bring to a boil over medium-high heat, and cook, stirring frequently, until the cherries are reduced by half.

Lower the heat to medium and continue to cook, stirring constantly, until the mixture has been reduced to about 1½ cups (most of the liquid will have cooked away). Cool.

To make the crust: In a large bowl mix together the flour, cinnamon, cloves, pecans, date sugar and lemon rind. With two knives or a pastry blender, cut in the butter to form a coarse meal.

In a small cup beat together the egg yolks and vanilla until they are just combined. Sprinkle over the dry ingredients. Continue to work the dough with the knives or pastry blender until all the ingredients are incorporated, and the dough is moist enough to form a ball.

Press two-thirds of the dough evenly onto the bottom and sides of a 9-by-1-inch tart pan with a removable bottom. Spread the filling over the dough and refrigerate.

Form the remaining dough into a rough rectangle about ½ inch thick; flour it lightly, wrap it in plastic or wax paper, and refrigerate until firm, about 30 minutes.

Roll the chilled dough between two sheets of wax paper to form a rectangle about 9 inches long and ¼ inch thick. *Either* cut it into small decorative shapes with a knife or small cookie cutters *or* slice it into strips about ⅜ inch wide by 9 inches long.

If you have cut the dough into shapes, arrange them on top of the filling.

If you have produced strips, place them in the refrigerator for about 30 mintues. When the dough is thoroughly chilled, carefully remove the strips from the paper one strip at a time using a long metal spatula, and fashion a lattice top over the tart. To achieve the classic look of a linzertorte, lay the strips diagonally across the pan.

Brush the dough with the glaze.

Place on a cookie sheet and bake at 350°F for about 35 minutes. Watch carefully so that the top does not burn.

To remove the pan sides, set the tart pan on top of a large coffee can, and carefully slip the sides of the pan down away from the bottom. Do not try to remove the bottom from the fragile tart.

Serve warm.

Makes 1 tart.

Gingerbread with Lemon Sauce

The Cake
2¼ cups whole wheat pastry flour
1½ teaspoons baking soda
1 teaspoon ground cinnamon
1 teaspoon powdered ginger
½ cup butter, melted
1 egg
¼ cup molasses
¼ cup honey
1 cup water

The Sauce
3 tablespoons honey
3 tablespoons lemon juice
2 tablespoons cornstarch
1 cup cold water
1 egg yolk
1 tablespoon butter
1 teaspoon grated lemon rind

To make the cake: Butter an 8-inch-square baking dish, or coat it with equal parts of oil and liquid lecithin.

Sift the flour, baking soda, cinnamon and ginger into a large bowl.

In a small bowl beat together the butter, egg, molasses, honey and water until they are smooth.

Pour the liquid ingredients into the dry ones, and beat with a wire whisk until smooth, about 15 seconds.

Pour the batter into the prepared pan, and bake at 350°F for about 30 minutes, or until a toothpick inserted in the center comes out clean.

Cool the cake in its pan.

To make the sauce: In a small saucepan combine the honey and the lemon juice.

In a cup combine the cornstarch and ¼ cup of water; stir until smooth.

Stir the cornstarch and the remaining water into the saucepan.

Cook the sauce over medium heat, stirring constantly with a wire whisk, until it clears and thickens. Remove from the heat.

In a small dish beat the egg yolk, and then gradually beat in a few tablespoons of hot sauce to warm the yolk.

Now, transfer the yolk mixture to the pan, and return to the heat. Cook, stirring constantly, for about 1 minute.

Stir the butter and lemon rind into the sauce.

Serve the sauce, either warm or cold, over the cake.

Makes 9 to 12 servings.

Flaky Apple Strudel

The Pastry

1½ cups sifted whole wheat pastry flour
6 tablespoons cold butter
1 egg yolk
1 tablespoon honey
2 tablespoons cold milk
½ teaspoon *Vanilla Extract* (see page 247)

The Filling

1⅓ cups finely chopped tart apples
2 tablespoons chopped pecans
2 tablespoons raisins
2 tablespoons honey
1 tablespoon lemon juice
½ teaspoon ground cinnamon
1 egg white beaten with 1 teaspoon water (as a glaze)

To make the pastry: Add the flour to a large bowl, and cut in the butter with two knives or a pastry blender until a coarse meal forms.

In a cup combine the egg yolk, honey, milk and vanilla. Sprinkle the liquid, 1 tablespoon at a time, over the flour, and, using two forks, toss the flour to moisten it. When all the liquid has been incorporated, gather the dough into a ball. If necessary, add a few more drops of milk to moisten all the flour.

Wrap the dough in plastic and refrigerate at least 30 minutes.

To make the filling: Stir together the apples, pecans, raisins, honey, lemon juice and cinnamon, and set aside.

To assemble: Turn the dough out onto a well-floured pastry cloth or place it between two sheets of wax paper and roll into a rectangle about 11 by 15 inches. Trim the edges, and save the scraps for decoration.

Spread the filling over the dough; leave a 1-inch border on the sides and bottom, and a 2-inch margin along one 15-inch side.

Roll the dough toward the 2-inch margin, and close the side seams. Transfer the roll to a well-buttered cookie sheet, and place it seam side down.

Brush it with the egg glaze, and, if you wish, use pastry scraps to decorate the top. Brush again with the egg glaze.

Bake at 350°F for about 45 minutes, or until the top is golden.

Serve warm.

Makes 1 strudel.

Sweet Cicely Tart

The herb sweet cicely looks like a giant chervil and has a similar anise flavor. (The seeds have a distinct licorice taste.) It is seldom available in markets so you'll have to grow your own to try this tart. The plant is perennial and will happily produce a bushy, feathery clump year after year. If cicely is unavailable, you may use mint, but the result will be a different dessert. Or you can omit the herbs altogether and stick with a filling of pineapple and almond.

The dough is quite delicate so handle it with care. Bake it in a shallow tart pan with a removable bottom for easier unmolding.

The Pastry

1¼ cups whole wheat pastry flour
1½ teaspoons *Baking Powder* (see *Index*)
6 tablespoons cold butter
5-6 tablespoons cold milk

The Pineapple Layer

8 ounces crushed pineapple, undrained

The Almond Paste

½ cup almonds
2 tablespoons honey
2 tablespoons reserved pineapple juice
¼ teaspoon almond extract

The Assembly

1 egg yolk beaten with 1 tablespoon milk (as a glaze)
¼ cup minced sweet cicely leaves

Sweet Cicely Tart—*continued*

To make the pastry: Sift the flour and *Baking Powder* into a large bowl, and with two knives or a pastry blender, cut in the butter to form a coarse meal.

Make a well in the center of the flour mixture, and pour in 5 tablespoons of milk. Stir with a fork until the flour is moistened. If necessary, add a few more drops of milk.

On a lightly floured surface, form into a ball, and knead about 10 times or until a smooth dough forms. Do not overwork. If the dough is sticky, dust it with flour.

Divide the dough into two unequal parts by cutting off one-third of it, and form the pieces into balls. Then, flatten both pieces, flour them lightly, wrap in plastic and refrigerate for 15 minutes (more if your kitchen is hot).

To make the pineapple layer: Drain the pineapple through a sieve placed over a bowl, pressing out all the juice with the back of a spoon; reserve the juice.

To make the almond paste: In a blender or food processor, process the almonds, honey, 2 tablespoons of the reserved pineapple juice and the almond extract until a paste forms.

To assemble: Between two sheets of wax paper, roll the larger piece of dough into a circle about 10 or 11 inches in diameter and ⅛ inch thick, and carefully peel off the paper. If the butter is soft and the dough sticks to the paper, slide a cookie sheet under all and refrigerate for 10 minutes until the butter firms and the paper peels off easily.

Transfer the dough to an 8-inch tart pan with a removable bottom. Trim the excess, but leave a 1-inch overhang. Now, fold the overhang in to strengthen the sides, and refrigerate.

Add the trimmings to the smaller ball of dough and roll it between wax paper to form a circle about 8½ inches in diameter and ⅛ inch thick.

Brush the inside and top edges of the tart shell with the egg glaze, and spread the almond paste evenly in it. Sprinkle with sweet cicely leaves, and top with the drained pineapple.

Fit the smaller circle of dough over the pan, trim off the excess and brush with egg glaze. Cut two or three steam vents into the dough with a knife.

Bake at 350°F for 30 to 35 minutes, or until the top is golden.

Carefully remove the sides from the pan, and serve warm.

Serves 4.

Molasses Spice Cookies

Date sugar and pastry flour keep these little morsels light.

1¼ cups whole wheat pastry flour
 1 teaspoon baking soda
 ½ teaspoon ground cinnamon
 ½ teaspoon powdered ginger
 ½ teaspoon ground cloves
 6 tablespoons softened butter
 1 egg
 2 tablespoons molasses
 1 tablespoon *Vanilla Extract* (see page 247)
 ½ cup date sugar
 ¼ cup currants

Sift the flour, baking soda, cinnamon, ginger and cloves together in a large bowl.

In a second large bowl, beat the butter, egg, molasses, vanilla and date sugar together until thoroughly blended. Add the currants, and stir in the flour mixture until all is thoroughly blended.

With floured hands form the dough into balls about 1 inch in diameter, and arrange them 1 inch apart on cookie sheets.

Bake at 375°F for about 12 minutes, or until the cookies are puffed and cracked on top. Cool on wire racks.

Makes 28 to 36 cookies.

Moroccan Rice Pie

This is my version of a classic Moroccan dessert I saw prepared in Paula Wolfert's New York City classes. The white flour phyllo dough of the original has been replaced with whole wheat crepes, and the white rice has made way for brown rice. The almonds and yogurt also make valuable health contributions to this unusual dessert.

The Rice
¼ cup almonds
1 cup hot water
1 cup uncooked short-grain brown rice
2 cups milk
1 tablespoon butter
1 cinnamon stick
2 tablespoons honey
¼ teaspoon almond extract
1 cup milk

The Nut Mixture
½ cup almonds
2 tablespoons orange juice
½ teaspoon ground cinnamon
1 tablespoon honey

The Assembly
12 8-inch *Whole Wheat Crepes* (see *Index*)
3 tablespoons butter, melted
1 egg beaten with ⅛ teaspoon ground
    cinnamon (as a glaze)
2 cups yogurt
2 tablespoons honey

To make the rice: Combine the almonds and ½ cup of hot water in a blender, and process until the almonds are ground. Strain the mixture through a sieve into a small bowl, pressing the pulp with a wooden spoon to extract as much of the liquid as possible. Reserve the liquid.

Return the pulp to the blender and repeat with ½ cup more water. Strain again, and then discard the pulp.

Combine the almond liquid, brown rice, 2 cups of milk, butter, cinnamon stick, honey

and almond extract in a heavy-bottom medium saucepan. Cover and cook over very low heat until all the liquid has been absorbed, about 1 hour. Stir occasionally to prevent scorching.

With the pan still over the heat, stir in ⅓ cup of milk, and beat vigorously to combine. Cook, uncovered, for a few minutes, or until the liquid is absorbed. Repeat the process twice more with the remaining milk to produce a thick and creamy mixture.

Remove the cinnamon stick, and allow the rice to cool.

To make the nut mixture: In a blender or food processor grind the ½ cup of almonds finely. Stir in the orange juice, cinnamon and honey.

To assemble: Butter a 9-inch-round cake pan, fit a piece of wax paper into the bottom and butter it.

Brush the spotty side of each crepe with melted butter.

Place a crepe in the middle of the pan, good side down. Take five more crepes and use them, spotty side up, to line the sides of the pan; overlap the top of the pan as you go. Take five more crepes and place them at the intersections of the first layer.

Spoon the rice into the pan, and sprinkle with the nut mixture. Fold the overhanging edges of the crepes over the almonds; brush each piece with butter as you fold it over. Cover the top with one last crepe, and brush it with butter.

Brush the egg glaze overall.

Bake at 425°F for 10 minutes and remove from the oven. Place a pizza pan or a 10-inch cake pan over the hot pudding pan, and invert them so that the rice pie is sitting on top of the cool pan. Remove the hot pan and the wax paper.

Return to the oven and bake for 10 more minutes.

To serve, invert once again onto a serving dish. Combine the yogurt and honey, and serve with the warm pie.

Serves 6 to 8.

Royal Strawberry Rice

Rice pudding with a French flair. Actually, I shouldn't call it a pudding at all, because the beaten egg whites make it light and airy like a mousse.

Be sure to cook the rice over very low heat in a heavy pot to prevent scorching; stir it frequently.

¼ cup uncooked long-grain brown rice
1¼ cups milk
1 cinnamon stick
1 tablespoon butter
4 egg yolks
1 tablespoon unflavored gelatin
3 tablespoons honey
1 cup milk
2 navel oranges
1 pint strawberries
1 tablespoon *Vanilla Extract* (see page 247)
4 egg whites

In a heavy-bottom saucepan combine the rice, 1¼ cups of milk, the cinnamon stick and butter, and bring to a boil over low heat. Cover, and cook over low heat until all the liquid has been absorbed and the rice is tender, about 1½ hours. Stir frequently to prevent sticking.

While the rice is cooking, combine the egg yolks, gelatin and honey in a medium saucepan. Now, slowly add 1 cup of milk, and beat with a wire whisk until combined. Cook over low heat, stirring constantly, until the sauce thickens enough to coat a wooden spoon.

Peel the oranges and section them, being careful to remove the membranes around each piece. Pat dry. Cut the strawberries in half lengthwise.

When the rice is cooked, stir in the custard sauce. Then, stir in the vanilla. Now, set the pan in a large bowl containing ice cubes and water to cool the mixture and set the gelatin. Stir occasionally until the mixture just starts to mound upon itself when dropped from the spoon. Remove from the ice.

Cover the bottom of a 6-cup ring mold with the orange sections and strawberry halves.

Coarsely chop any remaining fruit and fold it into the rice mixture.

In a clean bowl using clean beaters, beat the egg whites until stiff, and then fold them into the rice. Turn the mixture into the mold and refrigerate until set.

Serves 6 to 8.

Pumpkin Cheesecake

This cheesecake is higher in vitamin A and fiber and lower in fat and calories than many cheesecakes because of its pumpkin and ricotta cheese. If you wish, substitute mashed sweet potatoes or butternut squash for the pumpkin.

The Crust
- ⅔ cup wheat germ
- ⅓ cup ground walnuts
- 2 tablespoons butter, melted
- 1 tablespoon honey

The Cake
- 4 eggs
- 1 cup ricotta cheese
- 8 ounces softened cream cheese
- 3 tablespoons whole wheat flour
- 1 teaspoon ground cinnamon
- ½ teaspoon grated nutmeg
- ¼ teaspoon powdered ginger
- ½ cup honey
- 1 cup yogurt
- 1½ cups mashed cooked pumpkin
- 1 pint strawberries (as a garnish)

To make the crust: Combine the wheat germ, walnuts, butter and honey, and pat them into a 9-inch springform pan. Set aside.

To make the cake: Combine the eggs and ricotta in a blender, and process until smooth. Cut the cream cheese into ½-inch cubes, and add them to the mixture with the blender running; blend until smooth. Add the flour, cinnamon, nutmeg, ginger and honey, and blend until smooth.

Transfer the batter to a large bowl, and, with an electric mixer or a wire whisk, blend in the yogurt and pumpkin until they are well incorporated.

Pour the batter into the springform pan.

Bake at 325°F for 1 hour. Turn off the heat, but let the cheesecake remain in the oven for 1 hour.

Remove from the oven and cool on a wire rack. Finally, refrigerate the cake until it is thoroughly chilled.

Cut the strawberries in half lengthwise, and arrange on top of the cheesecake.

Serves 12.

Peachy Cheesecake Squares

The Crust
⅔ cup whole wheat pastry flour
⅓ cup ground pecans or almonds
⅓ cup date sugar
2 tablespoons wheat germ
½ teaspoon ground cinnamon
4 tablespoons cold butter

The Filling
2 eggs
3 tablespoons honey
2 tablespoons milk
2 tablespoons lemon juice
1 teaspoon *Vanilla Extract* (see page 247)
2 cups chopped peaches
8 ounces softened cream cheese

The Topping
1 tablespoon butter, melted
2 tablespoons wheat germ
2 tablespoons ground pecans or almonds
2 tablespoons date sugar

peach slices and mint leaves (as a garnish)

To make the crust: In a large bowl combine the flour, nuts, date sugar, wheat germ and cinnamon. With two knives or a pastry blender, cut in the butter until a coarse meal forms. Press the dough into an 8-inch-square baking dish.
Bake at 350°F for 10 minutes.
To make the filling: In a blender, combine the eggs, honey, milk, lemon juice, vanilla, peaches and cream cheese, and process on high speed for 15 to 20 seconds to combine well.
To make the topping: In a small bowl stir the butter, wheat germ, nuts and date sugar together with a fork until they are well blended.
Pour the filling over the baked crust, and sprinkle with the topping.
Bake at 350°F for 50 minutes.
Allow to cool completely, and then refrigerate until chilled. Cut into pieces, and top with peach slices and mint leaves.

Serves 9 to 12.

Woodruff

Woodruff's name may come from the French word for "wheel" and make reference to the spokelike appearance of the leaves. Woodruff tea is said to help relieve migraines and soothe the nerves, and the crushed leaves are said to help heal wounds.

Any-Way-You-Want Muffins

This all-purpose muffin recipe is adaptable to any fruit and season, because the variable ingredients are the bananas, blueberries and sunflower seeds. If you're out of bananas, use shredded zucchini, shredded carrots or shredded apples—even applesauce or mashed squash. And if blueberries are out of season, use chopped apples, strawberries, peaches or dates. Or try whole cranberries, currants or raisins. The sunflower seeds can also be omitted or replaced by grated coconut or chopped nuts.

Any old way you choose it, these muffins are loaded with fiber, vitamins and minerals.

Tip: Paper cupcake liners may stick to these muffins if you try to peel them off immediately. However, if you wait until the muffins cool, the liners will slip right off.

1 cup whole wheat pastry flour
1 teaspoon baking soda
¼ teaspoon *Baking Powder* (see *Index*)
1 teaspoon ground cinnamon
2 tablespoons wheat germ
2 tablespoons bran
¼ cup oil
¼ cup honey
1 egg
½ cup buttermilk
1 teaspoon *Vanilla Extract* (see page 247)
1 cup mashed bananas
½ cup blueberries
¼ cup sunflower seeds

Line 16 muffin cups with paper liners (or use butter or equal parts of oil and liquid lecithin).

Sift the flour, baking soda, *Baking Powder* and cinnamon into a large bowl, and stir in the wheat germ and bran.

In a smaller bowl beat the oil, honey, egg, buttermilk and vanilla together until they are well blended.

Stir the liquid ingredients into the dry ingredients until just blended. Do not overmix.

Fold in the bananas, blueberries and sunflower seeds.

Spoon the batter into the prepared muffin cups, filling them about two-thirds full. Bake at 325°F for 25 to 30 minutes, or until a toothpick inserted in the center of one comes out clean.

Makes 16 muffins.

Pumpkin Muffins

1¼ cups whole wheat pastry flour
¼ cup bran
¼ cup wheat germ
1 teaspoon baking soda
½ teaspoon ground cinnamon
¼ teaspoon grated nutmeg
1 cup mashed cooked pumpkin
¼ cup butter, melted
¼ cup honey
2 tablespoons molasses
1 egg
¼ cup orange juice
¼ cup chopped pecans

Butter 18 muffin cups or coat them with equal parts of oil and liquid lecithin. Set aside.

In a large bowl mix the flour, bran, wheat germ, baking soda, cinnamon and nutmeg together.

In another bowl thoroughly combine the pumpkin, butter, honey, molasses, egg and orange juice.

Add the liquid ingredients to the dry ingredients, and stir until just blended. Fold in the pecans, but do not overmix.

Spoon the batter into the prepared pans, filling them about two-thirds full.

Bake at 375°F for 20 minutes. Serve warm.

Makes 18 muffins.

Honeyed Pumpkin Pie

A whole wheat pumpkin pie for Thanksgiving, one that's brimming with vitamin A.

TIP: *Don't overfill the shell or your pie will overflow in the oven. If you should end up with too much filling, bake the excess in custard cups. To maintain its creamy texture, place the cups in a large pan of hot water, and bake until a knife inserted in the center comes out clean.*

  2 eggs
  1 9-inch *Whole Wheat Pie Shell,* baked (see
      Index)
1½ cups mashed cooked pumpkin
1½ cups half-and-half or light cream
 ⅓ cup honey
  2 tablespoons whole wheat pastry flour
 ¾ teaspoon ground cinnamon
 ½ teaspoon powdered ginger
 ⅛ teaspoon ground cloves
  1 teaspoon *Vanilla Extract* (see page 247)
      whipped cream (optional)

Beat the white of one egg lightly with a fork until frothy, and then lightly paint the inside of the pie shell with it.

Transfer any remaining white to a large mixing bowl, and add the yolk and the other whole egg. Now, beat in the pumpkin, half-and-half or light cream, the honey, flour, cinnamon, ginger, cloves and vanilla until the mixture is smooth.

Pour the filling into the pie shell, being careful not to overfill it; leave *at least* ¼ inch of space between the filling and the top of the shell.

Bake at 375°F for 50 to 70 minutes, or until a knife inserted in the center comes out clean.

Cool on a wire rack. If desired, serve topped with whipped cream.

Serves 6.

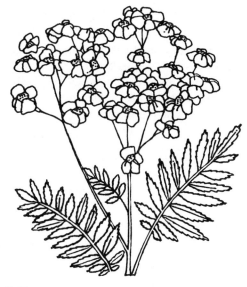

Yarrow

The ancient Chinese used yarrow stalks to foretell the future. Its old name, knight's milfoil, comes from its reputed ability to heal battle wounds. The tea is recommended by herbalists as a tonic to restore appetite, ease digestion and promote perspiration during colds and fever.

Soft Sauce

This is a nonalcoholic version of the hard sauce traditionally served with Plum Pudding, *but you can also use it with any sweetened bread.*

TIPS: *To soften the butter quickly, shred it through the large holes of a vegetable grater.*

If you don't have a pastry bag, use a spoon to drop dollops of sauce onto the wax paper.

¼ cup softened butter
¼ cup honey
½ teaspoon *Vanilla Extract* (see opposite page)
1 teaspoon grated orange rind
  few gratings of nutmeg
1 tablespoon boiling water (if necessary)

In an electric mixer or a food processor, beat the butter, honey, vanilla, orange rind and nutmeg together until smooth. If the mixture curdles, add some boiling water.

Fill a pastry bag fitted with a large star tube with the sauce, and pipe rosettes onto wax paper or parchment. Place them in the refrigerator to harden. When thoroughly chilled, carefully remove them from the paper, and return to the refrigerator in a tightly covered container.

Makes ½ cup.

Creamy Custard Sauce

Wonderful over spicy fruit compotes or sponge cakes.

2 tablespoons cornstarch
1½ cups milk
2 tablespoons honey
2 egg yolks
1 tablespoon *Vanilla Extract* (see opposite page)
½ cup heavy cream

Dissolve the cornstarch in a little milk. Add with the remaining milk to a 1-quart saucepan, and stir in the honey.

Cook the sauce over medium heat, stirring constantly with a wooden spoon, until it thickens enough to coat the spoon. Remove from the heat.

In a small cup beat the egg yolks, and then gradually stir in a few tablespoons of the hot sauce to warm the eggs. Now, return the mixture to the sauce and stir well.

Return to the heat and cook, *stirring constantly*, for 1 minute. Again, remove from the heat, stir in the vanilla, and strain into a bowl.

To keep a skin from forming, lay a piece of wax paper directly on the surface of the sauce, and chill.

In a small bowl whip the cream until stiff, and then fold it into the chilled sauce.

Makes about 2 cups.

Vanilla Extract

If you'd prefer not to use a commercial extract containing alcohol, you can make your own at home. Vanilla beans are available in gourmet shops as well as the spice section of many supermarkets.

1 vanilla bean
¼ cup boiling water
1 tablespoon honey
1 tablespoon oil
1 teaspoon liquid lecithin

Cut the vanilla bean into small pieces, place in a small bowl and cover with boiling water. Now, cover the bowl and allow to steep overnight.

The next day, process the mixture in a blender on medium speed until the bean pieces are pulverized, and then strain it through cheesecloth. Return to the blender.

Now, add the honey, oil and lecithin, and process on medium speed until well combined. Pour into a small bottle, cap tightly and store in the refrigerator.

Makes ¼ cup.

Appendix

Directory of Herb Sources

Herb seedlings and seeds—along with dried herbs and herb teas—are available from a wide variety of sources, so the following directory makes no claim to be complete. It is, however, a basic list of mail-order firms who deal in herbs. Some of the concerns carry nothing but herbs, others have a limited selection tucked among their other products, but all of them have catalogs. The list is as up-to-date as we could make it, but we cannot guarantee that by the time you read this all the companies will still be in business or will have all the items listed.

In your search for herbs and herb products, be sure to check out local sources first. Many nurseries, farmers' markets and large supermarkets carry seeds, plants and fresh-cut herbs. Some gourmet shops and cookware stores also sell fresh herbs as well as some of the more unusual dried herbs and herb teas.

ABC Nursery and Greenhouse
Route 1, Box 313
Lecoma, MO 65540
(314) 435-6389

Offers over 100 perennial and annual plants.

Applewood Seed Co.
P.O. Box 10761
Edgemont Station
Golden, CO 80401

A basic selection of herb seeds.

Attar Herbs & Spices
Playground Road
New Ipswich, NH 03071

A large selection of dried herbs and spices.

Borchelt Herb Gardens
474 Carriage Shop Road
East Falmouth, MA 02536
(617) 548-4571

Offers an all-inclusive selection of herb seeds.

Burpee Seed Co.
300 Park Avenue
Warminster, PA 18974

Offers seeds and plants for most popular herbs.

Calico Herbs, Inc.
P.O. Box 68
Old England Road
Ipswich, MA 01938
(617) 356-0437

Offers dried herbs and a few herb blends.

Caprilands Herb Farm
534 Silver Street
Coventry, CT 06238
(203) 742-7244

A large variety of plants, seeds, dried herbs, spices and some teas.

Carroll Gardens
P.O. Box 310
444 E. Main Street
Westminster, MD 21157
(301) 848-5422

An impressive selection of perennial plants, plus some annuals.

Casa Yerba
Star Route 2, Box 21
Days Creek, OR 97429
(503) 825-3534

A large selection of annual and perennial plants and some seeds. Catalog, $1.

Cornells Herb Farm
3908 Reforestation Road
Green Bay, WI 54303
(414) 434-2026

A selection of annual and perennial plants and a few seeds. Catalog, $1.

The Country Herbery
P.O. Box 1573
Auburn, CA 95603
(916) 269-0275

Offers dried herbs, spices and some spice blends.

Country Herbs
3 Maple Street
Stockbridge, MA 01262
(413) 298-3884

Offers a large number of annual and perennial plants, plus some seeds, dried herbs, spices and herb blends.

Cricket Hill Herb Farm, Ltd.
Glen Street
Rowley, MA 01969
(617) 948-2818

Offers over 250 herb plants, plus dried herbs, spices, teas and herb blends. Catalog, $1.

J. A. Demonchaux Co.
827 N. Kansas
Topeka, KS 66608
(913) 235-8502

A nice selection of annual and perennial herb seeds.

The Dutch Mill Herb Farm
Route 2, Box 190
Forest Grove, OR 97116
(503) 648-8202
Dried herbs.

East Earth Herb
Box 186, Route 3
Reedsport, OR 97467
Chinese herbs.

Far North Gardens
15621-P Auburndale Avenue
Livonia, MI 48154
(313) 422-0747
A few herb seeds. Catalog, $1.

Flintridge Herbs & Spindles & Things
Route 1, Box 187
Sister Bay, WI 54234
(414) 854-2423 or 854-2919
Offers an extensive list of annual and perennial herb plants, seeds, dried herbs and spices. Specify either the "Dried Herbs and Spices Catalog" or the "Plant Listing," each 50¢.

Fragrant Fields
Route 2, Box 199
Dongola, IL 62926
(618) 827-3677
Offers an abundant supply of perennial and annual herb plants, plus dried herbs, spices and teas.

Gurney Seed and Nursery Co.
Gurney Building
Yankton, SD 57079
(605) 665-4451
Basic herb seeds plus a few plants.

Joseph Harris Co., Inc.
Moreton Farm
Rochester, NY 14624
Offers a limited selection of herb seeds.

Harvest Health, Inc.
1944 Eastern Avenue, S.E.
Grand Rapids, MI 49507
(616) 245-6268
A wide selection of dried herbs and spices.

Hemlock Hill Herb Farm
Hemlock Hill Road
Litchfield, CT 06759
(203) 567-5031
Offers a good selection of perennial herb plants. Catalog, 50¢.

Herbal Effect
Box 6
Carmel Valley, CA 93924
(408) 375-6313
A large selection of dried herbs and spices.

Herbal Holding Co.
P.O. Box 5854
Sherman Oaks, CA 91413
(213) 765-5433
Offers dried herbs in bulk—mostly medicinal, some culinary—plus bulk tea blends. Catalog, $1.

Herbally Yours, Inc.
P.O. Box 26
Changewater, NJ 07831
(201) 689-6140
A nice selection of dried herbs, tea blends, herb and spice blends.

The Herbary and Potpourri Shop
P.O. Box 543
Childs Homestead Road
Orleans, MA 02653
(617) 255-4422

Offers a large listing of herb plants, dried herbs, spices, herb blends, and a few herb teas. Catalog, $1 (refundable with the first order).

The Herb Cottage
Washington Cathedral
Mount Saint Alban
Washington, DC 20016

Offers a nice selection of herb seeds, plus dried herbs and spices.

Herbiforous
Susan Puls
Route 1, Box 142
Elkhart Lake, WI 53020
(414) 565-2319

Offers herb seeds, as well as dried herbs and teas. Catalog, $1 (refundable with the first order).

Herbs, Etc.
26 Central Street
Ipswich, MA 01938
(617) 356-2947

Offers dried herbs, spices and herb seeds. Specify the "Herb Seed Catalog," $1 (refundable with the first order).

Herbst Brothers Seedsmen, Inc.
1000 N. Main Street, Dept. 2092
Brewster, NY 10509
(914) 279-2971

A fine selection of annual and perennial herb seeds.

Hickory Hollow Herbs
Route 1, Box 52
Peterstown, WV 24963

Offers many annual and perennial seeds, plus herb teas, dried herbs and spices. Send self-addressed, stamped envelope for catalog.

High Meadow Farm
P.O. Box 357
Hayesville, NC 28904
(704) 389-3495

Offers a small selection of annual herb seeds, plus a large variety of annual and perennial herb plants.

Hilltop Herb Farm, Inc.
P.O. Box 1734
Cleveland, TX 77327
(713) 592-5859

Offers an extensive selection of perennial herb plants, annual and perennial seeds, herb blends, dried herbs and spices. Catalog, $2 (refundable with the first order).

Horticultural Enterprises
P.O. Box 340082
Dallas, TX 75234

Offers seeds for over 30 varieties of domestic and imported peppers.

Indiana Botanic Gardens
P.O. Box 5
Hammond, IN 46325
(219) 931-2480

Dried herbs, spices and teas. Catalog, 50¢.

Internode Seed Co.
16 Pamaron Way
Novato, CA 94947
(415) 883-0822
Some herb seeds, plus dried herbs and spices (some in bulk).

Le Jardin du Gourmet
West Danville, VT 05873
A sizable variety of annual and perennial herb plants and seeds, and some herb teas.

Johnny's Selected Seeds
Albion, ME 04910
(207) 437-9294
Seeds for over 30 annual and perennial herbs.

The Lhasa Karnak Herb Co.
2513 Telegraph Avenue
Berkeley, CA 94704
(415) 548-0380
Offers an abundance of dried herbs, plus a large variety of herb tea blends. Catalog, 50¢.

Mellinger's, Inc.
2310 W. South Range Road
North Lima, OH 44452
(216) 549-9861
A small list of herb seeds and plants.

Misty Morning Farm
2220 W. Sisson Road
Hastings, MI 49058
(616) 765-3023
Offers over 75 varieties of annual and perennial herb plants and seeds; also dried herbs.

Mt. Vernon Farm Herbs
P.O. Box 1879
Nantucket, MA 02554
A sizable assortment of annual and perennial plants.

Nichols Garden Nursery
1190 North Pacific Highway
Albany, OR 97321
(503) 928-9280
A large selection of herb seeds, perennial herb plants, dried herbs, spices, herb blends and tea blends.

Geo. W. Park Seed Co., Inc.
Greenwood, SC 29647
A large assortment of perennial and annual herb seeds, plus a few perennial plants.

Penn Herb Co., Ltd.
603 N. 2d Street, Dept. 105
Philadelphia, PA 19123
(215) 925-3336
Dried herbs—mostly medicinal, but some culinary—herb seeds and teas.

Redwood City Seed Co.
Box 361
Redwood City, CA 94064
(415) 325-7333
An extensive list of herb seeds and many varieties of chili pepper seeds. Catalog, 50¢.

R.F.M. Publishing Corp.
P.O. Box 1299
Long Island City, NY 11101
Annual and perennial herb seeds.

Richters
Goodwood, Ontario, L0C 1A0
(416) 640-6677
A large selection of annual and perennial herb seeds. Catalog, $1.

The Rosemary House
120 S. Market Street
Mechanicsburg, PA 17055
(717) 697-5111
Offers perennial herb plants, a large selection of annual and perennial seeds, plus dried herbs, spices and herb teas. Catalog, $1.

Rutland of Kentucky
P.O. Box 16
Washington, KY 41096
(606) 759-7815
Herb plants and seeds. Catalog, $2.

Sanctuary Seeds
2388 W. 4th
Vancouver, British Columbia V6K 1P1
(604) 733-4724
Offers a large variety of annual and perennial seeds, dried herbs and some teas.

The Sandy Mush Herb Nursery
Route 2, Surrett Cove Road
Leicester, NC 28748
(704) 683-2014
Offers a bountiful selection of perennial herb plants, plus seeds for annuals. Catalog, $1 (refundable with the first order).

Smile Herb Shop
4908 Berwyn Road
College Park, MD 20740
(301) 474-8791
Dried herbs, spices, herb teas, herb seeds and plants.

Southern Garden Co.
The Gardenaires
P.O. Box 745
Norcross, GA 30091
(404) 449-3890
A selection of annual and perennial herb seeds.

Stillcopper Herb Farm
Route 1, Box 186-JR
Brookneal, VA 24528
(804) 283-5276
A large selection of annual and perennial plants, herb blends and teas. Catalog, $2.

Sunnybrook Farms Nursery
9448 Mayfield Road
Chesterland, OH 44026
(216) 729-7232
A large variety of herb plants and seeds, and a few teas. Catalog, $1.

Tatra Herb Co.
222 Grove Street, P.O. Box 60
Morrisville, PA 19067
(215) 295-5476
An extensive list of dried herbs (many medicinal), plus herb tea blends. Catalog, 50¢.

Taylor's Herb Gardens, Inc.
1535 Lone Oak Road
Vista, CA 92083
(714) 727-3485
A plentiful assortment of annual and perennial plants, plus seeds. Catalog, $1.

Tempco Industries
P.O. Box 6104
Philadelphia, PA 19115
(215) 728-5818
Herb teas.

The Tool Shed Herb Farm
Turkey Hill Road, Box 63
Salem Center
Purdys Station, NY 10578
(914) 669-5844
An assortment of perennial herb plants and
some annual herb plants. Catalog, 25¢.

Tusseyville Trading Post and Herb Farm
R.D. 1
Centre Hall, PA 16828
(814) 364-1206
Herb seeds and plants, dried herbs and spices
and their own tea blends.

Vick's Wildgardens, Inc.
Conshohocken State Road
Box 115
Gladwyne, PA 19035
(215) 525-6773
A modest list of herb seeds. Specializes in
wildflowers. Catalog 50¢.

Wayside Gardens
Hodges, SC 29695
(803) 374-3387
A few popular perennial herb plants. Catalog,
$1 (refundable with the first order).

Well-Sweep Herb Farm
317 Mt. Bethel Road
Port Murray, NJ 07865
(201) 852-5390
An extensive variety of annual and perennial
herb plants, plus some seeds. Catalog, 75¢.

Werner's Herbs
Route 1, Box 71
Letohatchee, AL 36047
Offers annual and perennial herb plants and
some dried herbs.

White Mountain Herb Farm
P.O. Box 64
Jefferson, NH 03583
Over 50 perennial herb plants. Send stamp
for catalog.

The White Pine Co.
Box 3512
Madison, WI 53704
(608) 251-2303
Offers dried herbs, herb blends and teas.
Catalog, $1.

Wide World of Herbs
11 St. Catherine St. E.
Montreal, Quebec H2X 1K3
Offers a sizable assortment of dried herbs
and spices.

Yankee Peddler Herb Farm
Route 1, Box 251A
Burton, TX 77835
(713) 289-3083
A large selection of herb seeds, dried herbs,
spices and a large selection of tea blends.
Catalog, $1.

Index

Boldface numbers indicate table entry.

G

H

About the Author

Jean Rogers was born and raised in eastern Pennsylvania, where she started cooking at an early age, at first under the guidance of her grandmother and later with the inspiration of Julia Child's TV shows. Since then, she has taken scores of cooking classes, both here and abroad, including the visitors' course at La Varenne Ecole de Cuisine in Paris and instruction at Roger Verge's Ecole du Moulin in the medieval town of Mougins on the French Riviera. She has also been a student in the classes of Judith Olney, Paula Wolfert and Julie Sahni.

In her professional life, Ms. Rogers was for eight years the copy editor of *Prevention,* the nation's largest health and natural living magazine, for which she also helped test and edit recipes, and since 1982 she has been the copy editor of *Spring,* a women's magazine dedicated to health and high-energy living. She is also responsible for editing that publication's food columns.

She lives in Pennsylvania with her husband, John Feltman, managing editor of *Prevention* magazine, and their dog, Ivy, who also enjoys home-cooked meals, herbed and otherwise.